BLACK BANNERS OF ISIS

BLACK BANNERS OF ISIS

The Roots of the New Caliphate

DAVID J. WASSERSTEIN

Yale

UNIVERSITY PRESS

New Haven and London

Yale University Press books may be purchased in quantity for educational, business, or promotional use. For information, please e-mail sales.press@yale.edu (U.S. office) or sales@yaleup.co.uk (U.K. office).

Set in Janson type by IDS Infotech Ltd., Chandigarh, India.
Printed in the United States of America.

Library of Congress Control Number: 2017931621
ISBN 978–0–300–22835–9 (cloth : alk. paper)

A catalogue record for this book is available from the British Library.

This paper meets the requirements of ANSI/NISO Z39.48–1992 (Permanence of Paper).

10 9 8 7 6 5 4 3 2 1

For Colin,
Eshes hayil
Prov. 31:10–31

Contents

Preface   ix

Map of Areas under Islamic State Control   xiv

INTRODUCTION   The Islamic State   1

1. Caliphate   27

2. Administration   56

3. Revenue   68

4. Religion   94

5. Women, and Children Too   121

6. Christians and Jews and . . .   146

7. Apocalypse Now   177

CONCLUSION   197

Notes   213

Glossary   257

Index   261

Preface

THIS BOOK BEGAN AS an attempt to clarify a superficially simple set of questions. What kind of Islamic state is the Islamic State (IS)? Is IS simply another terrorist outfit, splintering from al-Qaida, or should we see in it something different, something new, something with the potential to set off changes of world-historical significance? That is what the founder of IS Abu Musab al-Zarqawi means when he writes, "The spark has been lit here in Iraq, and its heat will continue to intensify—by Allah's permission—until it burns the crusader armies in Dabiq." How, other than in terms merely of terrorism in the Internet age, should we understand IS, and how should we think about reactions to it? How should the presence of IS affect Western, non-Islamic ways of relating to Islam and Muslims?

In the process of looking for answers to those questions, naturally I have found others and unearthed old debates about what it means to be Muslim and Islamic, as well as what it means to look at a religion, a culture, a civilization from the outside. The erudition and learning of the late Shahab Ahmed's recent publication *What Is Islam? The Importance of Being Islamic* did much to stimulate concern and illuminate what we Westerners do not yet know. But inevitably, especially given when the author was working on it, that book could not offer direct answers to questions specifically about IS. Other works, by journalists and scholars in particular, often seemed not to go deeply enough into the historical background of the issues involved, in part because of a perfectly understandable concern with day-to-day developments in the Middle East and elsewhere. The cost, perhaps inevitable, of that is a paring down of a concern with the non-immediate, the past.

My concern, by contrast, is with the past in the present, the present in its past. That past has two separate, if interlinked, elements. One is Western involvement with the world of Islam, an involvement that stretches from the beginnings of Islam to ongoing adventures in Afghanistan and Iraq. The term "crusader," deployed to great effect by IS and others as a label for Westerners, some of whom are Christians, reduces our understanding of that involvement to one of hostility and destructiveness, mutual ignorance and irreconcilable faith claims, power relations and intolerance and suspicion. The truth is that the connection has been far more complicated and messy—interesting, exciting, and rich, in both positive and negative ways—ever since the birth of Islam.

The other element is the larger Islamic past that feeds and forms IS as it does numerous other movements, ideologies, and cultures within the penumbra of Islam as a whole. In this book I have tried to look at IS as a phenomenon of the world of Islam, not in terms of alleged influences coming from outside or as a product of Western policies gone wrong. At least as a first step, it makes sense to look at such a movement as IS on its own terms, and those are at base those of the world of Islam.

My subject is a moving target. I have tried to keep up-to-date with events in the process of researching and writing this book, but inevitably, important changes and developments will have occurred between my writing of these lines and their appearance in print. As I write this IS is losing ground militarily, but the pendulum is likely to move to and fro for some time before IS is forgotten.

I have learned much in preparing this book. As a student of medieval Islam I have learned that the dead speak, and that the living listen. As a non-Muslim I have learned to see Islam as a living, changing faith in the world, and its faithful as members of a vital tradition with many mansions. Above all, in writing about IS, I have tried to lose the bogeyman approach thrust upon us by so many of our leaders and guides and to see through the veil to the reality within.

Along the way I have been fortunate to benefit from advice, help, and encouragement from a wide variety of sources. During the academic year 2015–2016, together with two Vanderbilt colleagues, I led an Andrew W. Mellon Foundation Sawyer Seminar on the subject "When the Fringe Dwarfs the Center: Vernacular Islam beyond the Arab World." It is a pleasure to thank the Mellon Foundation for its support of our endeavor; the Robert Penn Warren Center for the Humanities at Vanderbilt, which hosted us for the year; its director and staff; and in particular fellow members of the group and our guests for an enriching year that contributed enormously to shaping how I think about Islam in its non-Arab forms and how I write about Islam.

At Yale University Press, I have been fortunate in my editor, Jennifer Banks, who encouraged this project from the beginning. Her assistant editor, Heather Gold, shepherded me through the publication process. Julie Carlson, my copy editor, tolerated the transatlanticisms of a transplanted author. I am particularly grateful to Bill Nelson, of billnelsonmaps, for the map that graces this volume.

I presented versions of my thinking on this topic to the Vanderbilt History Seminar in January 2016, and subsequently to two other seminars. My thanks go to my hosts on those occasions and especially to those friends, colleagues, students—my teachers all—who attended and took part in the discussions following my talks. Family, friends, colleagues, and even total strangers on three continents and in the United Kingdom, Muslims and non-Muslims alike, have been unfailingly and instantly responsive to a stream of letters and calls demanding urgent assistance. I hope that they will accept this general expression of a gratitude that is deep in inverse proportion to the brevity of its expression. On such a subject as this, an unwonted anonymity appears preferable to an unwanted notoriety. Anonymity, however, gives way to notoriety in the greatest debt of all. That is expressed in the dedication to this book.

BLACK BANNERS OF ISIS

Map of Areas under Islamic
State Control

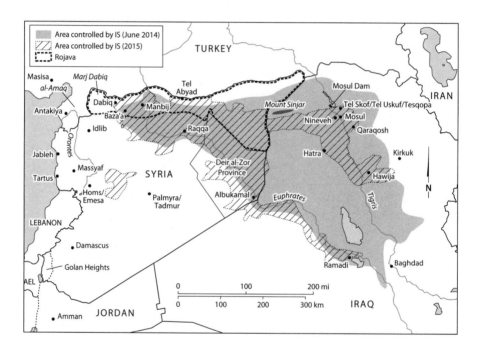

Introduction

The Islamic State

W E KNOW BOTH TOO much and too little about the Islamic State. The strategic use of violence and terror by IS, together with its ability to conquer—and, so far, retain—huge swaths of territory including major cities and frighteningly large populations in Iraq and Syria, have moved it, with tremendous speed, from the margins to the center of what is happening in the Middle East. Selfless individual bravery and skilled tactical maneuvering in the field by IS fighters, as well as a willingness by IS to sustain the losses required for multifront operations against the militaries of Iraq and Syria, and other non-state actors in these two countries, show that IS is not just going to fade away. Support from Iran and the United States and their allies does little to help Iraq and Syria. Western media accounts of knock-out blows against individual IS leaders, or seizures of computers and financial records, are being countered with reports of new victories and further conquests.

Yet the grandiose declarations from IS spokesmen about bringing the jihad of Islam to Europe; the call to Muslims everywhere to recognize the IS caliph, Abu Bakr al-Baghdadi; and the professions of loyalty that come from Islamist groups scattered from Nigeria and Mali via Libya all the way to Afghanistan, tell us little about the ideological basis of the movement. What does IS want? How does it attract so many recruits, not just fifteen-year-old schoolgirls who think that by running away to Syria and marrying a jihadi they will help to bring on the kingdom of heaven and get into Jannah, or Paradise (literally "Garden" in Arabic), but also older men who learn successfully how to kill and find in themselves the willingness to die for their cause?

We may follow the media, and see them merely as mindless fanatics. We may condemn their destructiveness and under-the-counter sales of antiquities in terms that present them as little more than Mafiosi of Islam, engaged in a permanent Valentine's Day Massacre and a long-term and larger-scale attempt to emulate Al Capone (without the attentions of the IRS). But all that, while possibly satisfying an instinct for classification and a desire to minimize a threat, is no more than a substitute for analysis and understanding. Even the use of such labels as "Sunni extremists" tells us little—what makes these Sunni extremists so different from other Sunni extremists?

Similarly, but more frustratingly, Islamic State's own calls for a return to the purity of the original form of Islam offer little more than conventional generalizations that avoid the central issue. Hostility toward the West, revival of a caliphal institution, and re-version to the practices of early Islam are all in their different ways surface features, epiphenomena that do not tell us much about the ideology or the thinking of the leadership or about its intellectual foundations. If hostility toward the West is the common fodder of new political movements outside the West, that does not explain what this new caliphal institution is about; what specifically is the desired early form of Islam; or why the answers to these questions matter.

Why should this particular movement be taking this particular shape? Early Islam, like early Christianity, can be understood and presented in many different ways, and for many different purposes. Does IS represent just a personality split in the higher ranks of al-Qaida, or should we see in it, and in its remarkable success since that split, something more substantial? It would be worse than na-ïve to imagine that the soldiers and supporters of IS, both those who fight and kill and die for it and those who wave it on and give it money and other kinds of support and welcome its victories, all do so without some idea of what IS means and some inkling of why they wish it well. Journalistic scoops, such as interviews with IS jihadis or surreptitious visits to Mosul or other places under IS control, too, for all their impressionistic value (and the undoubted courage of the journalists involved), have little to offer by way of the documented analysis of IS ideology that we need.

This book is intended to fill that gap. It is not aimed at recording outrages and horror—if it were it would be out of date long before it appeared in print. Nor is it aimed at documenting battles. Apart from serving those who find battle descriptions absorbing, or giving a Muslim aspect to what the late Sir John Keegan memorably labeled the "face of battle," that would do little to help us understand IS itself and the ideology that drives it as a movement. Further, we probably are not yet in a position, if we ever will be, to gather the testimonies and other materials necessary for such documentation. Nor is this book directly concerned with IS successes on the ground and the advance and retreat of IS control in vast areas of the Middle East. These are, at base, what make IS matter and what call for this writing, but in themselves they do little to help us understand IS. Nor again is it, except tangentially, concerned with the to and fro of political discussion about how to "deal with" IS. Internal successes and failures in the region, together with the influence of external interests, mean that study of such discussion is essentially about the interplay of Western, non-Islamic, and Islamic diplomatic activity rather than about IS itself, and so is far from the subject of this book.

Nor, finally, do I aim, at least not primarily, at recommending policy and military or political strategy. That does not mean that I avoid suggestions for action. But my main aim is knowledge and understanding, not advocacy and prediction. IS has clear ambitions and a patent strategy. These rest on a coherent ideology. Nothing about these is hidden or secret, though they are not as simple or as obvious as might be thought. The clues lie open to sight, scattered over the actions—not so much the horrific killings of propaganda purpose but quieter, more day-to-day activities that tend not to attract the camera—and the writings and sayings of its leaders. These can be put together to give us an understanding of what IS is about. Only with an informed understanding of what their ideology is, of why IS is what it is, of how it differs from other such groups, and of what makes it act as it does, can we move on to the vital next stage of thinking about how to contain and defeat it.

Old and New

All of this means that this book may to some wear an odd appearance. Its subject is the world of today, yet its author is a medievalist. It is about the twenty-first century, yet much in it is concerned with the seventh century and the Middle Ages. It is about warfare and political struggle, yet much in it looks at religion and matters of faith.

Two interrelated features of the pages that follow should stand out. The first is a heavy concentration on matters of religion; the second, not unconnected with the first, is a degree of dependence on pre-modern sources that may surprise in a work dealing with problems of the twenty-first century. As to religion and IS, the need for such concentration may appear so obvious as not to need remark. But it calls for explanation, for two reasons. First, IS and its followers take their religion, Islam, seriously. IS is not only a military-political but also, and primarily, a religious movement, so the involvement of religion in its identity and military-political activity calls for recognition. In one sense, religion can be viewed as a form of escapism. It offers a comfort zone into which the believer, or even one who is just a formal adherent of the faith, can withdraw to avoid the rough realities of the world outside—a world dominated by non-Islam. At the same time, religion functions as one element of the way in which the world works. That is, along with other forms of belief and action, religion underlies and helps to form what actually happens. That is not escapism.

Secondly, here in the United States we are historically and educationally so used to imagining (some might say conditioned to imagining) that there is a separation or firewall between religion and the public sphere, especially politics, that we also very often tend to imagine that such a division not only should exist but does exist, almost as a fact of nature, everywhere and at all times. Things, as they say, ain't necessarily so. What has happened is the opposite, not only in the developing world: a resurgence of Islam has gone more or less in parallel with a resurgence of Christianity, not least in the United States (and the former USSR); of Judaism in Israel (with lesser revivals in the United States and France); and more recently, of Hinduism in India.[1]

In the United States, of course, religion impinges on politics and the public sphere all the time, from quarrels and court cases about reciting the words "under God" in our schools or stamping "In God we trust" on our banknotes and coins to major election issues like whether abortion constitutes the killing of a human being for people who do not accept Roman Catholic teachings about the moment when life begins.

For Muslims—at least for many Muslims, and especially in the Middle East—the division that Americans try to cling to is inconceivable, and close to unacceptable too. Ideology, or what people think and how that helps to form their political attitudes and behavior, matters. It is convenient for many of us to imagine that we have no ideology, that we simply are and act without the straitjacket of some outside system of thought. But all of us, with or without a deliberate, self-conscious submission to such a system, do operate according to some thoughts, and when we put those thoughts together they constitute a form of ideology. For some, that ideology is clearer than others. And for many, religion is that system of thought.

Even in these post–Cold War, post-ideological days, ideology matters. In the form of religion, ideology matters far more in the modern world than we seem to want to imagine. A generation or so ago, when I was a student, standard teaching informed us that, just as religion was fading away in the modern West, so it was just a matter of time until it did the same elsewhere, in the benighted regions where it still held sway. The Islamic world in particular, thus the theory, would soon enjoy the blessings of freedom from the constrictions imposed by irrational faith and soar to the enlightened heaven of secularism brought by modernity and Westernization.

Things have not worked out that way. Nearly thirty years ago, the scholar of Islam William Shepard published a famous article in which he discussed the notion of "Islamic fundamentalism."[2] The central message of that article, and of studies by other writers— a message that makes for uncomfortable reading today—is that religion in the Islamic world is not like religion in the West. For Muslims, religion is not just for Fridays and attendance at the mosque. It applies to and finds its way into very many aspects of the daily life and activity of Muslims, from food and drink taboos through women's (and girls') attire to sexual attitudes and behavior. One feature that is of special importance here is the Quran. The holy book of Islam is not just a parallel to the Bible of Jews and Christians. Since the Enlightenment, many Christians and Jews have learned to see their holy writ as not true in the most literal sense in every detail. Discoveries of buried literary records of ancient civilizations, as well as modern scholarly research, have taught us that the stories of creation and the flood, along with the tales of the patriarchs, of Joseph and his brothers, and much else, can be looked at as metaphors, as beautiful and impressive narratives that have much to offer human understanding. But we no longer feel the same obligation to believe in their literal truth that our great-grandparents and their great-grandparents felt. This process has been helped, or made less difficult, for us because, whatever dogma tells us either about the truth of these texts or about the inspiration behind their composition, we are not compelled by traditional teachings to believe that they are God's literal speech. Consequently, as belief in the literal truth of the contents of Scripture has faded, other central aspects of Christian or Jewish faith have remained vibrant. It is perfectly possible to be a good Jew or Christian without feeling obliged to accept or assert that every word of the Bible is true. Fringe groups and sects who make such claims are just that, fringe groups.

For Muslims, by contrast, the Quran is the literal speech of God, delivered to mankind by Muhammad with the mediation of Gabriel. That is the dogma about the holy book of Islam. This brings with it other implications: God cannot lie; so the contents of the Quran must be true. Questions about the patriarchal narratives, about Abraham and Joseph, Isaac and Jonah and the rest, about creation, about the age of the Earth and about evolution, in consequence encounter different reactions among Muslims.[3]

Islamic Practice

The Islamic world remains far more religious than the vast majority of Western countries. This is confirmed not only by the surface impression conveyed through television and other media. Surveys carried out by such bodies as the Pew Research Center's Forum on Religion and Public Life tell us that Muslims everywhere are far more observant of their religious obligations than others; they are far more supportive of or acquiescent in the different ways in which religion is present and significant in their societies—most importantly in terms of law; and to a degree that is often insufficiently understood, they retain belief in and acceptance of the truth of the sacred text of their faith. Naturally there are great variations from country to country—Islamic territories emerging from communism tend, not surprisingly, to have lower levels of belief and practice—and generationally too, but overall Muslims remain closer to their faith than many non-Muslims.[4]

Islam lays greater obligations of religious practice on its faithful than does Christianity. The Quran tells us (*sura* 2:286) that God "does not burden a soul with more than it can bear," but Islam still loads more duties on its faithful than do other faiths. Partly for that reason, religion is more present and pervasive in Islamic contexts than in Western, Christian ones. The call of the muezzin goes out five times a day from the minarets that dot cities, towns, and villages in the Islamic world, reaching all ears nowadays thanks to loudspeakers that were unavailable to earlier generations.[5] In response Muslims can be seen everywhere downing tools and spreading a prayer mat unself-consciously in order to fulfill the duty of prayer. Daily prayers and fasting during Ramadan, with a joyful celebration as the fast is broken each nightfall, both typically take public form and not only draw people in but also discourage non-participation.[6]

Survey results show that Muslims pray and fast in huge numbers.[7] Figures for those attending mosque at least once a week vary considerably. In the ex-communist states attendance rarely reaches as high as 30 percent (the proportion for Bosnia-Herzegovina, part of the former Yugoslavia) and can go as low as 1 percent (in Azerbaijan).[8] The degree of communist repression of religion seems to play a role here. Sub-Saharan Africa, by contrast, has extremely high mosque attendance, running from 65 percent in Senegal right up to 100 percent in Ghana, while in the Middle East and South and Southeast Asia the figures run between 35 percent (in Lebanon, which has a mixed Christian-Muslim population) to a high of some 72 percent in Indonesia. Outside the ex-communist countries, tradition has kept Islam durable and resistant to change.

Muslims also pray outside of the mosque: in twenty-seven of the thirty-nine countries surveyed by the Pew Report, 50 percent or more of the population reported that they prayed once or more a day; not surprisingly, seven of the remaining twelve were countries emerging from communism.[9]

The Quran

The Quran is a constant presence for Muslims. They read or listen to passages of the Quran to a degree that puts most Christians and Jews and their acquaintance with their holy texts to shame. In the Arab world, roughly half the population read or hear the Quran every day; almost no one claims never to read it. In other parts of the Islamic world too, where Arabic, the language of the Quran, is not widely known, very high percentages of the population enjoy the Quran on a near-daily basis. Many TV stations, accessible via the Internet, offer a nonstop diet of the Quran. Even in such ex-communist countries as Kazakhstan and Uzbekistan, more than half the population still claims to read the Quran daily or occasionally.[10]

Frequent and deep contact with the Quran, through reading, via the radio and the Internet, and in sermons, marches with respect for its status, admiration of its style, and knowledge of its contents to make it a much more influential work among Muslims than the Bible is for most Christians and Jews. It is common to find Quran verses, often in beautiful calligraphy, displayed in people's houses all over the Islamic world. Among the territories surveyed by Pew, only in Albania was the figure for this kind of display as low as 18 percent. Kosovo, next door to Albania and ethnically largely Albanian but formerly part of Yugoslavia, was the next lowest, but it had nearly twice as high a percentage of people with such verses on display, at 34 percent. Albania's relatively low figure can be explained as a product of the fierce hostility to religion of the former communist regime. Meanwhile in other countries the figures rise from 42 percent in Kazakhstan and 49 percent in Kyrgyzstan (both ex-communist states) to as high as 95 percent in the Muslim-majority provinces of Thailand, and 96 percent in Morocco.[11] Whether or not the Arabic in such texts can be read and understood by those who put them on their walls, their very presence indicates something about the status of the Quran and of the faith that it represents for the faithful.[12]

Fasting

Placing a picture of a religious text on the wall is an essentially passive religious act. Fasting is extremely active. Ramadan requires the believer to refrain from food, drink, and sexual activity during daylight hours for an entire month. The fasting month, which can fall during the heat of the summer, is observed to a remarkable degree: in all countries covered by the Pew survey, astonishingly high percentages reported fasting. Even in ex-communist Albania, where religious belief and observance are otherwise low, 44 percent of Muslims fast during Ramadan. In sub-Saharan Africa percentages are far higher, ranging between 85 and 100, except in the Democratic Republic of Congo, where only 69 percent fast. But 69 percent is still more than two out of three people in the population. Elsewhere, percentages are similar: Thailand, Indonesia, and Malaysia offer near total observance; South Asia has observance rates in the 90 percent and greater range; and the Middle East and North Africa have rates between 86 percent and near totality.[13] Social and other pressures to conform prevent people from breaking the fast too early or from failing to fast at all. IS tries to compel observance of the fast, with punishments for those found to be breaking the rules.[14]

Sharia Law

Religious law—sharia—is reflected in the laws of many Islamic countries. Saudi Arabia proclaims that the Quran is its constitution.[15] Political arguments over the potential implementation of sharia law represent daily reality in many countries. In some this daily reality is not just a matter of political arguments but also translates into practice: in Qatar, for example, a report of a rape recently led to the complainant being charged with adultery, that is, engaging in sexual activity outside marriage.[16] One Pew survey, conducted in the spring of 2015, asked 10,194 respondents in ten countries (including the Palestinian territories): How much should the Quran influence our country's laws? It found that in "Pakistan, the Palestinian territories, Jordan, Malaysia and Senegal, roughly half or more of the full population says that laws in their country should strictly follow the teachings of the Quran. By contrast, in Burkina Faso, Turkey, Lebanon and Indonesia," all countries with either a large proportion of non-Muslims or, as in Turkey, a strong secular tradition, "less than a quarter agree." Four of these countries, Indonesia, Pakistan, Nigeria, and Turkey, are among the ten countries with the largest Muslim populations in the world.[17]

A Contrast with the West

The penetration of religion in the Islamic world today offers an instructive contrast with the West: in England and Wales, according to very recent reports, the number of people claiming that they have no religion at all is almost as large as all the rest put together. In 2014, 48.5 percent claimed no religion, a level that had almost doubled from as recently as 2011. All denominations of Christians together amounted to a mere 43.8 percent of the population.[18] In the United States figures for believers are higher, and their influence in such areas as education and law reform correspondingly greater, but irreligion is on the rise, and the constitutional separation of church and state in the United States, as in France, places real limits on the ability of believers of specific faiths to impose their beliefs on those of other faiths or none.[19] Religion is far less visible in all Western states than in Islamic ones. Belief in the literal truth of the Scriptures in the West is a fringe phenomenon, and even if the fringe occasionally manages to impose its will, as in Texas school textbooks, it remains a fringe.

The Islamic world is very different. The Pew results may be somewhat skewed in that respondents to their surveys may be disproportionately reluctant or afraid to admit to a lack of faith or to rejecting religious belief, but secularism, whether in keeping with the U.S. and French pattern or at a theoretical level, is absent or invisible virtually everywhere. Such skewing, in any case, is probably swallowed up in the huge number, occasionally over thirty thousand individuals, of the respondents to many of their surveys. Even in Turkey, whose constitution has since the birth of the modern republic asserted its secular character, and where opposition to making sharia the law of the land is much stronger than elsewhere in the heartlands of Islam, the current government is dragging society ever further away from no-religion toward the public recognition and practice of Islam.[20] Other countries, lacking the secular legacy of Turkey's founder Mustafa Atatürk, go much further still.

Commitment to religion, the continuing strength of faith and belief in the truth of the texts, and the penetration of religious practice and activity throughout society and into every corner of the individual's life are documented and corroborated by these surveys. Their findings are not random, nor are they cherry-picked from a mass of different or one-sided polls. As a "nonpartisan fact tank," the Pew Research Center has been conducting such surveys for more than a quarter century all over the world and justly enjoys respect for the independence, thoroughness, transparency, and reliability of its work. Its results confirm and point to one important difference between the Islamic world and the West. That difference, the role of religion and its vastly greater strength, matters because of the age-old link between Islam and politics. Just as religion can easily be politics for Muslims, so politics can easily be religion.

Religion, in this case Islam, makes promises that dwarf anything ideologies or states can offer: Paradise, filled with delights, many of them otherwise unavailable to the faithful Muslim—not just beautiful and well-watered gardens (particularly attractive in a desert environment), but also drink galore and women, perpetually virgin, in abundance—and everything for all eternity.[21] To those for whom Paradise is a metaphor or, worse, just a story, all this means little. Few among us in the West spend our time considering how we will spend the afterlife. (A billboard on a highway not far from Nashville, where I live, presses on passing drivers the message: If you died today, where would you spend eternity?) But for the believing Muslim Paradise is a reality, and every detail is founded in the Quran, where what is on offer is frequently made explicit. "Surely for the godfearing awaits a place of security, gardens and vineyards and maidens with swelling breasts, like of age, and a cup overflowing" (*sura* 78:31–34); "for God's sincere servants—for them awaits a known provision, fruits—and they high-honored in the Garden of Bliss upon couches, set face to face, a cup from a spring being passed round to them, white, a delight to the drinkers, wherein no sickness is, neither intoxication; and with them wide-eyed maidens restraining their glances as if they were hidden pearls" (*sura* 37:40–49); "Give good tidings to those who believe and do deeds of righteousness, that for them await gardens underneath which rivers flow; whenever they are provided with fruits therefrom they shall say, 'This is what we were provided with before'; and they shall be given the likeness thereof; and they shall have spouses purified; therein they shall dwell forever" (*sura* 2:25). For believing Muslims, such images are very real and compelling.

The Presence of the Past

The second feature of this book that will be strange for many readers expecting to learn about a major world issue of today flows from the first. It is the presence in it of so much that is very emphatically not of today. If the exploration of an important contemporary religious-political phenomenon is necessarily a kind of maze—one with no Ariadne's thread and possibly no real center—then it is equally true that, at least for this particular phenomenon, much of our evidence lies not in the horrors of IS killings and destruction themselves, but in the materials that we have to search to find their explanations. These reside, for the most part, far in the distant past, in the history of the first few centuries and the early development of Islam.

The past helps to form our present, and, as we are so often reminded, ignorance, bias, loyalty to lost causes, partial knowledge, as well as concern with current politics and the getting of votes all feed heavily into how that present is formed. Long ago now, in the middle of the twentieth century, the English novelist L. P. Hartley wrote that "the past is a foreign country: they do things differently there." If the past matters to us, then we should not underestimate its significance and relevance for the lives and actions of today's Muslims, for whom the distant past of the seventh century and the Crusades lives and remains meaningful in a way that most

Westerners find difficult to understand. What is true of Muslims in general applies with particular force to the followers of IS.

Our understanding of the thinking of IS derives necessarily from the documents, in a broad sense, that it has produced and that we can read and view. But we can understand these aright only if, first, we understand that they accept them sincerely. It is all too easy to suppose that the leaders and adherents of IS are as hypocritical and insincere about their ideology as the leaders of the Soviet Union were about their ideology as they approached the year 1989. But everything suggests that the opposite is the case. The evidence we have compels belief in their sincerity. This applies not only to the seemingly unlimited supply of volunteers for suicide missions but right across the wide range of those involved with IS. And secondly, and as a consequence of this, we can understand these documents only through the prism of the materials that underlie them.

The Islamic State draws us back deep into the past. If we want to comprehend the Islamic State, to understand why its followers are attracted to it and act the way they do, and where they find the sources for their thinking, then we need to follow it to its roots. Those roots are woven into the very fabric of Islam. Some of them go back to the beginnings, with Muhammad himself and the Quran; others accompany the history of Islam and of the Muslims down through the centuries. Seeking the roots of IS thus requires a journey through Islamic history, a Sherlock Holmes–like exploration of the religious and political past of the Middle East. It introduces us to a cast of characters largely unknown in the West, to patterns of belief and practice that remain alien to most Westerners, to legal ideas and norms that differ radically from our own, and to ways of reporting and talking about all this that are completely different from anything that we know in the West. Much in it appears medieval—because it is. Much about the behavior and ambition of IS followers has been consciously and deliberately modeled after the medieval past, and so offers a constant reminder that, at least for them, the past is not dead and forgotten but instead lives and is with us still.

Understanding IS is therefore a matter of exploration and reconstruction. We need to try to get behind the violent rhetoric and

the apparently casual bloodshed, not just to the textual sources that
influence IS and its followers but also to the tradition and the history that make those sources appealing and real to them, far more
real than the sources of the Judeo-Christian traditions are to most
of their followers today in the West. The Quran and other works
reaching back over a thousand years are mentioned here because
they have a living relevance to what is happening today. Even if
modern jihadists and others gain access to such texts via modern
renderings and modern readings, as they sometimes do, their contents come directly from the ancient sources. The written Arabic of
the Quran is essentially the same language as that of today's Arabic
newspapers, and modern media have made it and countless other
early and later texts easily available, literally at the press of a but-
ton, to the faithful. Linguistically and in practical terms, then, all
those sources are as accessible to modern Arab Muslims as today's
newspaper, and because of their antiquity many of them carry
more authority than yesterday's papers. To pretend otherwise is
willfully to ignore the religious and the political reality of the
world of Islam. To understand what such movements as the Islamic
State are saying and thinking, and why, then, requires us to use the
same access to those same sources.

This book is not, nonetheless, about Islam as such. It is about a
specific form of Islamic apocalyptic messianism and how it operates in the world today. This may appear to give this project a narrow focus. It describes no real battles, reveals no exciting details of
drone strikes taking out IS leaders or CIA accountants taking apart
their financial networks. There are no interviews with repentant
volunteers or families of dead followers of the cause.[22] There is no
analysis of battlefield successes and failures, no catalog of the endless supplies of U.S. war matériel that have fallen into IS hands, or
of the ways in which their middlemen (and those of others) shift
tens of millions of dollars' worth of oil daily onto the world markets or destroy the world's cultural heritage.

All of this is out there, and it makes for racy reading. Some of
it also helps, no doubt, to explain parts of what IS is about. But it
would be a mistake, I submit, to think that the narrowness of focus
here is an error. It is deliberate, and it has a purpose. Most members of IS and adherents and supporters of it as a cause probably

know as little about the details of its ideology's history as Roman Catholics, say, know about the doctrine of the Immaculate Conception. They probably care as little too. Like most combatants in most armies, of all stripes, ancient and modern, east and West, they are foot soldiers in what is sometimes a great enterprise, sometimes not so great, sometimes not so easy to categorize. They obey orders, because that is what soldiers do, or accept instruction, because that is what believers do.

This does not mean that the ideology is irrelevant. Quite the contrary. In the first place, for many, those outside the actual theater in the Middle East, it is possible simply to turn away—though how possible, how easy, is not as clear as one might think. Secondly, though, a glance at almost any of the great struggles of history demonstrates the varying ways in which ideology is important. This is not, probably, one of the great struggles of history, but the issues, and the attitudes and beliefs of those involved and attracted by it, are not on that account wholly different, not least because for one side this is precisely the great, final struggle of humanity. In particular, the central issue here can look like an example, the ultimate example, of the great struggle between east and West, in its latest major incarnation, the fourteen-century-long struggle between Islam and Christianity. One does not need to be a believer in Samuel P. Huntington's notion of a clash of civilizations—I am not—to see in what is happening an example, a version, of just such a struggle.[23]

Events move quickly in the Middle East. The Arab Spring began as recently as the end of 2010, but that seems definitively dead and buried by now. The events of 9/11, too, which are indelibly associated with the Middle East, took place fairly recently, in 2001— when next year's college students were being conceived and born. Syria collapsed into horrifying anarchy—five million displaced as I write, and the number continues to rise—after the Arab Spring began to fade. The Islamic State came into being more recently still—the formal declaration of the state under the name Islamic State occurred on June 29, 2014. Its successes and its advances on the ground are changing the map of the Middle East, quite literally, and, even if we can be confident that IS will be defeated, we cannot be sure how long victory will take or what the result will look like.

Change in the Middle East is rapid and deep partly because the region has been frozen politically for decades: at the time of the Six-Day War in 1967, Arab dictators and military coups seemed to be coming and going like next year's fashions. But in fact those who came to power around that time showed a remarkable resilience and staying power: in Syria the Asad family; in Iraq the group of revolutionaries around Saddam Hussein; in Libya Muammar al-Gaddafi; even in Egypt where Nasser was succeeded by one of his old revolutionary friends who was then assassinated for signing a peace treaty with Israel but was replaced very smoothly by another army colleague. All of these states, and others, actually displayed a high degree of political stability over some four decades. The price of that stability was, of course, dictatorship and repression, allied to massive corruption and associated economic and social underdevelopment, together with, at least in Libya, but with Iraq and Syria following behind, such ideological and cultural embarrassments as Gaddafi's *Green Book* and his Third International Theory.

The self-immolation of Mohamed Bouazizi in a small Tunisian town at the end of 2010 blew the top off the accumulated tensions. One after the other, Arab (and not just Arab) countries felt the effects of the new sensation of freedom that spread through the region. Very quickly, and not just because of the time of year when it got going, the movement acquired the name of Arab Spring, echoing and paying tribute to those springs elsewhere—the Springtime of Nations in 1848, the Prague Spring above all. And not coincidentally, it looked very much as though what was on the horizon, what was in the minds of the Arabs in the streets, was a set of societies governed according to the principles of liberal democracy. The Western model, which seemed to have been adopted by the communist bloc countries after 1989, appeared to be spreading to the one area of the world where major political reform was still awaited.

Where is the starting point of IS? Does it have some connection to the failure of the Arab Spring? For some in IS itself the beginning lies in the seventh century, when Muhammad received his revelations and brought Islam to mankind. But IS as a movement has its own beginnings, and they are amazingly recent. One of the most shocking features of IS is how young it is, and how rapidly its successes have been won. The obvious comparison for many is indeed with the Prophet Muhammad himself and his successors who in a single generation carved out an empire in the Middle East and beyond, one that was far larger than Alexander's and whose effects—the world of Islam—are with us to this day.

The real comparisons, however, lie closer to home, with al-Qaida and its peers. IS is different from all of them both in degree and in kind. It is far more extreme; and it pursues a different set of agenda: an Islamic state is not the same as what al-Qaida is aiming for. And despite its terrorist means, al-Qaida has proven itself to be less extreme an organization than IS.

IS is not unique. Its methods and especially its preference for extreme violence and terror as a tool have plenty of parallels; they make it stand out not least because IS has proven adept at using modern media to amplify their impact. More importantly, IS is not unique in the basic message that it seeks to get across. Dissatisfaction with current rulers; hostility to these rulers' cooperation with non-Muslim, Western, Christian powers; anti-Jewish or anti-Israeli rhetoric; opposition to other—especially Shi'i—versions of Islam; the desire to find a solution in a return to what it sees as the earliest and therefore best form of Islam: all of this has antecedents too. Even the use of violence to spread this kind of message is not new. In modern times, the most dramatic example is offered by the stunning takeover of the Grand Mosque in Mecca, the very heart of Islam, on November 20, 1979 (the first day of the Islamic year 1400) by Juhayman al-Otaybi. He apparently not only called for the overthrow of the Saudi ruling dynasty but also, more significantly, proclaimed the advent of a Mahdi.[24]

The writings attributed to Juhayman are of little help here. He himself is said to have been illiterate (possibly as a hint at a parallel with the Prophet?), but he had spent nearly two decades in the Saudi National Guard, and after that attended university lectures on Islamic religious topics in the country, so we should be hesitant about accepting this. The texts themselves show a wide-ranging acquaintance with the Quran, with hadith (traditions of the Prophet) and other religious literature, though they do not reveal very much originality of thought or novelty of ideas, in particular about the question of a Mahdi.[25] Nevertheless, though the claim is not sufficiently clear or confirmed, it was widely reported that he called for pledging of allegiance to his brother-in-law, Muhammad Abdallah al-Qahtani, as Mahdi, and the claim that he did so, and the apparent absence of any obvious reason to invent this specific charge, seems weighty in itself. It represents another step on the path toward what we have in IS.

To some, seeing IS actions as essentially a repetition or imitation of what the Prophet Muhammad and his Companions got up to in the seventh century may make it all look a little like a summer recreation popular in the United States and Europe—a reenactment. People love to dress up in medieval costumes and reenact great events. Something similar occurs also in the more serious scenes every year in various cities around Europe, when Jesus's final steps to the crucifixion are reenacted by the faithful as part of the Easter celebrations. The decennial Oberammergau play that acquired some notoriety in the 1960s and 1970s exemplifies this too. Both Easter commemorations and modern reenactments contain elements that parallel what is occurring here: in each the memory of what has happened in the past is perpetuated; in each that memory serves to strengthen a collective identity formed in large part by the events thus re-created; and in each what happened in the past offers a model for what is happening today and an inspiration for the future.

What IS is doing has roots in the past; it copies what was done in the past; it gains its justification from the past; and IS and its followers derive strength from such copying of that past. But this is not entertainment; it is not a way to fill a summer afternoon; it is not a replay of a religious event. At the same time it is a religious event; and it is modeled, very self-consciously, on things of great religious significance that happened in the past, in the lifetime and career of the Prophet, as part of his career. Repeating his actions, for the same purposes as his and under similar circumstances, validates both the actions of today and those who perform them. We should not make the easy mistake of simply ascribing everything that IS does to a love of violence, or a criminal indifference to rules. Here as elsewhere, IS is following rules, not making them; obeying standards, not ignoring them; and trying through such actions not to reenact, but to re-create a distant but ever-relevant past.

It is a curious paradox that a message that the end of the world is nigh succeeds mightily, yet fails to deliver, with the result, just as in Christianity, that measures need to be taken on one hand to explain or put off the end of the world scenario and on the other to make practical arrangements for the world for the time between the death of the founder and the arrival of the end, now far off in an indefinite future. Early Islam, like early Christianity, made its accommodation with reality, but here and there sects and other groups arose that rejected this accommodationism and sought to hasten the arrival of the Kingdom. The Islamic State joins a long tradition.

A related paradox is that the arrangements that are thus made almost of necessity bear little relation to what the founder decreed. The caliphate itself, that central and for Muslims so important institution, is born entirely out of the death of the founder. He never gave a thought, so far as we can see, to what might happen after his death—he did not imagine that there would be any need for such arrangements.

These—postponement of the end of the world and the resulting need for the institution of political arrangements—belong of their essence to a post-Muhammad time. They are both central to what happened in the years of conquest after 632. They were necessary features of the scene, but they were born of that scene. Neither was necessary or even, in some sense, conceivable, before 632, the caliphate especially. After 632 both were necessary.

The conquests themselves constitute a still more curious paradox. The Islam of Muhammad is an Arab affair, addressed to Arabs, just as Judaism was for Jews. The conquests were a post-Muhammad affair. Whatever their ex post facto explanation and justification, whatever the contribution of Islam to their success, they belong to the period after Muhammad and are not in themselves intrinsic to the message of Islam. Conquest, and together with it bringing Islam (and in its wake conversion) to others was emphatically not part of Muhammad's life or career. It would have been odd—other than in later Islamic salvationist rhetoric—if it were otherwise.

Alongside these paradoxes, two great illusions or misconceptions govern Western approaches to IS and its congeners in extremist Islamism. The first is that expressed by such Western outsiders to Islam as President George W. Bush and President Barack Obama: that IS and al-Qaida and others are somehow not Islamic, that their actions do not represent Islam, that the problem the West faces in these and other movements and their supporters is not inherent in Islam but concerns a ragbag collection of criminals and misfits who are misusing the name of a great civilization to attain their evil ends.[26] Few take such viewpoints seriously, but all seem to feel it necessary to mouth them ritualistically after every new terrorist outrage. Associated with these are sundry Muslims, scholars and others, who carefully analyze the actions and claims of the IS and others and show to their own satisfaction that they do not conform to the definitions of Islam and its beliefs that are accepted by these scholars.

The claims and assertions of both these sets of pundits have their strengths—they are highly attractive to their respective constituencies and their use provides a remarkable degree of feel-good self-satisfaction to all concerned. There are others, too, who for a variety of reasons lean toward acceptance of these points of view.

A second illusion is that put forward by those who ask—and often answer—the question what the West can do to deal with IS and its like. Here the problem, or the illusion, is the notion that what IS represents actually can be dealt with as other anti-Western, anti-American, anti-imperialist, or anti-fill-in-your-own-choice-here movements were dealt with in the past. The illusion in this case is self-serving for those who propound it because they are usually either mouthpieces for the military-political-economic complex that thrives on such activity, or elements of the chattering classes that live by discussing it.

Neither illusion gets us very far in understanding IS itself. In fact, it may well be that IS cannot be dealt with as effectively as we should like using conventional means. This is not a call for some superlative American Sniper, James Bond, or pre–World War I hero figure who would simply take out the leader of the movement and thus bring it all crashing to the ground. Assassination by drone has demonstrated both the potential and the limitations of such an approach.[27] It is, rather, a call for recognition that IS and what it represents are different from such other movements as the Vietnamese resistance, or the Algerian revolution, and that dealing with it may not be as easy as we imagine. IS may be with us for some time.

Sources

The Islamic State is not hermetically sealed. Because IS does not enjoy international recognition, border posts on the edges of the Islamic State exist only at places that happen to coincide with the international frontiers of Iraq and Syria (though not, of course, on IS-controlled territory between those two countries). People can and do go in and out. Volunteers for the holy war as well as some aid workers and the occasional intrepid journalist go in. Some of them make it back out. More locally, truck drivers and others make the journey across the line in both directions with some ease, bringing needed imports. Oil tankers cross the lines in the direction of Turkey. The frontier itself is not formalized or guarded along all its length, and military and related types of personnel cross it less visibly too, in both directions.

The relative openness and porousness of IS borders mean that our knowledge of what goes on inside IS is not dependent wholly on the Internet videos so plentifully produced for foreign consumption. During the last couple of years, a wide variety of documents from inside the Islamic State have become available. A number of them have been collected, analyzed, studied and summarized, translated in part or in full, and put up (some of them in the original Arabic too) on the Web, especially by Aymenn Jawad al-Tamimi, a student at Oxford University.[28] (Doubt has been cast on al-Tamimi's credibility and detachment because some of his posts appear to show him uncomfortably close to his IS sources, but the reliability of the material that he has put up on the Web seems to be unaffected by any such worries.)[29]

The Tamimi documents are in several collections. The largest of these, referred to here as the "Archive," contained by the end of 2015 some 301 documents.[30] They are a magnificent jumble, with official responses to questions about the legality of foosball mixed in with electric bills and texts of congregational prayers, and forms for registering oneself as a descendant of the Prophet appearing alongside receipts for oil and gas. Although they come from all over the lands of IS, there is a certain concentration on the province of Deir al-Zor, in northeastern Syria, as well as Mosul, in Iraq. This may suggest that Tamimi has particularly good connections in that area, but such an emphasis appears unlikely to have any special effect on the overall picture that the documents give. (There seem also to be a surprising number related to motorcycles—could this, too, offer a hint about his sources?)

Tamimi's documents and others give us considerable insight into everyday activities in IS territory and in consequence make it possible to know and, more importantly, understand many different aspects of daily life under IS rule. For those with both interest and experience in the history of the Middle East, the obvious parallel is with the Cairo Geniza, that vast medieval accumulation of the waste paper of centuries discovered at the end of the nineteenth century and still revealing its treasures, from receipts and laundry lists to drafts of petitions to the government and autographs of Maimonides.[31] These modern collections will be cited often in this book.[32]

Such documents inevitably raise important questions. How far can we rely on materials like these? Do they really emanate from IS? Are they genuine (not necessarily the same thing)? Or are they perhaps part of an elaborate scheme of disinformation, designed to give us a false picture? Are some authentic and others fake? Do some of them perhaps reflect black propaganda and come from enemies of IS, such as secret services operating on behalf of Western states? Do they retail only individual experiences or are they evidence of the more general way of life under IS rule in its vast territories?

Most of Tamimi's texts are printed documents, but occasionally they are handwritten. These raise particular problems of authenticity, for while printed documents exist in many copies, handwritten ones by their nature are individual, unique items. One such is Archive, Specimen 11E, apparently from early 2014. In this document, Omar al-Shishani, IS "General Military Commander, Northern Region," gives "the brother" Abu al-Layth al-Ansari the charge of a town on the border, instructing him to fortify and defend it.[33] How did Tamimi come by this letter? What happened to the piece of paper between the time it reached Abu al-Layth al-Ansari and the time it reached Tamimi (or his source)? Why was it not retained by al-Ansari, or destroyed? Are we to suppose that it was simply discarded and taken from an IS trash bin by someone who transmitted it to one of Tamimi's contacts? Who might have had such access? And who, having such access, would think it worth the heavy risk involved? It is hard, even impossible, to answer these and other such questions with confidence, and any answer we give concerning one may not be applicable for others. As with many of the printed texts that we have, although the investment in forging such documents seems higher than any potential gain, in the current conditions it is also hard to discern the significance of local and passing concerns that could motivate forgery.

Our knowledge of IS is of many different types and comes from or through many different sources. Apart from texts and videos emanating from IS itself, with the limitations and cautions mentioned above, we have material from governments, especially those of the United States and United Kingdom, and international organizations that are often but not always related to the United Nations. Mainstream media offer a good deal of information, too, though the pressure to provide a constant stream of sensational news often eclipses the drive to offer solid facts and helpful context.[34] Al-Hayat media center, the media outlet of IS, is another such source.[35] Neither fully part of the media nor fully part of IS, it occupies a gray zone between the two. In this sense, its products—not least among them *Dabiq*, the English-language Web magazine—are among the most primary of the materials that we have. Other documents in Arabic—for example concerning the status and lives of Christians under IS rule—have surfaced on the Web one way and another, and these too have been used, always with due caution as to their authenticity.

Some documents have been made available in English translation by various research organizations in the West. One important document of this type, entitled "Women of the Islamic State," was put out apparently by "women of the al-Khansa Brigade." Here we face complicated questions of authenticity: is this genuine? Does it come from inside the IS? If so, then, despite what it claims for itself, does it represent official IS thinking? Does it perhaps reflect such thinking but in a very unofficial or semi-official manner? Or is it no more than a production of some women who want to do their bit to help the movement, without official backing or support or even perhaps awareness of their action? If this last suggestion seems inherently unlikely, the others are not and they constitute a wide range of possibilities. Should we view the document as an attempt to present the situation of women in the Islamic State in a way that might prove attractive to potential recruits? Does it offer simply an ideal vision or does it reflect daily reality? Some of these questions can be answered on the basis of the documents and journalistic reports that we have, but the most fundamental questions, about authorship and background, must remain—for the moment at least—unanswered.

Similar problems attend "A Brief Guide to the Islamic State (2015)," by Abu Rumaysah al Britani ("the Briton"). Here the question of authenticity crops up again: is this a genuine piece of IS propaganda? Does it come from inside the Islamic State or from outside? Is it written by a sympathizer or does it represent some sort of official IS marketing ploy? With sections looking at food, weather, transport, and technology inside IS, the little pamphlet does not offer heavy reading, ideologically or in other ways, and it does not seem likely to attract many to vacation in the Islamic State. Like the text on women, it illustrates well the difficulties involved in assessing material claiming to come from IS. Unlike with them, however, we seem to have some additional information about the author. "Abu Rumaysah al-Britani," Abu Rumaysah the Briton, is also the name adopted by Siddharta Dhar, a Hindu from Walthamstow, in east London, who ran a business renting out "bouncy castles" before converting to Islam and jumping bail to flee the United Kingdom. Early in 2016, in a video released by IS, Dhar was identified as the probable killer of five alleged spies.[36]

The great bulk of the modern sources used here—paper, on-line videos, other online resources such as *Dabiq*, paper materials uploaded to the Web—come from within the Islamic State itself. From outside, journalism covers a wide range: some of it comes from traditional sources such as the *New York Times* and other major international newspapers and broadcasters like the BBC.[37] But the Web is now the home of a vast array of other types of journalism. Here, in the face of masses of material, some of it leaning in an assortment of ideological directions, I have tried to be selective, and in general I have not relied on such materials unless they can be confirmed from more traditional sources. Even though we often find as many as a dozen or a hundred or more reports on the Web dealing with a single event or fact in the story of IS, attention to what is written and where it claims to come from shows that most or all of them often depend on a single source. In looking at a phenomenon like IS such care seems all the more obligatory a precaution.

The Web as host for source material represents a further challenge, especially for the medievalist. Scholars who work on the Middle Ages are accustomed to complaining about the lack of sources for their research. The entire surviving textual base representing the history of the eight or nine hundred years of the existence of Islamic Spain, from 711 to 1492 and after, could be fitted comfortably onto a few bookshelves. Many other territories or topics are even less generously documented. For any modern topic, by contrast, the Web makes the source base potentially endless. While that is comforting in one sense, it means that it is not always easy to know if one has netted all that is relevant to one's inquiry. It also, just as importantly, means that sources that one has read online do not always remain online. Many disappear, for no obvious reason and without explanation. Thus the now standard "date of access" appended to many references; thus too the occasional note referring to such a disappearance and attempting to offer replacements. Medievalists may have fewer sources, but those they have at least (generally) stay.

In the end, though, some of the most important sources for this study are not Web-generated (even if some of them are now available on the Internet). Despite the very recent birth of IS, a great deal of its thinking and ideology draws on texts that go back, as we have seen, as far as the birth of Islam itself in the seventh century. Without an awareness of the meaning of those texts and of how they are used by IS, as well as the larger historical context in which that happens, the study of IS cannot go very far. The material used in this study has therefore been a combination of reliably sourced IS documentation and texts from the classical and medieval world of Islam. Because IS is both a modern and a medieval movement, drawing its intellectual sustenance and asserting its authority as much from medieval Islam as from the present or the recent past, we must employ our sources and our knowledge of that Islamic past if we are to understand the modern phenomenon of the Islamic State.

CHAPTER ONE

Caliphate

O N 2 RAMADAN 1435 in the Islamic calendar, corresponding to June 29, 2014, IS proclaimed the revival
of the medieval Islamic institution of the caliphate.
Describing it as "the abandoned obligation of the era,"
the movement asserted the need for the institution, and announced
the appointment of Abu Bakr al-Baghdadi as its first caliph.[1] The
caliphate is the preeminent political form generated by Islam, with
universal claims and a history going back literally to the moments following the death of Muhammad in 632. Harun al-Rashid, the ruler
who enlivens the pages of the *1001 Nights*, was caliph in Baghdad at
the end of the eighth century, belonging to the most famous caliphal
dynasty of all, the Abbasids. His claim to fame derives from the immense power of the Abbasid caliphs and the wealth of their courts,
whose elaborate, fabulous ceremonies were well known to east and
West alike. It was he who sent fantastic gifts, spices, monkeys, even an
elephant ("the only one he had at the time") to Charlemagne, "simply
because the Frankish king asked for it."[2] The Abbasids lasted for half
a millennium, from 750 through 1258, when the Mongols extin-
guished the last caliph, al-Mustasim, by rolling him up in a carpet and
trampling him to death, and with him the caliphate itself.

The words caliph and caliphate are strongly emotive. For
Muslims they evoke unity, power, greatness, a time long ago when

the empire of Islam was the only thing that mattered between China and the Atlantic. For many Christians, Jews, Europeans, Americans, non-Muslims in general, by contrast, their associations are darker and linked to more current events. Among Americans in particular they resonate in the way words like communism and communist did in the 1950s. Yet they should not be as unfamiliar as they are unwelcome. Anyone who recalls Jack Kennedy as a candidate for the presidency, rather than as president, or who has the slightest acquaintance with the history of Europe since the sixteenth century, will recognize the similarities with the papacy. The differences between pope and caliph, and between papacy and caliphate, are great, but the similarities are great too, as will become apparent, and are not without relevance here.

Caliphs had ruled an empire stretching from the Atlantic to India, and for centuries after the disappearance of the caliphate, the caliph and caliphal institutions represented an ideal of unity and magnificence that fed as it was fed by nostalgic dreams about lost power and glory and a consciousness of the declining significance of Islam and Muslims in the world. The announcement of a caliphal rebirth was met, therefore, with interest and in some quarters with enthusiasm. But the news itself took strange form. There was no great ceremony, or public act. The news came in the form of a press release issued by the IS media outlet al-Hayat. Thus the date of 2 Ramadan: it reported something that had apparently just happened at the start of the holy fasting month of Islam. And even this press release was actually a transcript of a thirty-four-minute speech given by the official spokesperson for IS, Abu Muhammad al-Adnani, posted on a Twitter account. It is not made clear what kind of speech this was, a radio or TV broadcast, an address before a live audience, one delivered in an open space or in a mosque; whether it was aimed at Muslims alone or at a more broadly universal audience; even precisely when it had been delivered.

The proclamation stands thus at one remove, possibly more, from the legal forms and instruments that lie behind this momentous development, momentous at least in the eyes of IS and its followers. Those acts are referred to in the speech. What are they? Is there some official document, formally agreed and approved, signed and archived somewhere, that confirms what happened? Was there in fact a ceremony—like a coronation perhaps, or an election in Saint Peter's, or a U.S. presidential inauguration—at which the choice of a caliph was made and where his installation took place? Who performed it? Under what authority? Do those who carried it out in any sense represent the community of Muslims as a whole, or even just in part? Or do they speak only for themselves?

Other questions present themselves too. Why did this happen at all? Why now? What is it about IS that causes or entitles it, unlike other Islamist movements, to revive the caliphate? Does its action represent anything more than an elaborate publicity stunt or power play (whether against internal or external foes) by the leaders of IS? And, from our point of view as much as from those of Muslims in and out of IS, why is this move of importance? What can it tell us about the thinking and ideology, as well as about the current situation, of IS?

A Foundational Document

Many of these questions are answered in the document itself. As we shall see, our text, entitled "This Is the Promise of Allah," is very carefully constructed; though it is wildly ahistorical, it is solidly rooted in what it presents as a historical understanding of Islam, including its origins and its relationship with the rest of the world; it is arranged in such a way as to present a watertight legal argument for its claims; and that argument is aimed at a very specific and highly ambitious target. The text repays attentive analysis, then, not least because it reflects and reveals the ideology of a large and very dangerous movement.

As a document, however, this is an odd text. It does not read like a typical press release, and even as a record of a speech, it wears a special, not easily definable appearance. As a whole, it looks like a combination of several different types of document, but its closest resemblance is to a religious address. Consisting mainly of exhortations, like a sermon addressed to the believers, it repeats the expression "This is the Promise of Allah" numerous times.[3] Fully twenty-seven quotations, from fifteen of the *suras*, or chapters, of the Quran, represent the first 90 percent of that book. And the text concludes with holiday wishes, IS-style, for the month of Ramadan: "In conclusion, we congratulate the Muslims on the advent of the blessed month of Ramadan. We ask Allah (the Exalted) to make it a month of victory, honor and consolidation for the Muslims, and make its days and its nights a curse for the *rafidah* [here, Shi'is], the *sahwat* [the Awakening—pro-government groups in Iraq], and the *murtaddin* [apostates]."

Along the way, we find religious admonitions, historical tales used to uplift the hearer or reader, quotations from hadith (traditions of the Prophet), commentary on hadith, formal announcements, as well as descriptions of how low the Muslims have sunk, of how this is their own fault, of how the work of IS has raised them up and restored the honor of Islam. The text also includes calls for unity among Muslims, cautions of troubles to come on the path to final victory and the coming of God's judgment, and reassurance that if Muslims can just remain united in loyalty to the caliph and active and courageous in his service, victory will be certain.

Sermon, history lesson, religious exhortation, homiletics, political and legal announcements and military warnings, social analysis of a sort, even predictions—all this is woven into "This Is the Promise of Allah." Nevertheless this text is not just a jumble of literary genres. It has a shape that fits with its purpose. At base, it is a religious document. But this does not keep it from being also a political text. As we shall see, in the Islamic context it is hard to separate the two spheres. The political message adumbrated here is simultaneously religious, the religious message at the same time political. Each implies the other; each is supported and justified by the other; each is adduced to justify and give meaning to the other. More precisely, each is the other.

Sandwiched in the middle, between the religious sermonizing and historical morality tales of the beginning and the end, we find the real message of the speech. Here Adnani makes a series of announcements that carry the religious-political and legal message of the movement forward. They all concern the reestablishment of the caliphal institution.

Islam: Religion and Politics

Islam makes different demands, and has different aims and ambitions for the believer, from Christianity. Born under very different circumstances from Christianity, it grew very fast. While Christianity took several centuries to take over the political world in which it lived, Islam did so in a single generation; and it also created its own political world, one coextensive with Islam itself. By the time of the Prophet's death, in 632, the state incarnated in him dominated most of the Arabian Peninsula.

The death of the Prophet, however, cast into doubt the continued existence of that state, and of the religious system preached by its founder. According to the earliest biographies of the Prophet, at first the news of his death paralyzed the believers. But once the truth of his going was understood, the two main groups among the Muslims began jockeying for power. The great fear was that the community would fall apart. Muhammad's followers had constituted a political entity as much as a religious community. Who would lead them and keep them together now that he was gone? How would he be chosen? Would the new leader come from the original believers, those who had "migrated" with him from Mecca to Medina, in what is known as the *hijra*, ten years earlier, in 622? Or would he emerge from the "supporters," those Medinans who had welcomed Muhammad and enabled him to build his small group of believers into a locally important state identified by its common faith?

In the end, Meccans and Medinans alike chose to reject chaos and the dissolution of Muhammad's legacy, preferring to unify around the figure of one of the Prophet's earliest converts, his father-in-law, Abu Bakr. He became the first caliph, with the support of other Meccans, and the Medinans rallied to him as a counter to the fissiparous tendencies of traditional Arabian society.

Muhammad was dead. He had been the last, the "seal," of the prophets. Revelation had ceased with him. But a religious community, one defined by the common faith of its members, could not easily forgo religious as well as the existing political leadership. The twin role of the Rasul Allah, the Messenger of God, as founder both of a faith and of its associated state, made the ruler of the Islamic world-empire that grew out of his legacy within a single generation also, at least potentially, a religious figure.

History works in odd ways, however. The caliphs were unable to combine a truly religious role for themselves with their real political tasks as rulers, and they quickly lost virtually all their religious significance. Their religious role was taken over by religious scholars of different types, with the consequence that the religion of Islam, as distinct from the political entities that grew up within the areas of the conquests, far from becoming a monolithic structure on the pattern of the Roman Catholic church, became very varied. The immense expanse of the Islamic empire, and the difficulty of communicating across huge distances in the pre-modern period, help to explain how this happened. At the same time, an impressive historical tendency to accept diversity helped to maintain Islam as a vast religious tent (at least in what became the Sunni world)—one that tolerated a wide range of religious ideas and practice within the overarching unity conferred by, among other things, the institution of the caliphate.

By the tenth century, the caliphs themselves had become nonentities, superseded even in their political role by generals of their armies. At that time, they succeeded in creating, or re-creating, a more symbolic but historically more useful religious role for themselves: that of supreme leaders of the Islamic world. This makes their role not wholly different from that of popes, apart from the authoritative features of the papacy as a source of religious teaching and validation of doctrine.

The Proclamation

The formal purpose of the new IS document is to proclaim the revival of the caliphate, and it achieves this through a series of formal announcements, which appear in the middle of the text. Such a positioning makes the document look long, and even rambling, but this is not a legal brief or a company report. It is a political-religious document, with legal implications, and because of this it is deliberately constructed to appeal to its proper audience on all three levels: political, religious, and legal. Thus, while the announcements are measured and calibrated, building their own

argument as they proceed, they are preceded and followed by sermonizing of various sorts, and they themselves express their
legal and political message in religious terminology and form. The
announcements take their place within a religious message, are
part of a religious message, and derive their authority from being
part of a religious message.

The long religious introduction to "This Is the Promise of
Allah" is part of this, for its function is to make the point that God
Himself promised Muslims "succession"—*khilafa* in Arabic, from
the same root as the word *khalifa*, "caliph"—together with their
safety and the establishment of their faith. This promise, which is
conditional on Muslims worshipping only Allah and submitting to
His commands, great and small, is confirmed by a quranic quotation (*sura* 24:55):

Allah (the Exalted) said: Allah has promised those who have
believed among you and done righteous deeds that He will
surely grant them succession [to authority] upon the earth
just as He granted it to those before them and that He will
surely establish for them their religion which He has preferred for them and that He will surely substitute for them,
after their fear, security, [for] they worship Me, not associating anything with Me. But whoever disbelieves after
that—then those are the defiantly disobedient.

Following a historical digression, about the miserable condition of
the Arabs before Islam, whose purpose is also to make the audience
understand that everything happens according to a divine plan, the
text tells us that things are now changing for the better. "The flag
of *tawhid* [monotheism] rises and flutters." "The *hudud* [Sharia
penalties] are implemented." "Crosses and graves are demolished."
Only one thing is lacking, "forgotten," a "collective obligation" of
the entire Muslim community. It is "the abandoned obligation of
the era," the caliphate. Another quotation from the Quran (*sura*
2:30), complete with commentary, explains what that is: "Allah (the
Exalted) said, 'And mention when your Lord said to the angels,
"Indeed, I will make upon the earth a *khalifah*."'" Just in case anyone is unsure about the applicability of this passage to the caliphal

institution—it seems from its context actually to refer to mankind, in the person of Adam, who is mentioned immediately afterward— we are given a passage from a medieval Quran commentator in which we learn that "this verse is a fundamental basis for the appointment of a leader and a khalifah who is listened to and obeyed so that the *ummah* [the Islamic community] is united by him and his orders are carried out."[4]

The Influence of the Quran

We should recall here the significance of the Quran in Arabic and Islamic culture. Unlike the Bible in the Judeo-Christian world, in the Arab and Islamic world the Quran is omnipresent. In the West, quotations from and allusions to the Bible occur in literature and in speech, and many phrases from the biblical text have become common currency. This is especially the case in the English- and German-speaking worlds, thanks to the immense influence of the English King James version and that of Luther in German. Nevertheless, quotations and allusions are not so very frequent in daily use today, and biblical phrases for the most part have tended to lose their biblical identity on their way into the daily language. This reflects in part the decline in Western countries of active participation in religion, as well as the vitality of the living languages.

The Quran by contrast is probably the first text that many Muslim children learn, often by heart, even when they do not learn to read. The famous blind Egyptian writer Taha Husayn (1889– 1973) devotes much of the first volume of his autobiography to accounts of how he memorized and forgot the Quran in a *kuttab*, or traditional school, several times during his childhood.[5] A special way of reciting the Quran, similar to music but not considered as music in the Islamic world, makes the holy text instantly recognizable and familiar too.[6] Muslims hear the Quran in the mosque and in sermons, on radio and TV; it is available online in recordings by famous reciters; and expressions and passages from it are part of the daily language of educated and uneducated Arabs alike in a way that even the English Bible cannot parallel.[7] The former Egyptian president Gamal Abdel Nasser—a secular nationalist—sprinkled quranic quotations and allusions liberally throughout his speeches. So did Yasser Arafat, the Palestinian leader.[8]

The Quran is a written text. Its language is classical Arabic, which is very different from the varied forms of spoken Arabic. Yet it was delivered by Muhammad as speech and its content has the character of speech—because it is all in the form of direct address from God to Muhammad or the believers. The combination of direct-address style, religious content, and sonorous high classical Arabic makes the Quran extremely effective as spoken word, especially in semi-formal contexts like sermons and even political speeches. The use of quranic quotations and allusions, or of quranic style, in such contexts, compels admiration in itself. It also commands respect for the Islamic credentials of the user.

A Call to Action

Following the long religious introduction, whose main purpose was to demonstrate that the caliphal institution is a necessity authorized by God Himself in the Quran, the text turns to the future, asking who will be responsible for these important developments. We learn that, responding to the necessity in the quranic text, the Islamic State "represented by *ahl al-hall wal-aqd* (its people of authority), consisting of its senior figures, leaders, and the *shura* council" have made the relevant decisions.

Who or what are the *shura* and the *ahl al-hall wal-aqd*? Both terms wear an antique appearance. A *shura* is a consultative council, with roots going back to traditional practice in pre-Islamic times. It was a *shura* that chose the third caliph, Uthman, following the assassination of Umar in 644, and the notion of election that it implies survived throughout the Umayyad period and even later, down to modern times, as a significant element in Islamic political thinking and practice.[9] The idea of election encouraged the notion that the caliphal throne was not simply a personal or dynastic possession to be passed on automatically by inheritance from father to son. As we shall see, a caliph must have certain personal qualities to be a proper candidate for the office. The membership of a *shura* is generally fluid, and in the present case we are not told who the members are.

Ahl al-hall wal-aqd is a larger category. It includes the *shura* council, and it refers also to the "senior figures" and "leaders." Together, these constitute the totality of the leadership of the Islamic world relevant for IS. Hence it is the body qualified, and at the same time obliged, to make the decisions and claims that follow.

Making the Case

Having established what needs to be done and who they are, the authors of the document move on to their argument. First they assert that all the prerequisites for the reestablishment of the caliphal institution are in place. More than that, there are no reasons that might argue for delay in setting it up: "The Islamic State has no legal constraint or excuse that can justify delaying or neglecting the establishment of the *khilafah*." It can be done now. Here as throughout the entire document, IS displays a legalistic concern to lay out and establish the groundwork for what is to come in carefully structured points: something needs to be done; the situation is ripe; now is the time; we have no reason to put off what must be done. This covers all the bases. The rest follows inevitably and in logical sequence.

The first logical step is the reestablishment of the caliphal institution, which in turn implies the need for a caliph and a pledge of allegiance to him. This is what the first five or six pages of religious discussion and quranic justification have been leading up to. Quite suddenly, in a rush, this is the message of the text:

> Therefore, the shura (consultation) council of the Islamic State studied this matter after the Islamic State—by Allah's grace—gained the essentials necessary for khilafah, which the Muslims are sinful for if they do not try to establish. In light of the fact that the Islamic State has no shari (legal) constraint or excuse that can justify delaying or neglecting the establishment of the khilafah such that it would not be sinful, the Islamic State—represented by ahl al-hall wal-aqd (its people of authority), consisting of its senior figures, leaders, and the shura council—resolved to announce the establishment of the Islamic khilafah, the appointment of a khalifa

for the Muslims, and the pledge of allegiance to the shaykh (sheikh), the mujahid, the scholar who practices what he preaches, the worshipper, the leader, the warrior, the reviver, descendant of the family of the Prophet, the slave of Allah, Ibrahim ibn Awwad ibn Ibrahim ibn Ali ibn Muhammad al-Badri al-Hashimi al-Husayni al-Qurashi by lineage, as-Samurra'i by birth and upbringing, al-Baghdadi by residence and scholarship. And he has accepted the bay'ah (pledge of allegiance). Thus, he is the imam and khalifah for the Muslims everywhere. Accordingly, the "Iraq and Sham" in the name of the Islamic State is henceforth removed from all official deliberations and communications, and the official name is the Islamic State from the date of this declaration.

We clarify to the Muslims that with this declaration of khilafah, it is incumbent upon all Muslims to pledge allegiance to the khalifah Ibrahim and support him (may Allah preserve him). The legality of all emirates, groups, states, and organizations, becomes null by the expansion of the khilafah's authority and arrival of its troops to their areas.

Claims

This short passage contains a great number of key claims: in just a few lines, set in the middle of a very much longer document, it proclaims (1) the need for the caliphate, (2) the re-establishment of the institution, (3) the appointment of a new caliph, (4) a pledge of allegiance to him, (5) his identity, complete with a string of complimentary adjectives, (6) his acceptance of that pledge, (7) that he is in consequence the imam and caliph for all Muslims everywhere, (8) that as a consequence of that the Islamic State is no longer territorially bounded, so that "Iraq and Sham (Syria)" are to be omitted from its name, (9) that all Muslims are obliged to give the new caliph their loyalty and allegiance, and (10) that all other Islamic political entities and organizations are made void as the caliph's authority expands.

This is a great accomplishment for just a few lines and a couple of sentences. As can be seen, each step depends on the preceding one. Together they build up a complete scenario for the re-creation of the caliphate and the reign of this caliph. The individual steps are all necessary and they all need explanation or justification.

The Rise, Fall, and Revival of the Caliphate

A document of this sort is a rarity, for obvious reasons. But the institution it describes is actually not so rare. A surprising number of caliphal institutions have come and gone. The revival of a caliphate is exceedingly infrequent, however. It implies that a caliphate has died, disappeared, or been abolished, something that is very hard to conceive. If the caliphate as an institution is part of Islam, and is prefigured in the Quran, then its abolition, or disappearance, raises conceptual problems. A divinely created institution should be everlasting. How can humans disestablish something established by God?

The answer is that only one caliphate has been formally abolished. This was the caliphal institution to which the Ottomans, who ruled most of the Middle East for four centuries before the end of World War I, laid claim as distant successors to the Abbasids. When Mustafa Kemal Atatürk built a new Turkish nation on the ruins of the Ottoman state after World War I, he abolished the empire, in 1922. The caliphal institution, as a religious office with transnational significance, remained in existence. But a couple of years later, in 1924, even that was abolished by the Turkish Grand National Assembly. That is, a modern, secular, national institution in Turkey (no longer the heart of a great Islamic empire), formed and acting under the influence of the Westernizing ideas of Mustafa Atatürk, found it conceptually possible to abolish a religious, universal institution that had been founded in Arabia at the birth hour of Islam and with no end anticipated except that augured by the Day of Judgment. It is that notion of the caliphal institution, interrupted rudely by Atatürk, that IS is seeking to restore.

IS is not altogether original in seeking to revive a caliphate. After the 1924 abolition several Muslim leaders proposed something similar, but without success. A more impressive example comes from al-Andalus, Islamic Spain, in the tenth century. The Umayyad dynasty in Damascus was almost wiped out by the

Abbasids who deposed them in 750. One young prince, however, survived and managed to get as far as Spain, which had been conquered for Islam just a few decades earlier. Safe there if only because of the distance from Baghdad, where the Abbasids had built a new capital, signaling their turn to the east, he established a dynasty that derived its legitimacy from its connection to the Umayyads of Damascus, and lasted, with mixed fortunes, until the early eleventh century.

At first, these new Umayyads were hesitant about claiming the caliphal title. Because they were isolated in an obscure and distant corner of the Islamic world (the real Wild West of the day), lacked control of the two holy cities of Mecca and Medina, and had no very impressive Islamic credentials of their own—or even, at first, any substantial Andalusi Islamic culture to justify caliphal claims—they could mount no credible challenge to the Abbasids.

By the tenth century, however, just as the Abbasids entered into what would be a terminal decline, others attempted to snatch the caliphal dignity from them. The Umayyads in Cordoba joined the rush, and in 929, taking up their Damascene inheritance, they called on their subjects, and, by extension, other Muslims, to recognize them as caliphs:

> We are the most worthy to fulfil our right, and the most entitled to complete our good fortune, and to put on the clothing granted by the nobility of God, because of the favor which He has shown us, and the renown that He has given us, and the power to which He has raised us, . . . He has made our name and the greatness of our power celebrated everywhere . . . We have decided that the *dawa* (the call of religion) should be to us as Commander of the Faithful and that letters emanating from us or coming to us should be [headed] in the same manner. Everyone who calls himself by this name apart from ourselves is arrogating it to himself [unlawfully] and trespassing upon it and is branded with something to which he has no right. We know that if we were to continue [allowing] the neglect of this duty which is owed to us in this matter then we should be forfeiting our right and neglecting our title, which is certain.[10]

Here the caliphate is being claimed as an entitlement of the Umayyad dynasty, one that the usurping Abbasids have interfered with but that should be revived given the renown and the power that God has given the Umayyads (even if they are now living far from the centers of the Islamic world). The Islamic "call" to which the Umayyads refer is here a very general term for spreading the faith; the Friday sermon with its prayer for the sovereign is the most easily and frequently heard measure of a ruler's status because it includes his name and titles. The Abbasids are now openly derided as trespassers, "branded" by their treachery to the Umayyads. Most importantly, this announcement stresses the obligation laid on the Umayyads not to neglect this "duty that is owed to us," lest they forfeit thereby their indisputable right.

The Umayyad caliphate lasted for just a century after this declaration in 929. During that time, they sank from being masters of much of the western Mediterranean to, by the end, scarcely controlling even the environs of Cordoba, their capital. In 1031, the inhabitants of Cordoba decided they had had enough of them, and the last Umayyad was unceremoniously expelled from the city.

Despite its medieval obscurity and ultimate failure, the Iberian case is instructive here. It shows that a caliphal title can be reclaimed; deprivation, as in this case, can be undone even generations later by those with a claim that they can make stick. Abolition of a caliphate, similarly, as in the Turkish case, can be ignored or used as a basis for revival. In the Spanish case, the decline of the Abbasids and the real strength of the Umayyads made it possible and, in local terms, realistic for them to stake their claim. What counts is the sort of argument that can be brought to bear. The Umayyads' political success in the western Mediterranean, together with the growth of a locally significant Arab-Islamic culture there, gave them the status that was needed to justify the august title.

The Iberian case also adds context to an important feature of the IS claim: the Umayyads did no more than assert their personal claim, as a dynasty, to the title held by their ancestors. They had been caliphs in the seventh and eighth centuries; the caliphal institution had existed then and still existed in the tenth century; and it belonged by right to the Umayyads. IS by contrast exists in a different world: the caliphal institution no longer exists; for it to be viable and usable, IS needs to be able to argue that it not only may but must exist and enjoys quranic, hence divine authorization. Only on that basis can IS make any further claims. That is why we find so much space devoted at the start of our document to the quranic proof-texts for the caliphate. IS does not mention the Turkish abolition explicitly, but its insistence on the quranic roots of the institution constitutes recognition of the need to justify, in religious terms that trump the political action of a Turkish political assembly, its re-creation of that earliest political institution of Islam.

Who Is the Caliph?

Who is the leader of this renewed institution? The post of caliph represents, at least in the eyes of IS followers, leadership of the world's Muslims, as well as sovereign authority over Islamic territory and potential rulership of the entire world. The new caliph, therefore, must be someone with the necessary qualifications. The proclamation by Adnani tells us something about him: it says that the electoral college has chosen "the shaykh, the mujahid, the scholar who practices what he preaches, the worshipper, the leader, the warrior, the reviver, descendant of the family of the Prophet, the slave of Allah."

These words breathe three qualities. First, the caliph possesses religious qualifications: he is pious and learned (the speech describes him as the scholar; one who practices what he preaches, the worshipper). Next, he has martial attributes in the service of the faith (he is a *mujahid*—one who engages in jihad; he is the leader, the warrior). Thirdly, his genealogy fits: he is a descendant of the family of the Prophet. A number of tribes in Iraq claim descent from Muhammad, so this is less surprising than it might appear.

Together with these, the document asserts that the new caliph must be a reviver and slave of Allah. "Slave of Allah" is a title given to all caliphs, and it appears frequently in documents and on coins throughout the Middle Ages. Sometimes, because it can be a name in Arabic, "Abdallah," it even appears alone in the absence of a named caliph.[11] As to reviver, this has both a religious and a martial tinge: it echoes Adnani's central theme throughout this entire document, that Islam has sunk into a dark age of oppression by non-Islamic forces, religious and political, and stands in need of a revival that must be both religious and political.

A similar attitude has existed in the past: thus the great scholar al-Ghazzali (1055–1111) was regarded as the reviver of Islam in his time; and other scholars have been considered as revivers of Islam at the start of various centuries in the Islamic calendar. What makes this case different is that revivers in the past have generally been religious scholars. In the present case, while Abu Bakr al-Baghdadi is certainly credited with both piety and learning, it is his military qualifications, rather than his religious ones, that seem to be in play here.

The description that we have here is certainly impressive. But does it suffice? A caliph, like any other leader, must possess certain qualifications. In the eleventh century, when the office of caliph had already lost much of its real significance, a jurist called al-Mawardi (972–1058) composed a work on government in which he listed the qualities necessary in a caliph. They are not all that different from what we find here: he must be just; he must have knowledge relevant to decision-making; he should have good vision, hearing, and speech, "so that perception can serve as a sound basis for action"; he must be physically fit and not suffer from any handicap; he should have prudence so as to handle his subjects and their interests wisely; he needs courage to defend the territory of Islam against its enemies; and finally, he must have the nobility of Qurashi descent, "a matter indisputably settled by explicit text and by general consensus."[12] All of these, apart from those relating to lack of physical blemishes, are covered by the present account of Abu Bakr al-Baghdadi. Reports since his election to the effect that he has been wounded do not make clear whether any of his faculties have been affected, but if they have, the apparent desire by IS to cleave close to classical requirements may lead to a change in leadership even during his lifetime.

But who is Abu Bakr al-Baghdadi? We are given his identity: Ibrahim son of Awwad son of Ibrahim son of Ali son of Muhammad al-Badri al-Hashimi al-Husayni al-Qurashi by lineage, al-Samurra'i by birth and upbringing, al-Baghdadi by residence and scholarship. And we learn that he is also known as Abu Bakr. What can we learn from this string of names?

In accordance with the traditional naming pattern of the culture, we do not see a surname, but rather the father's name and those of paternal ancestors (those being the ones that count in this society) going back to his great-great-grandfather. This is a very respectable four generations of ancestors. And whether or not the genealogy is true, the caliph has the same name as his grandfather in this list, a very common pattern, and the names Muhammad and Ali both resonate as the names of the Prophet and of his cousin and son-in-law, one of his first converts. If nothing else, this solidifies the Islamic credentials of the new caliph.

The next four elements in the name, al-Badri, al-Hashimi, al-Husayni, and al-Qurashi, go much further: each of these lays claim to different sorts of Islamic prestige. Badri seems here to refer to the first important victory won by Muhammad, in 624, shortly after his move, or *hijra*, from Mecca to Medina.[13] Hashimi ties al-Baghdadi to the Prophet's family, the Banu Hashim. Al-Husayni denotes descent from al-Husayn, a grandson of the Prophet, and thus also from his father Ali. And al-Qurashi, like the other names he bears, indicates a further link to the Prophet. Al-Qurashi points to the ancient Arab tribe of Quraysh, of which the Prophet Muhammad was a member. There is no such tribe today, but the use of all these labels by Ibrahim points not to genetic descent—which would be impossible to demonstrate and unbelievable if recorded—but to another feature of leaders of his stripe: the desire to legitimate himself through the assertion of a physical link with, in this case, the founder of the Islamic faith. The claim does not warrant any greater credence in this case than it does in many others.

Caliphal Names

The new caliph's names suggest meaning and intention. Ibrahim is indeed, so far as we know, his name, but it is at the very least a happy coincidence that this happens also to be the name of Ibrahim (the biblical Abraham), the father of Ismail/Ishmael and hence of the Arabs, and commonly identified as the first Muslim.[14]

Yet Arabs tend not to be known by their given names. They are usually known by an honorific, or nickname, a name-form known as the *kunya*, in the form "Abu X," "Father of X," or "Possessed of X," which often refers to a son, a source of pride and honor for an ancient (and not just an ancient) Arab.[15] A *kunya* very often does not refer to an actual son, but to personal qualities (generosity, wealth, height, ignorance); or to sons who do not exist (many men are childless, or have not yet fathered offspring, or have only daughters; to deny them a *kunya* on that account would expose them to the shame that the possession of a *kunya* conceals); and men's *kunyas* are thus not automatic keys to the identity of one male among their offspring. Partly because of that, many *kunyas*, especially of people whose given names are those of well-known figures of the biblical or ancient Arabian past, simply refer to supposed "sons" whose names reflect that biblical or ancient Arabian past.[16]

The caliph of the Islamic State is frequently referred to not as Ibrahim but as Abu Bakr. Accompanying the name Ibrahim, Abu Bakr looks at first glance like a *kunya*, and is indeed found used as a *kunya*, but it is far more commonly used as a proper name in itself.[17] More importantly, as we have seen, Abu Bakr was also the name of the very first caliph, or successor. A close friend and also a father-in-law of the Prophet, he ruled as caliph for two years, from the Prophet's death in 632 until his own death in 634.[18]

Caliphal Titles

Most medieval caliphs are known to us not by their personal names—Muhammad, Abdallah, and so on—or by their *kunyas*, but by titles, known as throne-names, chosen on their accession. These tend to express what was, or what was hoped for as, a characteristic of the ruler—wisdom, right guidance, help from God, victory, power, and so on. They typically take the form of an adjective or another word plus an expression such as "with the help of God," or "in God," or "by God." Thus we have al-Mansur billah, "he who is helped, or given victory, by God," hence, "The Victorious"; al-Muqtadir billah, "he who has power through God," so "The Powerful"; al-Mutamid ala Allah, "he who relies on God"; al-

Mustasim billah, "he who takes shelter with God" (unfortunately this did him little good—he was the last Abbasid caliph, the one who ended up trampled to death in a carpet in 1258); and so on.

As the prefix al-, "the," shows, these are descriptions, like titles, reminiscent of such titles as Alfred the Great, or Ivan the Terrible. The difference is that the personal name is usually not remembered; only the title is preserved in later memory (Harun al-Rashid, Harun the Rightly Guided, is an exception, with both his name and his title remembered by posterity); and of course the change, or the addition, comes not following the death of the ruler but upon his accession.[19] The sources even preserve occasional anecdotes about how a ruler would choose a throne-name of this sort.[20]

Very often, because the "God" element is understood to be present in all such cases, and partly just to make it simpler to refer to someone, that part is left off. Consequently we find the great second caliph of the Abbasid dynasty, al-Mansur billah, "he who is helped/given victory by God," referred to simply as al-Mansur, "the Victorious." In formal contexts, however, in official documents or inscriptions, or on coins, such titles retain their florid fullness.

When a different kind of ruler, not a caliph, wished to impress, he faced a problem: he could not take such a title because it was reserved for caliphs. The solution was to take such a title nevertheless, but without the "God" element. Thus in Islamic Spain, the powerful dictator who took over toward the end of the tenth century adopted the title al-Mansur—this particular title was popular because of its meaning—but he did not tack on the caliphal addition of "with (the help of) God," in recognition of the fact that he was not a caliph.[21] Indeed, part of the political savvy, and success, of this ruler lay in his strategy of leaving the sitting caliph in Cordoba, the capital of Islamic Spain, in place with his full honors, taking away just his political power, but leaving his ceremonial privileges intact and his titles untouched. A son of this al-Mansur tried to take the caliphal title away for himself a little later, with fatal results all round.[22]

Much later, in the dying years of the twentieth century, and of his regime, Saddam Hussein also took on this title, but this time with the suffix, describing himself as *al-sayyid al-rais al-qaid al-mansur billah*—"Mr. President, the leader victorious by the will of God." In this case, the expression served more as an adjective than as a formal title, but because of the way the Arabic language works, the difference is slight. Its purpose here was, as in the eighth century, not only to magnify the ruler, but also to do so by suggesting the support of heaven.[23]

The Arabic language is rich in expressions like this, partly because of the ways in which the language is able to generate words from roots with related meanings. As a result such titles are varied and almost endless, so much so that one writer in the Middle Ages, the famous Ibn Hazm, collected a list of "titles for caliphs that have not yet been used." Some duly were used after his time.[24]

Abu Bakr Ibrahim al-Baghdadi, the new caliph, has not taken on any throne-name. Is this because he thinks that such titles are outmoded? Does he perhaps think that the moment to call himself by such a title has not yet arrived? Or maybe there is some other reason? Not all caliphs actually did adopt such titles. It will be interesting, in the context of the names and titles that he and IS have adopted and used so far, to see whether Abu Bakr al-Baghdadi or his successors choose to follow these precedents and adopt titles of their own. If they do, the question of importance will be whether they do so in imitation of the Abbasids, for whom these titles were little more than political trophies, rather like all those medals and military decorations that kings and princes wear today, self-awarded and with little real meaning or reference to actual achievement but rather reflecting simply their rank and desire for adornment, or whether they follow the pattern of the Umayyads, in the very first century of Islam, who did not take such titles at all.

One later writer, the famous historian al-Masudi, actually reports a couple of traditions—which he roundly and rightly rejects as inventions—to the effect that the Umayyads did take throne-names. As an invention, the claim is clearly intended, by the pro-Umayyad who must have invented it, to magnify that dynasty in retrospect and to place it on a par with the later dynasty that had displaced them and dishonored their memory. It is of more than passing interest here to note that the titles conferred on the Umayyad caliphs by this source are otherwise unknown. With one exception, they were not used by any Abbasids before al-Masudi's own time, or, for that matter, afterward. That single exception is the title al-Mahdi, which has messianic, salvationist implications. This will be of relevance later on. Our source gives this title to the Umayyad caliph Sulayman, who ruled briefly from 715 to 717.[25] Strikingly, we learn from this same source that Sulayman also bore another such invented title, al-Dai ila Allah, "he who summons to God," which is itself a suitable title of this type. Should we understand that the original invented tradition gave Sulayman this latter title, and that a subsequent writer, knowing—and approving—of another, messianic tradition attached to Sulayman, somehow inserted the phrase into the text along with the title al-Mahdi? As we shall see, this is not an empty speculation.

The Choice of the Title of Caliph

Why has IS chosen to make use of the title of caliph? At first sight the answer may look obvious: the successors to Muhammad were called caliphs and Abu Bakr al-Baghdadi wishes to be viewed as one in that line, reviving a dormant institution and giving it renewed glory. But two features of the history of the caliphal institution make this choice of title less obviously appealing. First, the institution dates back to the moments following the Prophet's death, but it did not exist during Muhammad's lifetime. As we have seen, it has been argued that the roots of the institution can be seen in the quranic text. The word khalifa, "successor," "deputy," occurs twice in the Quran. We find it in sura 2:28: "And when the Lord said to the angels, 'I am setting in the earth a viceroy (khalifa).' They said, 'What, wilt Thou set therein one who will do corruption there, and shed blood, while we proclaim Thy praise and call Thee holy?' He said, 'Assuredly I know that you know not.'" And it occurs again at sura 38:25: "'David, behold, We have appointed thee a viceroy (khalifa) in the earth; therefore judge between men justly, and follow not caprice, lest it lead thee astray from the way of God. Surely those who go astray from the way of God—there awaits them a terrible chastisement, for that they have forgotten the Day of Reckoning.'"

Is this a statement of the origin of the caliphal institution? It seems, far rather, to resemble Christian use of the famous New

Testament story about Jesus and Peter and the birth of the church as an institution: "On this rock (*petra* in Greek) I will build my church" (Matthew 16:18). Jesus cannot have conceived of the myriad ways in which Christianity and the Christian church would develop after his death. Similarly a couple of occurrences of the word *khalifa*, "successor," "deputy," "viceroy," in the Quran can scarcely be used to explain the birth of such an institution as the caliphate and its history over the centuries after Muhammad. At best, they may offer a model for parts of what happened later. The character of the caliphal institution and the way caliphs were chosen show the gulf separating them from whatever the quranic passages describe. However useful it is for homiletical purposes, a quranic root for the caliphal institution is belied by the way in which the caliphate is reported actually to have come into being after the Prophet's death.

Secondly, the institution does indeed go back very far, and had its glory days—the period of vast conquests between 634 and about 720, and the next couple of centuries when the Abbasid caliphate was the greatest empire west of China—presiding over the birth and massive development of a new world culture. All that came to an end, however, by about the middle of the tenth century. Thereafter the history of the caliphate, whether as the ruling institution of a great empire or as a focus of religious significance and attachment for Muslims worldwide, is one of terminal decline. As an institution, indeed, and looked at over the longer term, the caliphate, like other very long-lived institutions, should be seen as a failure, a failure with a distinguished history, to be sure, but a failure nevertheless. After the middle of the tenth century, the Abbasids were largely puppets of their generals, and in 1258 the last caliph was killed. Since then, title and institution alike have been sites of nostalgic idealization rather than political, or even religious, reality.

It is that nostalgic idealization, however, rather than any recent reality, that IS seeks to build on and exploit. And in ignoring problems concerning the origins of the institution and stressing the historic role of the caliphs, in particular the early Umayyads, in the conquests of Islam, they have tied them to themselves as fighters for jihad and new conquests. In this sense their choice of the title caliph highlights the importance they attach to the unity of Islam and to the exclusive rights—and duties—of caliphs as distinct from other types of ruler. The Islamic world has had kings and sultans, and more recently presidents for life, even regular presidents, and all sorts of other rulers (Muammar Gaddafi called himself at one stage Revolutionary Chairman, and later on Brotherly Leader), but none has enjoyed the same type or range of authority as a caliph. Only the title of caliph is so redolent of Islamic authenticity and historic justification. Only the title of caliph resonates as specifically Islamic in a religious as well as a political sense.

The IS document of 2014, then, not only is a political text, but is also rooted deeply in religious thought and heavy with quranic language and style, making claims and demands that appeal at a very basic level to the Muslim as a Muslim. The related ideas of re-creating the caliphal institution and rebuilding a caliphal state are highlighted by the reminders in the document of the sunken state of Islam and the Muslims in the world and the presentation of the world as divided, us and them, between Islam and Muslims on one side and their enemies on the other. This focus on the caliphate is designed both to attract support from Muslims and to provide a kind of justification for IS strategy and policies: it was thus once; it should therefore be thus again; it can be so again—but only if Muslims give their support to those endeavoring, in their names, to make it so.

Recycling an Ancient Saying

The same religious-cum-political ethos is what lies behind the selection of the phrase to be used on coins that IS proposes to issue. Instead of quotations from the Quran or references to Muhammad or the *umma*, there will be a reference to a *khilafa ala minhaj al-nubuwwa*, a "caliphate on the pattern of prophecy/prophethood."[26] This too is a very strange expression. Superficially it seems to be simply another call to return to the Islam of olden days. But the expression looks a little wooden. What exactly is intended by it?

Khilafa is an abstract noun denoting the institution of the caliphate, rather than the state ruled by a caliph. We do not find the term on classical Islamic coins. And even the word *khalifa*, "caliph" (as distinct from other titles), rarely appears on coins of the early caliphs.[27] The Prophet never used the word *khilafa* or *khalifa* to describe his political entity or himself—not surprisingly, for it was only those who came after him who invented the institution and used the title caliph, which means, literally, "replacement."[28] And the noun *nubuwwa*, "prophethood," "prophecy"—also anonymously abstract—rather than *nabi*, "prophet," similarly strikes an odd note here.

This strange expression seems intended to suggest an Islamic state on the pattern of the entity created by the Prophet Muhammad, but the absence of his name here (or anywhere on the proposed coins), together with the oddity of the word *nubuwwa* itself, is striking. It seems to open up the possibility of a very different understanding of the expression.

While the phrase *khilafa ala minhaj al-nubuwwa* does not appear on coins, it is found in ancient Islamic sources. It occurs, twice, in hadiths, traditions or anecdotes attributed to the Prophet Muhammad, in the huge collection by Ahmad ibn Hanbal (780–855) entitled the *Musnad*.[29] Both hadiths are said to derive from Hudhayfa ibn al-Yaman, a Companion of the Prophet who died in 656 "at a great age."[30] In the first hadith, he reported that Muhammad "summoned people from unbelief to faith and from error to guidance ... The truth that had been dead lived (again) and the falsity that had been alive died. Then prophecy departed and there came the caliphate on the pattern of prophecy/prophethood."

This seems pretty clear: the Prophet came and did his work; then, though they were not prophets, but caliphs, those who succeeded him worked in accordance with the patterns set by him. The second hadith is more complicated. It looks rather like a transformation of the first in a messianic direction. In the first hadith what we have is little more than a pedestrian account of a golden age followed by an age of imitation. In the second one, transmitted by al-Numan ibn Bashir, another Companion of the Prophet, decline following the death of the Prophet is succeeded by a return to his standards.[31]

In this little text, al-Numan ibn Bashir relates an occasion when Hudhayfa ibn al-Yaman reported that the Prophet said:

"Prophecy will be among you as long as God wishes it to be; then he will take it away when he wishes to do so; then there will be a caliphate on the pattern of prophecy and it will last as long as God wishes it to; then he will take it away when he wishes to; then there will be cruel kingship and it will last as long as God wishes it to; then he will take it away when he wishes to; then there will be kingship of insolence/haughtiness; and that will last as long as God wishes it to; then he will take it away when he wishes it to be away; then there will be a caliphate on the pattern of prophecy." Then he was silent. And Habib related: and when Umar ibn Abd al-Aziz came to power (Now Yazid ibn al-Numan ibn Bashir was one of his associates), I wrote to him with this hadith, reminding him of it and I said to him: I hope that the Commander of the Faithful—meaning Umar—will be (the one) following the cruel kingdom and the insolence; and my letter was brought to Umar ibn Abd al-Aziz and he took pleasure in it and it pleased him.[32]

How should we understand these hadiths? Are they just simple anecdotes without any particular meaning, the table-talk of an admired leader? Or do they possess special significance for a community used to seeing every action, every utterance of its founder as full of import, with predictions in particular possessing the weight that derives from their deliverer's direct tie to the Almighty? Obviously the latter.

We should not imagine that such stories necessarily record genuine utterances of the Prophet. Like many that foretell the future, these are to be seen as prophecies *post eventum*, prophecies made after the event that they foretell. The second hadith virtually tells us that this is so by the form that the story takes—it looks too suspiciously like something invented to flatter the caliph Umar ibn Abd al-Aziz.

Flattery can be found everywhere and can take many forms, including predictions—which in turn can be made by anyone. But placing a prediction about the quality or the character of a particular caliph's reign in the mouth of the founder of the Islamic faith goes beyond mere flattery toward certain prophecy and implies something more than mere human excellence about that caliph.

What the Prophet declares will happen is a sure statement about the future. This means, among other things, that the details listed in this hadith should be taken as pointing to what those who invented the hadith wanted us to understand about different periods of rule in the *umma*, the world of Islam. And since it was invented after the event, when it refers to periods of rule in a future, we should understand that it does so on the basis of what the author or authors know happened in the past. In particular, the hadith describes five periods, with their different characters:

1. Prophecy
2. Caliphate on the pattern of prophethood/prophecy
3. Cruel kingship
4. Kingship of insolence, haughtiness
5. Caliphate on the pattern of prophethood/prophecy

The first of these, prophecy, is clearly the period of Muhammad. The second period, "Caliphate on the pattern of prophethood/ prophecy," must refer to the era of Muhammad's first four successors, the "Rightly Guided" caliphs, from Abu Bakr through Umar and Uthman to Ali, who was killed in 661.[33] Period three, "Cruel kingship," refers to the caliphate of Yazid I (who reigned from 680 to 683). This caliph was responsible for, among much else, the slaughter of the supporters of a son of Ali at Karbala in the year 680 (one of the events that fed into the martyrology of Shi'i Islam), as well as the siege and destruction of Madina together with the bombarding of Mecca and the burning of the shrine of the Kaba in 683–684. The fourth period, "Kingship of insolence, haughtiness" is less clear than we might like. Does it refer to a particular Umayyad caliph in the period after Yazid? Or does it refer to the Umayyads in general? In referring to kingship, not to a king, the language certainly permits the latter interpretation: the later Umayyads were a wicked lot; they were haughty, abandoning the egalitarian tradition of the desert (followed ostentatiously by the founder of the dynasty, Muawiya). If so, that leads naturally to the fifth period, "Caliphate on the pattern of prophethood/prophecy," which as we have seen is made to refer to Umar (II) ibn Abd al-Aziz, who was caliph between 717 and 720. He virtually alone among the Umayyads enjoys a high reputation, so high that when the Abbasids supplanted that dynasty and destroyed the tombs of the Umayyad caliphs, they spared his.

Succession to the Caliphate

What will happen when the caliph Abu Bakr al-Baghdadi dies? He may indeed already be dead by the time this book appears in print, but unless IS has been totally defeated when he dies, the institution he led will not perish with him. Now that IS has revived the caliphate, it cannot permit it to disappear: it is central to the justification, the identity, and now the very being of IS. The specific identity of the caliph is far less important than the institution itself. Nevertheless, the death of a caliph must be followed by the selection of a successor. Who will that be? How will he be chosen?

We can say several things on this with confidence: first, he will not be a member of Abu Bakr al-Baghdadi's family. Dynastic succession on the pattern of the Umayyads or the Abbasids is a thing of the past. Whatever else he desires, Abu Bakr al-Baghdadi is certainly not attempting to make the caliphate a family inheritance. That much accommodation to modern realities is inevitable. Second, related to this, election of some sort, something that was at least theoretically inherent in the institution from the start, is likely. What about the chosen candidate? He will almost certainly be described in terms very similar to those used for Abu Bakr al-Baghdadi—that is, as a man of vast learning, deep piety, military skill, and above all with a tie, like his predecessor, to the tribe of Quraysh, that of the Prophet. Even if dynastic or family ties no longer possess real religious or political meaning, the force of tradition and its use in this case are too strong to permit the choice of a caliph who cannot lay claim (genuine or otherwise) to such descent.

Who will the electors be? Will we know anything about them or about the larger process of selection? Probably not: IS is unlikely to succeed in going beyond the building of a territorially large state to giving it stability and acceptance among other states in the region. Its ideology effectively prevents that, and it is difficult to imagine it abandoning its ideology very quickly. As a result, major events such as the election of a leader will not happen in the open. We should instead expect another announcement on the pattern of "This is the Promise of God."

Why Does the Caliphate Matter?

Why does this revival of the caliphate matter? Four reasons suggest themselves. First, IS itself matters. It is not just another rebel group fighting against regional governments. It dominates a huge territory, substantial populations, extensive resources; it threatens its neighbors, far and near; and local and international opposition is not succeeding, nor does it appear likely to succeed very soon, in getting rid of it completely. IS will be around for some time, possibly well beyond the lifetime of its first caliph.

Second, in choosing to use a caliphate as its governing institution, IS has made a powerful appeal, on many levels, both to its core constituents and to what it sees as its larger constituency, the universal community of Muslims today. It offers a deliberate echo of the caliphate as a vast and powerful state in the Middle Ages. In addition to being a state, the caliphate was also the central vehicle for the birth and massive growth of medieval Arabic culture. Without the empire built by the early Muslims, the existence of a major world culture based in Arabic and replacing the Greek and Persian cultures of the past would have been inconceivable. The memory of that political and cultural richesse is inflected through its roots in the early development of Islam not just as a political entity but also as the political expression of the religious message of Muhammad. The caliphate is not simply one political institution of Muslims—it is the political expression of Islam.

Third, against this background, the caliphal institution and the state that it governs represent explicitly, as we have seen, a revival of an Islamic world that is sunk under the weight of Western, especially Christian, political domination. A caliphal Islamic state would be more than the reassertion of political selfhood and independence by a state of Muslims. In making a demand for recognition as the heir to the caliphal state of the past, IS is attempting to restore the honor of Islam and the Muslims in a world that seeks to dishonor and to trample Islam and its adherents.

Finally, and growing out of these three points, one of the main ideals guiding IS is that of jihad, and with it the desire to conquer new lands, to spread Islam—by force in their case, unlike most Muslims throughout history—and to bring about the Islamic apocalypse and the Day of Judgment. This is a real ambition for IS. It is not like the vague and unreal commitment to a day of judgment or a final hour that we find among most Jews and Christians today. For that to be possible, for the apocalypse actually to arrive, certain conditions must be fulfilled. Among these is the creation of a powerful Islamic state. An Islamic state is one ruled by a caliph.

CHAPTER TWO

Administration

I T IS VERY EASY, looking at the computer screen or TV, or reading the papers, to get the impression that IS is no more than a group of unruly bandits running amok, inspired by a fanatical vision of Islamic dominance in the world, whose aims and joy lie in killing and destruction. The movement and its members act with cold and apparently random savagery toward those they conquer: they loot captured towns; they rape and enslave their captives; they shoot many in the towns that they take; they steal from their subjects; they dictate to women how they should dress and behave; they deny political, religious, and personal freedoms to those they rule; they effectively deny even the rights they supposedly grant to those minorities that they permit; they impose their own version of correct religious behavior; they ban smoking; they destroy precious and irreplaceable antiquities and records of the history of humanity; they regard most other Muslims as apostates and treat them in accordance with a traditional view of what that entails; they preach unending violence against their neighbors and the rest of the world; and they encourage suicide bombings and other acts of terrorism. Above all, they seem to act with a complete lack of discipline or order.

Such a picture has much truth in it. But it is important to remember, first, that IS is in the primary stages of setting up its state.

We should not be surprised, therefore, to find here as in other such situations (like the early days of the French Revolution, the so-called Reign of Terror; the years following the 1917 Revolution in Russia; or the period following the fall of the communist regime in Afghanistan) a certain degree of lawlessness and, still more, disorder. And secondly, despite the barbarism and the apparent randomness of much of the killing, IS fighters generally display a remarkable degree of discipline and obedience to their own laws and rules. IS now controls a territory the size of the United Kingdom and a population of some eight million. Regardless of how IS behaves, that population needs not only to be kept under control and prevented from resisting IS, but also to be supplied with food and other necessities, and offered something approximating a normal existence. That is what a state offers its citizens and that is what IS, in its own way, claims to be providing.

Law and Order

Terror is a tool of limited use. It can be very effective in conquering and pacifying, "but a reign of terror cannot be effective through terror alone. The most effective tyrannies are characterized by their excellent powers of organization."[1] Terror is not a reliable substitute for an administrative system. Terror will not fill holes in the roads or provide midwifery services; it does not offer a stand-in for traffic lights or medicines; nor does it provide driver's licenses or birth certificates, teach children in schools and authorize exams, organize universities and medical schools, keep gas stations supplied, run a judicial system, or, except in a most extreme and literal sense, keep bakeries and shops open. All of these are functions of a state, and for many people under IS rule, as for many people around the world, the specific identity or character of the state is less important than its existence in some form.

IS not only recognizes this; it is keenly aware that IS needs a state organization, both to keep its territory under control and to attain the final aim of IS ideology, the apocalypse. Only a caliphate, according to IS thinking, can reach that goal, and a caliphate consists not just of a caliph. A caliph requires a caliphal state.

IS behavior here lays bare a cardinal difference separating it from most other Islamist or terrorist outfits. Merely establishing a state along Islamic lines is not the IS ambition. For IS an Islamic state is more than just an ideal for this-worldly life. An Islamic state is a necessary step along a road leading to the end of days and the final judgment. That is what IS has set up. As a result, while IS benefits from being able to show that it can control its territory and its subjects, and that it can do so on Islamic lines, it needs, more importantly, to show that an IS-run state actually works as a state. Anything short of that would confirm the failure of IS as an ideology. Each side, therefore, both those under IS rule and IS itself, has an interest in the existence of some stable form of state structure. In consequence, IS territory is characterized by the workings of a normal state, far more than it is by the brash pronouncements from IS media outlets about crusaders and Jews, or the movement's barbaric killings. The work of the state and its offices is inflected in accordance with an Islamic, even an IS, pattern, but the functions it fulfills are by and large those of any state.

Beyond Sykes-Picot

Geography and history are tremendously influential in the Middle East. For millennia, northern Syria and Iraq have functioned as a transit zone at the meeting points of great empires, marking for many the line separating a civilized West from a savage and threatening east. Alexander versus the Persians, Romans versus the Parthians, Umayyads versus the Abbasids, Ottomans versus the Safavids; these and other such pairings confirm the eternal significance of the area as a frontier region.

Boundaries between states and those inside them, demarcating both political and administrative divisions, are the hallmark of states' existence and identity, and over the millennia those in the Middle East, not just those between empires, have remained remarkably constant. IS pronouncements about the wickedness of the 1916 Sykes-Picot Agreement, by which England and France imposed imperial boundaries in the region, represent a propaganda position far more than a genuine intention to change realities on the ground. The administrative arrangements of earlier empires offer built-in benefits that successor states have learned, in long succession, to exploit. Prime among these is that conferred by continuity: existing arrangements present the attraction of already existing. Resources are always at a premium, so it makes good sense administratively and for the ease of everyone involved to stick with existing systems. A rapid return to normalcy following rude conquest also offers welcome reassurance to those conquered. Thus the administrative divisions of vast areas in the Middle East have remained largely stable and little changed over many centuries, passing from the overall control and suzerainty of one empire after another, right down to the present. IS is not the first, nor will it be the last, to appreciate the value of retaining this kind of vestige of even a hated past. Whatever its ideological claims and propaganda assertions, IS actually does impose internal boundaries in its territory: the Islamic State, like the states it replaces, is divided into *wilayat*, governorates, provinces, and while Islamic law in its IS forms applies throughout IS territory, it issues many administrative decrees and regulations at the local level, for individual provinces. Administrative convenience, especially in a time of hostilities, naturally trumps the dictates of ideology.

The administration set up in IS territory represents continuity in a variety of ways. Not only the basic geographical divisions of administrative units have remained fundamentally the same. Many of the institutions, departments, offices, ministries, and so on have retained their basic functions and occasionally even their names (though IS has chosen, very deliberately, to use the old-fashioned Arabic word *diwan*, rather than *wizara*—both of them originally loan-words in Arabic from Persian—as its term for ministry). Similarly, IS has taken over the offices of government institutions everywhere and by and large assigned them similar roles under its own rule—though the functions fulfilled by these offices have sometimes been renamed or reidentified in accordance with IS ideology, and IS has been careful to decree the elimination of all references to the preceding regimes on its documentation, as well as everywhere else. The functions themselves, however, also remain much the same as before, if only because the requirements and demands that states make on their subjects, like the needs and expectations that subjects have from their rulers, tend to remain largely similar and unchanged from one regime to the next. Finally, little has changed in the character of the personnel in most of these institutions. Whether from a desire to calm the population, or from a lack of trained personnel of its own, IS has recalled those who had abandoned their posts in governmental and public institutions, often with threats of dire alternatives for those unwilling to serve IS. Again this follows a pattern from the past. The result is that for many in IS territory, most aspects of life—electronic communication may be the most obvious and most immediately sensed victim of IS disruption—have returned to relative calm.

As we have seen, we are fortunate to possess several hundred documents emanating from IS territory. Most of these represent official actions taken by IS in its role as a state, as a replacement for the Iraqi and Syrian states. Unlike the political pronouncements shown in the IS videos, these documents take us inside the world of the Islamic State and show us how the subjects, not the soldiers, of IS actually live. They deal with all sorts of topics, from health care and education to public cleansing and garbage disposal, from shop opening hours and provision of bakeries to road-mending and Internet cafés. Many of them are also very local in scope, not because IS has abandoned its dreams of a universal state, but because the irregular character of IS conquests means that the imposition of rules and regulations often responds to local needs.

All of these documents bear visible reminders of the Islamic State. IS wishes its subjects to be aware of who rules them and to feel appropriate gratitude for IS care. Every such document identifies who issues it. Thus an order in late 2013 (shortly before the creation of IS itself) to close shops for twenty-five minutes during times of prayer in a town near Aleppo is headed not only by the traditional expression "In the Name of God the Compassionate the Merciful," but also by the expression "Islamic State in Syria and al-Sham," while the text itself begins "The Islamic State in Iraq and al-Sham in the town of Baza'a announces . . ."[2] Atop many of the documents appear the slogan and the banner of IS, which proclaim and confirm the new dispensation's dominance, even at the level of electricity bills. Anyone, even if only semi-literate, who looks at these documents can see at once who issued them. Dates are given according to both the Islamic and the civil calendars or just in

Islamic form. And the language used, here as elsewhere in IS publications, is coded in ways that are easy to learn but highly effective as a kind of shorthand for IS ideology and condemnation of their opponents: as we have seen, Crusaders are a stand-in for Westerners and Christians (occasionally even Jews); Rafidi (Arabic for "rejecter," or "apostate") is used as a label for Persians (in their quality as Shi'is); Nusayris—a reference to their sectarian identity—identifies the Syrian regime of Bashar al-Asad; "mujahideen" is the IS term for its soldiers—it means literally those engaged in jihad; "diwan," rather than the standard "wizara," as we have seen, serves as the name for "ministry"; and "Muslim brothers," less complicatedly, refers to fellow Muslims—though the use of the term acts as a cover for a hugely important issue: who, for IS, is a Muslim?

Mens Sana

A state offers education to its young. It also requires its young to receive education. The state's population, too, expect the state to provide education for their young. Education also offers a state, whether IS or any other, the opportunity to take children away from their parents for many hours every day and inculcate in them its own attitudes and ideals. IS is no exception in desiring to influence the minds of its children. While IS has retained much of the existing structure of the education system in the territories it has conquered, it has invested great efforts in re-shaping the contents of the system to comport with its own ideas about sexual segregation, about curriculum content, about behavior in schools, about teaching, and about teachers. The documents that we have provide copious information about schools and teaching in IS, from kindergartens right up to university-level institutions.

At Mosul University, according to a notice from the "Islamic State, Caliphate on the Program of the Prophets, Diwan al-Tàlim (Ministry of Education)," dated 24 Dhu al-Hijja 1435 (October 19, 2014), a number of fields of study have been suppressed, because "they are not legitimate according to Sharia." These include "College of human rights, political sciences and fine arts. Archeology, physical education, and philosophy department. Department of management of tourism and hotel institutions," along with the following subjects: democracy, culture, freedoms, rights, and "fiction and theatre in the English and French language and in translation departments." Nor is it permitted to teach "special questions on usury interests, principles of nationalism, racism, pseudo-historical events or geographical divisions that also contravene Islamic Sharia."[3]

Another document, this time from the Province of al-Kheir (Deir al-Zor), cancels all programs issued by the "apostasy" government (*hukumat al-ridda*—the Syrian government), and eliminates the name of the previous regime from all documents. It announces that "the main subjects in the programs of the Islamic State" are "Islamic Sharia, principles of tawheed [monotheism], and the Arabic language." At the same time, "all theories of shirk [idolatry] that speak about the beginning of man and the Sun are to be done away with. The laws of nature are from God's will."[4] And just in case students are unaware of what has been happening around them, "maps of the Islamic State are to be put in the history and geography programs."[5] In the Province of Homs, similarly, the IS Ministry of Education issued a statement "that must be implemented to the letter" canceling teaching of the "doctrine of shirk (polytheism) that the Nusayri regime cultivated in the minds of the people of the town." It decrees establishment of "correct Islamic doctrine free of shirk, apostasy, and sanctifying of idols" and "making children aware that one remains for God alone without the mushrikeen [idol-worshippers] and their idols."[6]

Apart from showing what subjects ruffle IS feathers, the above list shows us interestingly something of what could be studied in earlier days. But the real point is that the space created by the elimination of these subjects makes room for subjects more in line with IS thinking and aims, that is, topics of religious content. Such decrees also mean that in the long run, students will emerge from IS educational institutions lacking much of the foundational knowledge and many of the basic skills necessary to thrive in a modern society that is part of the world economy. This gutting of the secular educational system by IS will affect the future of the area for generations and may well have more dire and lasting effects than the physical destruction it has caused in the territory it controls. The Arab Spring and the ideals that it nurtured have been wholly rejected in this view of what education should be for and about.

The Islamic State's concern with education has taken it deep into the details of educational administration too. It has been active in the routine aspects of public education: issuing examination timetables, registering children for kindergartens and schools, setting dates of terms, opening (or re-opening) kindergartens, publishing application forms for universities and medical schools, and even distributing booklets of helpful advice about how to fill in such forms. Further, in striking testimony to awareness of the dangers that lurk in unrestricted access to schools, "it has been decided not to allow any person to enter the schools on pain of being held liable, except with written permission from the Ministry of Education." "But the Diwan al-Hisbah [a kind of morality police] is exempt from this regulation."[7]

In Deir al-Zor province, in early 2015, detailed regulations provide that uniforms are not compulsory; "no introduction or teaching of any [Asad] regime book is allowed"; students are not to stand up in line when the teacher comes in, "and no prior slogans are to be repeated"; students study every day of the week except for Friday, and "the use of the bell in the school is absolutely forbidden"; classes begin at 8.00 a.m.; and a class lasts for forty-five minutes, with a break after every two classes. Above all, "prayer is to be observed at its time, the call is to be raised for it, a place is to be designated for prayer, and students who wish to pray in the mosque and undertake the remaining duties can do so."[8]

IS has issued directives about the content of textbooks, even at the first-grade level. The cover of one elementary school reader, entitled *I Am a Muslim*, shows a small Islamic State banner in the corner. The rest of the cover is occupied by a composite picture showing the minaret of a mosque; the Kaba, the great shrine in Mecca; and a banner underneath the Kaba bearing the IS slogan "la ilaha illa Allah" (there is no god but Allah). Along the front is what appears to be a depiction of the skyscrapers of New York, including a stylized representation of the Empire State Building, with, to the right, what looks like the façade of a Greek temple, and little boys apparently throwing stones at these symbols of Western decadence and worship of idols.[9] The syllabi of IS schools superficially resemble others, but a heavy emphasis on Islamic subjects is also visible: first-grade schoolbooks in Mosul deal with such subjects as math, sciences, and physical education, but they also look at the Quran, the life of the Prophet, hadith, Islamic creed, Arabic language, and Arabic handwriting. By the time the child reaches fifth grade, the subjects studied have expanded to include English, history, and geography, but the religious subjects are an even more prominent part of the curriculum.[10]

Not all the residents of IS are local. Some are new arrivals, often from Western countries, who have brought their children with them. In recognition of the role played by such immigrants and of the distinctive educational needs that their arrival creates, IS has also worked to establish a special school for the English-speaking children of foreign recruits to IS.[11] This may point to large numbers of English-speaking arrivals. If it does, then that suggests that IS will need to devote considerable resources to building a parallel English-language network of schools, teachers, and textbooks. At the same time, however, IS seems to be ignoring the needs of non-English-speaking children from other regions—Chechens, for example, who are reported to be oddly numerous among IS recruits and volunteers, or immigrants from France. This gap suggests that IS does not anticipate that these children will learn Arabic, and may reveal a trace of reluctance to encourage the mixing of foreign children with locals.

Teachers present a major challenge for IS. As elsewhere, teachers are tremendously important in forming the adult citizen. Hence they also represent the soft underbelly of a regime dedicated to changing society. Teachers themselves must be formed—or sometimes re-formed.[12] Those who worked for the previous regime are clearly dangerous—they may have unapproved ideas and try to inculcate these into their young charges. At the same time, the supply of teachers is not infinite: they cannot all be discharged and replaced with new ones. Allowing some teachers to stay also gives IS a chance to demonstrate that it is not simply a bloodthirsty gang of killers. Teachers in IS territory have typically been summoned to repent their past misdeeds in the classroom and pledge to adhere to the IS ideology.[13] Yet not all teachers are willing to show penitence, while some may not show it sufficiently

well. Thus we hear of teachers being fired, and of new teachers being sought, presumably to replace those lost in this way.[14]

In Corpore Sano

Like education, health imposes massive demands. Costs are enormous, demands limitless, expectations unceasing and often hope-
less, resources always inadequate. In both its Iraqi and its Syrian
areas, IS has inherited the institutional networks and personnel of
the preceding regimes—hospitals, medical schools, pharmacies
and colleges of pharmacy, doctors, nurses, and other supports. As in
the educational sector, continuity of service has been complicated
by the need to repair the physical damage caused by conquest
and war; the falling away or flight of employees; a lack of access to
supplies from outside; not to mention the collapse of educational
institutions. In addition, IS ideology has added special requirements.

On May 18, 2015, three days after the city of Ramadi had
fallen to IS forces, Dr. Abu Othman of the Ramadi Teaching
Hospital issued a statement on behalf of the new authorities "to
our brothers and our people in the beloved Wilayat al-Ramadi." It
announced the resumption of regular hours at the hospital, and
called all those working in the hospital—technicians, administrators, service and health staff—to return to their jobs "in the interest of all our sick."[15] It is not clear if all the workers heeded the
summons, but other such calls have been made, one notably for the
province of the large city of Mosul. Medical personnel and their
role in society bulk large in IS propaganda too. In a long announcement by the IS Ministry of Health in October 2015, we are
reminded of the attacks on IS by the Western crusaders, with
Barack Obama at their head, and of the Prophet Muhammad's account of "a division of the world into two camps with no third way
for the two." The message goes on to "call on all medical cadres
who abandoned the land of Islam after the rise of the state and the
announcement of the Caliphate or those residing in the abode of
disbelief to return and migrate to the land of the Caliphate and the
abode of Islam, a land of glory for the believers, and to join the
medical cadres in all the provinces of the Islamic State—may God

make it mighty—to enjoy security, safety and glory under the rule of Islam."[16]

Supplies of medical goods are also a problem. IS has stressed that medical supplies cannot be used if they come from Iran—the land of the "Rafidis," or "rejecters," that is, Shi'is. Even the import of Iranian food is forbidden, because "they found that the watermelon was contaminated with poisonous substances," and there was a "lack of trust in Iranian medical treatments/goods etc., for these are a people of treachery and betrayal who are not to be trusted, for this is their habit."[17] Similarly, a decree of May 2015 forbade the continued operation of medical aid organizations in Tal Abyad and ordered the takeover of their operations, together with all their equipment. The danger from foreign, non-Islamic involvement in IS medical activity was too great. Autarky, self-sufficiency, is preferred. Thus in October 2014, the General Supervisory Committee of IS announced the opening of a factory to make synthetic body parts. Anyone who needs such an item should "go and register with the Ministry of Health to send for the desired part by writing to the factory." And there was a postscript: "Notice: please do not send any ill person to Turkey to have a part made."[18] Iran is not the only foreign Muslim country viewed with suspicion and hostility.

Not all body parts can be made in a factory. Sometimes they can be taken from cadavers, or in certain cases from living donors. One of the documents apparently brought back by U.S. special forces from a raid in eastern Syria in May 2015, in the form of a fatwa, or legal opinion, even authorizes taking body parts from living captives who are non-Muslims in order to save a Muslim life.[19] While the authenticity of this document is not completely above suspicion, its general tenor and approach do not conflict with IS behavior in other areas.

Sexual and moral norms present special difficulties. Segregation of the sexes is an old Middle Eastern and Mediterranean practice that was absorbed early on into Islam. Men and women may not be in contact unless they are *mahrim* (non-marriageable)—that is, people who because of close family relationships and the like may not marry.[20] For medical practitioners and their patients, this rule created real problems. Doctors need to be able to examine their patients, to talk to them and even to touch them. Medieval and early modern Islamic sources tell many stories of how doctors—always men—dealt with the problem of access to female patients. They might talk to them with a curtain drawn between them; a hand might be slipped out, possibly with a thin silk covering, through a slit in a curtain for a doctor to see, or a portion of a female body could be made visible through a hole in a coverlet.[21] Many female patients endured the medical attentions offered by women practitioners who possessed even less training or medical education than most male doctors.[22] Modernity did little to change things. Although women doctors became available as early as the middle of the nineteenth century, responding to the ambitions and the investments made by Muhammad Ali and his successors in Egypt, their patients were principally also women, and the sexual divide remained largely unaltered.

Not surprisingly, given its concern with women's status and behavior, IS has returned to this divide within the medical sphere. A fatwa issued on December 17, 2014, answered a question about "the presence of the nurse with a doctor in the same clinic without a mahrim in the town and some of the villages." The answer was unequivocal: "It is forbidden for a woman to be left alone with the man who is a stranger." All jurists agree on this. The Prophet even said, "A man is not to be left with a woman unless their third is Satan." The only possible way in which a female nurse can attend a male doctor is if a group of other women is present as well.[23]

CHAPTER THREE

Revenue

NONE OF THE NEEDS or desires of IS as a governing organism can be accomplished without revenue, and like any state, IS depends on a variety of sources to fund its operations. Health services and education, road-building, sewage and water services, salaries for soldiers and the leadership, to say nothing of military supplies, all cost money. If newspaper accounts are to be believed, IS is the richest and most financially successful terrorist outfit in history. It appears to draw funding both from regular, normal sources—taxation, and fees paid for services including water, gas, and other utilities—as well as from more irregular sources, including plunder, seizure of gold and other valuables from Christians migrating out of IS-controlled territory, simple theft and extortion, black-market sales of antiquities, and oil sales on a very gray international market.[1] Money is also said to flow to the group from sources in Saudi Arabia and the Gulf, both private and at least somewhat public. The Islamic State may have an annual income in the hundreds of millions of dollars, and reserves that would make many a small country envious.

Gray, however, is the dominant color in our knowledge here. We seem to know a great deal about the less normal revenue sources of IS. The media provide a constant stream of reports about IS seizure of property from those it conquers. The argument used to justify this is that it is permitted under a traditional Islamic (and not only Islamic) view of the rights conferred by conquest. Occasionally, hints surface in the documents available to us about how this works. For example, in what looks like an attempt to control undisciplined or overenthusiastic seizure of property by supporters of IS, on 18 Ramadan 1436 (July 5, 2015), in the province of Raqqa, the IS capital, an announcement made it "absolutely forbidden for [the mujahideen brothers] to attack the homes and properties of the Kurds under any justification or pretext." Violators were to be punished.[2] Discipline applies even to the act of plundering in the IS.

The taking of plunder, in the form of wealth or of slaves, has a long history, and it is no surprise to find IS encouraging its soldiers to grab the spoils of its conquests. Apart from any historical, or quranic, justification, the historical basis offers those doing the plundering the feeling that their booty enjoys religious sanction. Confiscation of gold, money, and jewelry from those Christians permitted to depart from IS territory (which recalls Nazi seizure of property from Jews permitted to leave Germany in the 1930s, or Soviet charges on emigrants in the 1970s and 1980s) is a slightly different form of plundering, but a similar principle seems to be at work.

In the context of revenue or fund-raising for a state apparatus, however, these stories should not be exaggerated. Picturesque as they are, if disagreeably reminiscent of medieval stories of conquests and battles lost and won, the real financial import of these essentially one-off sorts of plunder by IS cannot have great significance in the context of a territory as large as that controlled by IS and with the ongoing needs of a population in the millions. While IS makes a point of seizing the caliph's "fifth" of any plunder that is taken, the income generated in this way is by definition unpredictable.[3] Especially today, when the stream of conquests has slowed more or less to a halt, the amounts generated by these sources must be greatly reduced. Larger and more reliable sources are needed.

Such sources are found, according to the reports we have, partly in donations from Saudi Arabia and the Gulf. About these, once again, little is known, and we have next to no idea of their possible size. Their real importance may lie less in their amounts than in their indication of occasionally widespread quiet support for at least parts of the ideology and aims of IS. Here as elsewhere a muddy opacity obscures the distinction between the ideas and practices of IS and those of other groups that are more acceptable to the West or to conservative circles in the Islamic world itself. The amounts raised in this way, like the routes that they take to get to IS, cannot be known. Similarly, there is no way that IS can know that such donations will continue to arrive. Something more reliable is needed.

Taxes

Taxes, with their promise of a regular, predictable delivery of income, must be the foundation of a workable revenue system for a state. Taxation, therefore, should be the most interesting category of revenue for IS. In this area, though, for IS as an Islamic state, religion can prove both a boon and a bane. The Quran recognizes the need for and the permissibility of taxation. At the same time, however, it lays down, and hence limits, what taxes may be levied.[4] The corollary of that is that other taxes are non-quranic and therefore impermissible. A great many populist and religious movements in Islam through the past fourteen centuries have sought to justify their opposition to existing regimes with the complaint that they are levying non-quranic taxes. Only quranic taxes may be raised in a state that claims to be Islamic. A state that levies non-quranic taxes cannot claim to be run on genuinely Islamic lines. Unfortunately, as reality all too often demonstrates, practical immediate needs frequently outrun a state's income, and the usual solution is to ignore the quranic prohibitions and invent new taxes that will raise the additional revenue required.

We do not yet possess enough solid information to judge whether IS is following the traditional pattern, and in this initial, idealistic phase is levying only quranic taxes, or at least what it defines as quranic taxes. For the moment it seems to be practicing a fuzzy approach, raising taxes as it needs them but combining them with other sources of revenue. We do know that *jizya*, a kind of tax levied on Christians, is being employed, because it is mentioned in documents concerning Christians under IS rule. In addition, we can assume that IS charges fees for driver licenses, birth and death certificates, and the like; and we know also that it charges, less formally, truck drivers delivering produce along roads into and out of IS territory. But the real impact of the sums raised by such charges must be small.

In this sphere as in some others, IS apparently recognizes that the world has moved on since the time of Muhammad. IS seems to consider itself bound, as a state, to provide certain services to the public under its rule that were not provided in the seventh century, including some that did not exist at that time. Modern reality demands this, and the needs of the Islamic State, like those of any state, demand it too. Health and education are foremost among these, both to ensure that the subjects of IS are in good health and to provide for the future personnel of IS operations, military and nonmilitary. Acceptance of this important change may go along with a revised interpretation of what taxes should be considered quranic and permissible in a state in the twenty-first century, or at least a revised understanding of how such taxes should be defined and presented in an Islamic context.

This leaves many questions unanswered: Is a form of sales tax permitted? And if one is being levied, can IS devise a formula that will bring it into the circle of quranically permitted imposts? Other questions are still more obscure—can we be sure that our sparse documentation presents a single unified picture of taxation across the entire IS territory? Are former Iraqi territories being taxed in the same way as areas taken from Syria? How are taxes being assessed and collected? It is hard to imagine tax collectors for IS going door to door for the money. But it is even harder to imagine some sort of direct deduction at least for income and sales taxes. At some point, documents emanating from inside the IS will probably give us an indication of how IS defines and determines taxes, tax rates, and the like, and then we shall know more about how the movement views taxation in the modern context.

The Past as a Resource

Apart from private donations from the Gulf, the Islamic State is said to rely heavily on huge illegal sales of antiquities and oil. Here again, though, fuzz and gray dominate our knowledge. The pictures showing enthusiastic volunteers wielding hammers and drills on imposing ruins, especially statues, from antiquity at such sites as Palmyra that fill our TV screens and newspapers are accompanied by stories about IS agents infiltrating masses of smaller pieces of loot onto the international black market. We have only a limited understanding of the scale and seriousness of the problem, however.[5]

In this area the international community has attempted to do more than indulge in ritual hand-wringing over its inability to stop or control IS. The United Nations and other national and international bodies have passed worthy resolutions outlawing trade in stolen antiquities and forbidding their transport into member states' territories. Following the release of a video by IS showing the destruction at the Mosul Museum, the British Institute for the Study of Iraq said that it "greatly regrets the appalling damage that has been done" in Mosul, Nineveh, Nimrud, and Hatra, describing the situation as "a cultural disaster of the greatest magnitude."[6] Archeologists and museum curators around the world also denounced the damage, with the head of Unesco, Irina Bokova, calling for an emergency meeting of the Security Council of the United Nations to discuss how to protect Iraq's cultural heritage.[7]

In truth, however, the international community could do as little to stop IS from destroying cultural artifacts as it could to stop it from killing its enemies in ever uglier fashion. In May 2015, the General Assembly of the United Nations condemned "the barbaric acts of destruction and looting of the cultural heritage of Iraq," pointing out that such acts "may amount to war crimes"; it called for all states to join in fighting against trafficking in antiquities; and it expressed support for the Security Council's resolution, passed in February of that year, that aimed to stop IS financing, in particular through a ban on trade in oil and in antiquities.[8] Months later, in September of 2015, at yet another international conference called to discuss the problem, Irina Bokova said, "Culture has always been a victim of war, but what we're seeing today is new."[9] What was new was both the scale of the destruction and that it was being carried out deliberately and publicly, as part of a policy that aimed to wipe out an entire culture and to publicize the destruction as widely as possible.[10]

In the interim, the United States had acted too. On June 1, in a unanimous vote, Congress passed legislation that "would make it illegal to sell looted artifacts from Syria, dealing a blow to the Islamic State's finances and agenda."[11] The executive branch of the U.S. government also took aim at this illicit trade. It hosted a meeting at the Metropolitan Museum in New York, in late September 2015, attended by government officials, antiquities professionals, international civil servants, and others, at which it presented details of materials seized when Abu Sayyaf, a senior IS official, was killed, along with information about the secret illicit trade in the heritage of humanity from Syria and Iraq. Speakers at the meeting came from the UN Office on Drugs and Crime as well as the State Department and elsewhere. The meeting was an international, internetwork assembly devoted to finding ways to strengthen cooperation and stifle the financing of IS through the illegal trade in looted antiquities.

Andrew Keller, a deputy assistant secretary for Counter Threat Finance and Sanctions in the State Department's Bureau of Economic and Business Affairs, gave a PowerPoint presentation in which he argued that antiquities were "just another resource" from which IS raked in huge profits. He showed pictures of some of the items retrieved in the U.S. raid on Abu Sayyaf's compound, including pieces of sculpture, jewelry, and coins, together with a handful of documents translated into English. His conclusion was that the trade helps fund IS, and because the supply is hard to control, it is necessary to "address demand."[12]

The International Council of Museums, possibly responding to that sentiment, has also produced at varying times an "Emergency Red List of Syrian Cultural Objects at Risk," together with another one for Iraqi objects.[13] In the space of just a few pages, these offer pictures and brief descriptions of some thirty or so remarkably varied (and often very beautiful) ancient and medieval objects of types that are subject to looting and theft in these two countries. (These lists themselves belong to a larger series of publications covering also African, Latin American, Afghan, Cambodian, Haitian, and other items at risk.)

The magnitude of the investment by the State Department and others in the meeting at the Metropolitan, like the actions in the

U.S. Congress and the United Nations, as well as the production of the Emergency Red Lists, demonstrate that everyone concerned is aware of the gravity of the situation and is taking it seriously. Professionals and scholars, as well as administrators, government officials, and international civil servants, are showing their shared commitment to defend the heritage of these two countries, which they see, rightly, as the common heritage of all of humanity. Even so, their investment may not be paying off, and the results may be less impressive than they appear. Just as importantly, they may also reveal less about IS and its attitudes and activity than they appear to.

The Emergency Red Lists are beautifully produced. They are each eight pages long, though four pages of each of them are devoted to title pages and introductions and lists of useful addresses. Only four pages in each list are given over to pictures and descriptions of actual objects, some thirty or so in each list. And although it appears at the top of the list itself in each publication, one scarcely notices, as one's eye moves down to the pictures beneath, the "IMPORTANT NOTE" that tells us that "The Red List is NOT a list of actual stolen objects . . . The cultural goods depicted . . . serve to illustrate the categories of cultural goods protected by legislation and most vulnerable to illicit traffic." And then one observes, from the captions, that most of the pictures show objects from Syrian (or Iraqi) collections such as the National Museum of Damascus or the Idlib Museum, while others show objects from the collections of the Bavarian State Archeological Collection, Munich; the British Museum; or the Royal Museums of Art and History, Brussels.

Far from being true "Emergency" lists of stolen goods, of hot property that is flooding the insatiable, under-the-counter international market in antiquities, these attractively produced pamphlets are in fact nothing more than guides to the sorts of objects that might be offered for sale, and that might be of illicit background, and that might be of Syrian (or Iraqi) origin. Or not.

The international market for antiquities, of all sorts and sizes, of all dates, from all parts of the world, is large and greedy. As with famous paintings by modern artists, collectors are eager to snap up whatever they can find and, often, to spirit it into private collections away from the prying eyes of others, whether the interested public or the law. Much is stolen, both from established collections (generally at times of civil stress, as in Syria today or in Iraq following the U.S. invasion—who can forget the disdainful boorishness of the remark by the then U.S. Secretary of Defense, on being told of the plundering of the National Museum in Baghdad, that "stuff happens"?) or via illegal excavations. And the Red Lists do indeed illustrate what kinds of objects may become available. But that is all they do. Illegal trade in antiquities is an everyday problem; the Red Lists are part of the everyday response. It is a puzzle whom they are aimed at—professionals, such as museum curators, will not need them; traders in antiquities and the rich collectors who are their clients will ignore them except as indicators of what kinds of stolen items they should be on the lookout to buy; and others will not know about them or will have little access to the kinds of objects they show.

Coins

Not all such objects, however, are vastly expensive or rare. One of the participants in that meeting, Ute Wartenberg Kagan of the American Numismatic Society, wrote a short paper outlining the unique problem posed by looted coins.[14] Coins are small and easily transportable; because of their value as precious metal and their premodern use in international commerce, their source—where they were discovered in modern times—is often difficult to ascertain; and they generally do not command astronomical prices. These same characteristics, moreover, make it unusually hard to identify coins that come from IS-controlled zones.

Wartenberg Kagan was able, despite this challenge, to show very neatly that it was fairly likely that some ancient coins were entering the market from IS sources. By looking not at the cheaper end of the market—ancient coins and coins of medieval Islam can be bought in this country for as little as ten or fifteen dollars—but at a small selection of coins of greater rarity and importance, she was able to track an increase in their availability in the market over the last few years.

She looked at three types of rare coins. The first was a special coinage that Zenobia, the famous queen of Palmyra in the third century, along with her son Vabalathus, had minted during three months in the year 272 at Antioch. Such coins are extremely rare: in the years 1800 through 2010, only some 125 had become known. Since then, a further twenty-seven specimens have come to light, with a surge in that (still very small) number coming in 2012–2015. It is tempting to see this increase, and especially the surge in the first half of this decade, as connected with IS. But as Wartenberg Kagan points out, there is no necessary link: a variety of other explanations are possible. First, it is possible that the outbreak of the Syrian civil war in 2011, not the arrival of IS, was what generated the collapse in security leading to an increase in the discovery and marketing of these coins. Secondly, the trade in ancient coins, fed by both legal and less legal sources, carries on all the time, and changes in small numbers of known specimens of rare types need not be attributed to some large external influence like a civil war; they could just as easily result from the chance discovery by a peasant working his fields of a hoard of coins buried many centuries ago. And thirdly, coins travel. They exist in order to make commerce possible, and so they can and do turn up all over the place: for example, an Abbasid coin reached England in the eighth century where it was imitated by Offa the king of Mercia between 757 and 796; and enormous hoards of silver coins minted in what is now Iran in the eighth and ninth centuries turn up nowadays along ancient trade routes in Scandinavia. That is the character of silver and gold coins. Thus even though these coins of Zenobia were minted in Antioch, in Syria, then under Palmyrene rule, there is no reason to assume that the specimens coming to market in recent years must come from that region. A link with IS, though possible, is far from sure, and certainly not provable.

Wartenberg Kagan performs a similar exercise using two further well-chosen types of coins. One is another rare type, this time of coins minted in the second century before Christ, from mints in what is now western Turkey. She chose these because the rare specimens of this coin type that we have today turn up mainly in the Syrian region, very far from where they were minted. Once again, that coins travel is relevant, but in this case, it is not where they are made, like the coins of Zenobia, but the findspots—where coins get to—that is relevant. It seems not unreasonable to expect that a sudden growth in supply of such coins on the antiquities market may have a connection with findspots in the area where such coins normally turn up, in Syria. Again, she notes a peak in supply of new coins coming to market in 2014, but her table also shows a gradual increase over the last fifteen years. The year 2014 is an upward blip in a rising market. As she points out, a newly discovered hoard or two could easily be responsible for the increase in supply. Once again, a role for IS is possible, but we cannot say more than that.

The third case concerns a large hoard that was apparently found at Masyaf in Syria, around 1961. But though it was found in Syria, the bulk of its contents were coins that were manufactured all over the eastern Mediterranean region. As she writes, this "is one of many hoards from the Near East and Egypt that illustrate the circulation of early coinage in this region."

While the numbers of coins involved in Wartenberg Kagan's demonstration were very small, and the likelihood that a few of them originated in IS-controlled territory is great, it cannot be shown with certainty that any of them actually come from there. Some coins, like those in her first example, were manufactured in areas now under the control of IS; others, like those in her second class, made elsewhere, generally turn up in areas now associated with IS rule; and others again, as her third example demonstrates, can easily turn up anywhere. Gold and silver coins have value not just as money but also as bullion. It is virtually impossible to know, if one does not have outside knowledge of the findspots of individual specimens or hoards, where coins coming to market derive from.

Coins are antiquities; they are small and easy to transport; unlike larger objects that are more obviously one of a kind and therefore identifiable, they were made in their thousands and are, particularly to the non-specialist, more or less indistinguishable from each other; they are relatively cheap, compared with large statues or the like, and therefore find a market more easily than larger objects; and for similar reasons they can easily disappear once sold. For all these reasons, even with careful investigative work like that by Wartenberg Kagan we cannot be sure what kind of impact IS control, as distinct from the more normal kinds of civil upheaval and general illicit plundering, is having on the market. The figures suggest that whatever impact it is having is slight.

Other Archeological Treasures

Coins are not the only surviving remains from our ancient past. All sorts of objects, from bone needles to oil lamps, and on up to huge statues and sarcophagi and stones bearing inscriptions, turn up in excavations, both those conducted by archeologists with licenses from local governments and those carried out in the dark by local enthusiasts whose aim is personal profit. Like coins, these objects are not always easy to identify as coming from the conflict areas of Syria and Iraq, though an original area of manufacture in such a region can often be confirmed. And like coins, they are special objects of interest to those who wish to stifle IS funding derived from illicit smuggling and sale.

Yet here again, as with the coins, puzzles remain. While antiquities stolen by IS can be sold to buyers from anywhere, the United States is clearly a market of choice for such sales. It is the heart of the international market and it has the most potential buyers. But the United States is also a highly bureaucratized country, and statistics are available for almost anything one wants to know. A group devoted to cultural heritage law, Red Arch, suggested one way of using government statistics to study the flow of conflict antiquities from IS territory in Iraq into the United States. Its conclusion was that "more antiques [were] imported from Iraq than goods like lambskin leather, dates and figs, fruit juices, and even spices."[15] At the same time, though, they estimated the amounts involved to be very low: less than $4 million worth of illicit antiquities were imported in 2014.

The Red Arch study used figures from the U.S. International Trade Commission to support these conclusions. Another set of figures, from the U.S. Census Bureau, offers similar results. Taking Iraq and Syria together, these show imports of numismatic coins in 2014 as amounting to some $457,000. This is a high for the decade; only in 2011 did the figures reach even $330,000. The amounts differ for the various years, with Syria sending a lot more coins than Iraq to the United States. Yet the salient point is that only a very small total amount is involved.[16]

If we turn again from coins to the larger category of archeology and antiquities more generally, the picture remains similar. In

2014, Syria sent antiques valued at just under $5 million to the United States, while Iraq sent just over that sum. But here too, as with the coins, the figures have varied dramatically, for both countries, over the past decade: for Iraq the amounts were under a million dollars until 2007; thereafter, they fluctuated between $1.5 million and a little over $8 million. There seems to be no clear pattern, just an up-and-down movement within low levels of trade; and a figure of $5.2 million for 2014 (which is rather higher than the Red Arch figure of just under $3.4 million) should not appear either as very large or as indicative of intensive activity by "archeologists" backed by IS or related groups. Syria, similarly, with a low of just under $2 million in 2005, fluctuates thereafter, at a higher level than Iraq, between $2.4 million in 2006 and $11 million in 2013, then falling to just under $5 million in 2014.[17] Once again, these are not amounts that a state-sized organization can rely on to run a state, especially when we remember that IS or other such groups are certainly not receiving these amounts. At best, these are the amounts that those middlemen who sell these objects to the United States receive. IS would receive much, much less for them.

Finding the Loopholes

Critics will point to problems with such an approach—the United States is not the only market for illicit antiquities; government figures, even U.S. government figures, are patchy and far less reliable than they look; more narrowly, figures for these particular types of imports are likely to conceal a great deal, for instance, antiquities may well be entering under other headings (though a glance at the available import categories suggests that "toiletries and cosmetics," or "hair, waste materials," may not offer easy ways to hide them); antiquities may somehow not be listed at all; records may have been incorrectly filed or not submitted; smuggling may bring much more into the country than we can know; or illegally traded goods such as conflict antiques may be exported first to countries that are less observant of their own laws and then re-exported on to the United States.[18] Lending credibility to the suspicion that other countries may be laundering these goods, some countries on the lists appear to be exporting, or perhaps re-exporting, vast amounts of goods to the United States that they do not even produce. Monaco, for example, which is less than one square mile in size, is one of the most crowded states on Earth, and has no agriculture, apparently sent $125,000 of fruits and frozen juices to the United States in 2014.[19]

Yet although government statistics are notorious for their inexactitude and though it can be easy to categorize imported products under different headings, these figures are nonetheless indicative of the general situation, and over time offer fairly dependable indications of trends and of relative amounts.

Numismatics, coins, are not a bad guide here. It is very easy to smuggle a couple of ancient coins picked up on a foreign trip. You can just put them in your pocket along with your small change. But that has little or no effect on the figures. Even if a thousand tourists do that, it does little or nothing to change either the statistics or, more significantly here, IS finances. The only way IS can benefit from large-scale illicit trade in coins is through otherwise legal imports of large numbers of coins. The official figures have a separate category for numismatics, both from Iraq and from Syria. And these show, as we have seen, totals that, while higher since the rise of IS, are not dramatically higher than in previous years. As with the evidence for a small number of very select coins examined by Wartenberg Kagan, this rise is another blip. More significantly, and again as with Wartenberg Kagan, the overall totals involved are tiny at best, in the context of a movement as large as IS. Even taking into account the figures for Syria and Iraq together, and those not only for coins but for antiquities, they amount to no more than a few million dollars. Further, IS is certainly not getting all that money—middlemen and other costs along the way all demand a share of the pickings. And while IS is certainly trying to sell to markets outside the United States too, such markets are smaller than that of the United States. Illegal sales of antiquities from IS territory make very good newspaper and TV copy—though a careful examination of that copy suggests that most of it relates in fact to destruction rather than sales—but verifiable information gives no support to the view that IS is cornering a market or raking in real money from such sales.

Illicit Trade in Antiquities: The Reality

Beyond all that, it is far less clear either that such movement or trade is even taking place—scarcely any evidence seems to have been picked up by the authorities of Western countries—or, if it is, that it is occurring on a significant scale. If such sales were generating meaningfully large sums in terms of IS and its operations, then we can be sure that we would see more evidence, in the form of confiscations by customs agents and reports by journalists and scholars. The news stories we read are compelling, and they appeal to the universal urge to do something to help protect and conserve irreplaceable records of our common past, but while the destruction appears to be all too real, and important, the surreptitious stealing and sale of smaller pieces remain just out of sight. If they are happening at all, they probably merge into the (not inconsiderable) general illegal trade in antiquities that the international community is always trying to curtail, with varying degrees of success.[20]

Iraq and Syria are not alone in offering rich pickings to the looters of antiquities. One recent report, looking at the situation in the West Bank, where security is lax and law enforcement in this area understandably light, reports the existence of some twelve thousand archeological sites of all periods, with many hundreds, possibly thousands, of them already picked at by treasure-hunters.[21] IS territory is just as rich in ancient sites, and probably equally subject to plundering, with the effects of such illegal digging probably not much worse, even though IS appears to have made special efforts to take control of archeological exploration for commercial purposes. IS contributions to this trade, whether of coins or of other larger types of antiquities, have not depressed the market, and few if any items identifiably from IS territory grace our museums or, apparently, our customs storehouses.

Black Gold

As with antiquities, oil too represents a problem. It is oil, so we are given to understand, that, more than anything else, makes IS "the richest terrorist outfit in history."[22] The movement supposedly makes $1 to 3 million a day from illegal sales of oil on the international black market.[23] Its cash reserves of half a billion or a billion dollars, if they really exist, apparently come largely from this source, dwarfing everything else the group has except perhaps the scarcely credible amounts—as much as half a billion dollars—reported for paper money taken from banks at the time of the capture of such towns as Mosul.

When IS seized control of oil fields in eastern Syria, the price of a barrel of oil was more than a hundred dollars. At the time of writing the first draft of these lines, it is less than half that price. Whatever oil IS manages to sell is affected by that fact. The world is suffering from, or enjoying, a glut of oil, thanks in part to U.S. oil from shale and in part also to the refusal of OPEC countries, headed by Saudi Arabia, to cut back production in the face of collapsing prices. The return of Iran to the oil market in early 2016 has only made the overproduction worse, and so lowered crude prices even further. At the end of January 2016, the benchmark price of Brent crude had sunk to twenty-seven dollars, its lowest price since 2003.

Naturally, IS has to spend money from its reserves—there are plenty of stories, true and invented, confirming the wisdom of spending reserves to preserve power ("you cannot have an army without money; and you cannot have money without an army," according to the eighth-century Abbasid caliph al-Mansur)—but the income from oil sales should more than cover such expenditures. Even the generous payments made to foreign volunteers fighting in IS ranks—at one time as much as a thousand dollars per month—seem unlikely quickly to drain such coffers.[24]

The numbers we read are nevertheless worth a closer look. A century ago, the German war historian Hans Delbrück gave a series of lectures in London, subsequently published in 1913 as *Numbers in History*.[25] Delbrück made two central points that are of enduring relevance and have special application here. The first concerns the sheer credibility of large numbers, and the second applies to logistics, to what is possible in a given space or situation. Whether our sources are ancient historians or modern writers makes no difference. The lessons are the same.

First, numbers, in particular large numbers, and in particular large numbers that cannot easily be checked, should arouse our wariness and our skepticism. For example, Napoleon claimed that in his first campaign, of 1796, he conquered 80,000 Austrians and Sardinians with 30,000 men; but in truth he was only a little weaker than his opponent, some 40,000 against 47,000 men.[26]

Delbrück stresses that the numbers given by commanders, as in this case, are frequently false, not least because a general wishes to give the impression that he has defeated a huge enemy force with numerically very inferior soldiers of his own. Small numbers on the conquering side magnify the effect of the victory and, still more, burnish the successful general's own reputation. Inflated "body counts" in Vietnam a couple of generations ago impressed this lesson anew on a country's attention.

Secondly, whether it is ancient Greece or modern Iraq, movements and supplies exist in a world of real possibilities:

> It is impossible to form a judgment about any act of fighting if you do not picture to yourself the size of the armies. A movement that a thousand men would make forthwith is for twenty thousand already a strategic movement; for 100,000 a masterpiece, for 300,000 an impossibility.[27]

And:

> Herodotus tells us quite exactly that 5,100,000 men was the strength of the army of Xerxes, including all the servants that followed the warriors. Seldom in these 2500 years has this number been doubted, and even up to date it has found defenders, although, if it were true, one may calculate that, marching through paths, often very narrow, between the mountains, the last men could only have left Susa, beyond the Tigris, when the first arrived before Thermopylae.[28]

Here, too, Delbrück is telling us that if a vast number of men just could not have fit on a battlefield of a particular size, or if the carrying capacity of a set of roads is too small for the numbers asserted in our sources, then we have to doubt our sources, not insist on blind acceptance of what they say.

The lessons here are simple: we need to consider the credibility of our sources, and we need to do so with an understanding of the real context in which things are happening. This is just as true whether it is a battlefield at Thermopylae, in ancient Greece, or the parking area for oil tanker trucks at the border between Turkey and Iraq in 2016; whether it is soldiers twenty-five centuries ago or truck drivers today.

In the present case, it is not just that a billion, whether dollars or anything else, is a very round figure—much easier to throw about than, say, 870,000,000, or 1,137,000,000. A billion is also extremely large. You can buy a lot of oil for that sum. How much, precisely? Clearly, that depends on how much it costs. At the end of 2014, when IS was going strong, the benchmark price for oil hovered around a hundred dollars a barrel. A year later, at the end of 2015, it was less than half that, thirty-six dollars per barrel. And in early 2016, as we have seen, it was at twenty-seven dollars a barrel, before lifting to forty-five dollars a barrel in the fall of 2016.

Numbers matter. How much does IS get for its oil? It gets as much as it can, like everyone else who has something to sell. But its reach is constrained by a variety of factors, some of them unusual. First there are the regular costs involved in extracting oil from the ground and getting it to market, in tanker trucks sent to the Turkish border. The basic initial costs of development, buying equipment, and boring wells have already been met by the oil companies that opened up the oil wells now controlled by IS. But that does not mean that IS gets its oil completely free. The workers in the oil fields, who have been summoned back to work by IS often under dire threats in the case of failure to appear, earn normal amounts, possibly increased somewhat at the moment as an encouragement to obedience. Nonetheless, the oil fields are large, numbers of workers are not small, and the total cost of their pay is high, even for an organization as large as IS. A report quoted in *Business Insider* mentions 253 wells under IS control in Syria, though only 161 of these are operational, and 275 engineers and just over 1,100 other workers. The same report describes Iraqi oil engineers receiving a daily rate of pay of $300, "rising to nearly $1,000 when they deal with technical problems."[29] Keeping oil wells operational can be complicated. Similarly, while the drivers probably do not earn much individually, in large numbers their pay adds up; and the cost of trucks, whether bought or hired, is far from insignificant. Related costs, gas charges for the tankers themselves, security for the tankers, payments (including bribes) to people along the way, border crossing, and so on, cannot be ignored.

Above all, IS is operating in a gray zone in terms of oil sales. Some of the oil is sold in the region where it was pumped, whether that is under IS control or nearby. But the bulk is aimed, has to be aimed, at a different, international market, with higher prices. Yet IS cannot sell its oil directly on that international market. Local hostilities and international sanctions, as well as proclaimed IS attitudes to trade with the enemy, all prevent open sales. IS has to operate through a number of shady middlemen on a very dark black market. It is they who get the oil into the international arena where oil carries no "Made in the Islamic State" label and obscure its origins so that even we here in the United States cannot know whether what we are putting in our gas tanks comes from the United States, Kuwait, or IS. These middlemen do not pay IS $100 per barrel, at the price levels of late 2014. They do not pay even the $36 per barrel that oil cost in late 2015. They are certainly paying IS very much less than that. IS may be paid initially—but not, of course, because of the costs involved, netting—as little as $10 or $15 per barrel. It may be getting much less even than that.[30]

At a price of ten dollars a barrel, it would take 100 million barrels to yield a billion dollars for IS. How many tanker truckloads is that? Tanker trucks vary in capacity, but they can carry somewhere between roughly 131 and 276 barrels per truck. One hundred million barrels at somewhere between 131 and 276 barrels per truck means somewhere between 362,000 and 764,000 trucks. And the lower the price, the more tanker truckloads would be required to reach the billion-dollar mark.

That does not mean actual trucks of course. It means truckloads. And that brings us to the twelve thousand trucks reported to be waiting patiently on the Turkish border.[31] Twelve thousand trucks, with twelve thousand truck drivers, and possibly a large number of substitute drivers and miscellaneous other colleagues and camp followers, is a lot. Does IS have so many truck drivers? It is not necessary, of course, for IS actually to have so many truck drivers in its forces. Drivers may be sympathizers, and IS and its middlemen may also be using otherwise inactive, unemployed drivers in northern Iraq and Syria, who have no connection to IS or to any other such movement, to transport trucks bearing oil to the Turkish border. Such a large number of driving jobs must have an effect on unemployment figures in a region not oversupplied with jobs. Their wages must have an effect on the economy of the area.

However unpleasant IS is to those under its rule, its borders are notoriously porous when necessary. But twelve thousand trucks in one place raise other problems. In the first place, who owns them? Where do they come from? Do they carry some sort of insurance? Secondly, the logistics of twelve thousand men in a single place who were not there a day before and are staying, possibly for some time, even through attacks by pinprick accurate Russian bombing (presumably no more accurate in reality than such bombing by others) and the subsequent explosions and firestorms that that causes, because they have to stay until they have unloaded their oil and can safely leave, are enormous. What about toilets? Water? Food supplies for twelve thousand men? We hear nothing at all of any of this. Twelve thousand people are the population of a small town.

The very number, twelve thousand, is suspiciously large. It becomes still more largely suspicious when we hear a more precise figure from a Russian spokesman, Lieutenant-General Sergey Rudskoy. His figure is 11,775.[32] That number could, of course, be not only precise but accurate and true. But for it to be accurate and true calls for exact counting of some sort to have taken place, whether on the ground or from the air. The latter could certainly yield good approximations. But the number seems just a little specious. The careful observer would like more detail.

Other questions intrude: what is the production capacity of the oil wells controlled by IS? What was it before the takeover, and what is it now, following what must be a high degree of degradation caused not only by bombing but also by wear and tear and the normal effects of the activity of oil production on the plant? Related to that, further, can we know whether IS possessed and was able to maintain the storage capacity for such a vast amount of oil at its oil production facilities until, suddenly, twelve thousand trucks became available to take the oil to market?

The figure of twelve thousand, like that of 11,775, comes from Russian sources, and clearly is aimed at a Turkish audience. Russia has accused Turkey of colluding with IS to push illegal oil onto the international market. That should make us even more cautious about accepting these figures. Rejecting them, however, creates further problems, not least in identifying the possible routes and methods adopted by large numbers of trucks and truckloads of smuggled oil, or the pipelines occasionally suggested as channels for IS oil sales. In particular, it makes for problems in estimating IS oil revenues at any very high figure. For IS as for legally operating oil companies, there could easily come a point where it makes no economic or any other kind of sense to bring oil to market. Because of the pricing system that IS has to use and the extremely low prices that it can now command for its oil, that point is likely to be reached sooner for IS than for regular sources. And that makes it all the more difficult to identify the sources and quantities of IS funding.

All of these puzzles may have solutions, and some of them may be both true and acceptable. But until we have those answers and can assess them against what we know, it would be unwise to grant too much credence to the reports of IS growing rich on the oil of northern Syria and Iraq.[33]

Recently a number of documents connected to oil production has become available as part of the archive posted by Aymenn Jawad al-Tamimi. They shed a little more specific light onto the subject of IS oil production and sales. What emerges from them is that, to the extent that they are authentic and reliable, and to the extent that they offer coverage of the entirety of IS oil production, they confirm much of what has been described here. The figures for income from sales in early 2016 suggest a maximum of roughly $30 million a month, or $1 million per day, from these sales. These figures are likely to reflect something like total IS oil income, which means a maximum of some $365 million a year. But several considerations come together to suggest that we should see this figure as in all probability an all-time high: the costs involved in getting the oil from underground to market, and in receiving the income from the sales, will remain constant or grow; allied attacks on the oil fields and the supply networks will continue to degrade productivity and sales; Iran's return to the international oil market in early 2016 and the determination of other producers not to scale back production in the face of low prices will make IS oil unattractive on a glutted market; sales are unlikely to maintain their level so far; and at least for the next couple of years, oil prices are likely to suffer continuing volatility.[34] Oil may therefore not be quite as profitable, or more importantly, reliable an enterprise for IS as some have thought.

IS has taken care to seize control of archeological and oil resources in the areas under its rule, and it is doing its best to monetize both. Neither, though, seems to be a truly big contributor to IS coffers, or to offer reliable, predictable supplies of money. Profits from sales of antiquities are small, at best, and those from oil have been eaten away by the costs involved and the current low price of the commodity, as well as the likelihood that not all that much IS oil is actually getting to market. Instead, any steady income for IS almost certainly comes from taxation, which as we have seen, is not very high.

FATF

The Financial Action Task Force, or FATF, is an "independent inter-governmental body that develops and promotes policies to protect the global financial system against money laundering, terrorist financing, and the financing of proliferation of weapons of mass destruction." Its remit includes IS, and it gathers information and makes recommendations for blocking IS access to funding and to the international financial networks. Because FATF is essentially a preventive organization, it is impossible to know how much success it has had. In its recent report, it stresses that not all sources of IS funding have yet been stoppered.[35] Not all the methods traditionally used to deprive terrorist movements of funding can be used effectively against IS. And above all, a great deal in our knowledge remains unclear, especially concerning the amounts of money to which IS has access.

Burning Money

That IS needs money in large amounts is clear. It pays its fighters and uses money for many other purposes. It depends on money to survive, and it runs through large sums every month. Many of its financial transactions and payments take place in cash, of necessity because of IS exclusion, to the extent possible, from the international banking system. Various kinds of foreign interdiction are in operation to prevent IS from acquiring money internationally. FATF is doing its best to turn off the faucet of international donations and other transfers. Oil deliveries are being hampered by air strikes and sanctions. Sales of antiquities of all kinds have been largely banned. These efforts have had an effect: by some accounts IS fighters' salaries have been cut by 50 percent.[36]

Despite those salary cuts, IS is still flourishing. So the coalition has tried a new tactic. Rather than—or in addition to—trying to cut off IS funding at its sources, the allies have moved to attacking IS funds directly, by "literally blowing them up."[37] In January 2016, for example, the United States bombed some IS warehouses in Iraq where cash was stored. A video released by the U.S. army showed what it said were plumes of paper money flying in flames from the bombed buildings.

Destroying IS reserves of cash, as distinct from cutting off its supply of money, is an innovative way to cause damage to the movement. It can also be very effective: burning cash means that the efforts invested in getting the money in the first place have been completely wasted. But how effective a tactic is it? How much money has been destroyed in this way? It is not clear from the reports we have how many sorties were made, or how many stockpiles of cash were destroyed. One suggestion is that some nine depots were attacked, another that just two two-thousand-pound bombs did much of the work. And no further such attacks have been reported. Regardless of the details, the U.S. army publicity was very self-satisfied—so much so that the story gained traction and was reported again and again in the media over the succeeding months.

Although there is no indication of how the figures are arrived at, early reports suggested that the bombing destroyed very large amounts of currency. The attacks apparently took place on January 11. Four days later, on January 15, the (London) *Daily Mail* reported that "It's unknown exactly how much money was being kept in the depot, but officials estimate the amount to be 'millions.'"[38] Curiously, given the *Daily Mail's* liking for extravagance, on the day of the attack itself NBC had spoken of "tens of millions of dollars" going up in smoke.[39] The *New York Times*, similarly, quoting "Col. Steven H. Warren, a spokesman for the American-led coalition," referred to "nine depots where the group is believed to have stashed tens of millions of dollars in cash."[40] A month later, when the story was taken up again in the media, the figure had inexplicably shot up to "more than $500 million" plus twenty kilograms of gold.[41] (Those twenty kilograms, at a price then of just under $1,100 per ounce, or roughly $38,800 a kilo, do not affect the total much, coming in at a mere $776,000.) By April *Time Magazine* and the *Daily Mail* were reporting a figure of a staggering $800 million (the gold had apparently been forgotten).[42] And one of the earlier estimates of $500 million had called its figure "plausible" based on "intelligence estimates" ranging from $200 million to $1.3 billion.[43]

The constant in almost all versions of the story is that millions of dollars were destroyed, making the strikes extremely damaging. A figure of $800 million, unlike a vague "millions," is clearly in the same ballpark as the $1 billion to $2 billion that IS is regularly credited with possessing. A movement with $1 billion to $2 billion in the bank is not going to notice a few "millions." But the loss of $1.3 billion, or even just $800 million, or even as little as half a billion, matters.

Damaging or not, however, the action raises other questions. For example: is it legal for the U.S. to destroy American currency, knowingly and deliberately, in this way? It is one thing to engage in action against IS in which fighters are killed and in the process American dollars are perhaps destroyed. That is collateral damage and of no great significance alongside the other benefits. But setting out deliberately and knowingly to destroy American currency—whatever the ultimate motive of such destruction—is another matter. It may in fact contravene U.S. law. It certainly skirts an interesting legal issue.

The reports we have, both those in the media and that coming from the U.S. military itself, suggest that the cash in question is likely to have been in Iraqi dinars or in dollars or in a combination of the two. Dinars are foreign and therefore do not matter. But dollars are a different matter. They are protected by U.S. law. Title 18 Crimes and Criminal Procedure, of the U.S. Code, chapter 17, section 333, states explicitly: "Whoever mutilates, cuts, defaces, disfigures, or perforates, or unites or cements together, or does any other thing to any bank bill, draft, note, or other evidence of debt issued by any national banking association, or Federal Reserve bank, or the Federal Reserve System, with intent to render such bank bill, draft, note, or other evidence of debt unfit to be reissued, shall be fined under this title or imprisoned not more than six months, or both."

All That Glistens

The sale of artifacts and oil challenges the ideological purity of IS. At a basic level, it constitutes trading with the enemy. Islam, like other cultures, has a long tradition both of doing precisely this and of agonizing over its permissibility. Where there are clear enemies, the decision is usually to forbid such trade, so as to deprive the enemy of the benefits of whatever is being traded. But it is easy to see that an opposing argument could have weight too: trading with the enemy may, it is true, give him something that he wants (sometimes even, as we know from medieval examples, arms and weaponry), but at least it will make him part with his money. Such disputes are rarely fully resolved.[44]

Yet oil and archeological artifacts also represent two different kinds of cracks in IS's ideological wall. Archeological artifacts are not just beautiful objects; they also very often feature images of infidels, men and women, gods and goddesses. An entire tray of coins seized by U.S. commandos when they killed Abu Sayyaf showed, as can be seen clearly in the picture released by the State Department, the heads of emperors. Not only have IS soldiers destroyed a good many such images, and filmed themselves doing so for the edification of the faithful and in order to shock the infidels, but the movement also insists that such destruction is the only way to deal with these remains of ancient cultures. Its proclaimed model here is Muhammad himself, who destroyed 360 idols in the Kaba in Mecca when he returned in triumph to take over his native city near the end of his life. Abraham too, the first real Muslim according to Islamic tradition and builder of the Kaba, did the same to his father's idols.

These are the models for IS. Preservation of ancient idols and images is anathema to IS. Going beyond that, to sell them to infidels, Westerners, is still worse. Doing so actively undermines not only an age-old and respectable Islamic tradition, though one often honored in the breach; it also stands in direct contradiction to the propaganda of IS itself and to the most fundamental elements of its thinking. The apparently limited scale of such sales notwithstanding, this presents a logical problem for IS. This problem is then compounded by the fact that regardless of the small income that they produce, archeological materials; sites; excavations; and licenses for excavation, storage, selection, and actual sales all appear to be under the formal cloak of the IS administration. This is not being done under the table.

Oil sales offer a different kind of problem. Unlike oil production, sales of oil seem to be less openly administered by IS, though we can be sure that IS knows exactly what goes on—how, how much, where, at what price, and so on. Oil sales are probably a necessity for IS, in that they bring in possibly the major portion of its hard currency earnings. Foreign trade, however, of any sort, with any state outside IS territory, is also a problem for an Islamic state that claims to be the only legitimate state in existence.

There is more to this: unlike archeological remains, which need only to be located, dug up, and somehow brought to market, oil is a highly complex industry, involving not just many specialists but also huge amounts of technical equipment and materials that need to be looked after, maintained, and kept up-to-date and functioning. Feeding these needs consumes precious financial resources. More than that, it also demands frequent contact with the outside world in order to obtain the necessary supplies, and, still more important, to acquire the necessary current scientific knowledge and information.

For IS, this like so much else amounts to another contradiction. In the areas of religion, politics, science, and culture, IS rejects everything that the West stands for, but IS needs certain products of Western culture that it cannot produce internally. An autarkic self-sufficiency, on the pattern of the early Soviet Union, or of Ceauşescu's Romania, or North Korea, will not work. It did not work for those states either. No society, and especially not one that seeks to use the weaponry of the West against the West, can be wholly self-sufficient. And no society that inveighs against everything Western can acknowledge its dependency on that same West without falling into an ideological contradiction.

These two difficulties are set off by yet one more: all sales to the outside world earn dollars, euros, or yen for IS. The foreign currency that they earn may actually not be delivered in dollars, but in pounds or euros or yen. Nonetheless, they are foreign currency, and IS, in this area too, has set up its own standards, decrying the Islamic world's subservience to the almighty dollar and Western currencies in general and calling for change. Selling the family silver, in the form of archeological artifacts that it proclaims should be destroyed, and in the form of oil that fuels the Western economy that IS claims to be seeking to bring down, for foreign currency that should not be used ("worthless paper"), presents IS with an ideological problem. That problem derives from the fact that IS calls itself, claims to be, and operates as a state of religion.

CHAPTER FOUR

Religion

"We will get you to paradise, even if we have to drag you there in chains."

—A TUNISIAN PREACHER IN RAQQA

RELIGION IS AT THE heart of the IS enterprise. Earthly power, brutally exercised, is its ever-present manifestation, but it is religion that feeds the Islamic State and justifies as it nourishes that brutality. IS sees and presents itself as Islam on Earth for today. It is in religion, therefore, as understood by IS, that we can see some of the most characteristic features of IS as a movement.

The Islamic State is not a new revolutionary movement. It emphatically does not offer an original ideology. It is not seeking to attract followers to something novel. It rejects the notion of fresh ideas. All of these suggest innovation. Innovation is anathema to IS. It implies adding something new or extra to what Muhammad brought. If Muhammad did not bring it then by definition it is to be rejected. Rejection of whatever is new or innovative, *bida* in Arabic, has deep roots in Islam. Medieval Muslims devoted entire treatises to listing and denouncing "innovations," much as early Christian writers produced accounts in loving detail of the heresies that they urged their followers to avoid.[1] In both cases, by condemning them in such detail, the writers have preserved for us valuable evidence, often the only surviving evidence, about such "innovations" or heresies. Conversely, something that is disliked or disapproved of in Islam, even if it is not actually new, easily acquires the label of *bida*, innovation, as a marker of rejection. Novelty is unnecessary and worse. Did not God Himself say, "Today I have perfected my religion for you" (*sura* 5:3)? Islam is here and it is complete.

The Islamic State seeks therefore only to realize what might otherwise remain abstract. It calls for all Muslims to fulfill all the obligations of their faith, however trivial and however apparently unrelated to religion, in order to help bring about the final apocalypse that lies at the end of IS ideology. But IS also has political and military ambitions and along the way to achieving them it has acquired practical responsibilities. Regardless of its own pronouncements, it is a revolutionary movement that has seized power in a large territory and needs to hold on to it and control it. In managing that IS uses every means available. Among these is the religion of Islam, with which IS identifies itself. Just as Islam reaches into every aspect of a Muslim's life, so IS too is a totalizing movement, with very clear and explicit aims that involve everyone and every aspect of people's lives, from the most exalted to the most trivial.

The primary method of control is violence, applied as terror, but while this works best as an introductory mechanism of rule, it is Islamic law—including the judicious, and public, application of violence—that offers the framework best suited to spread submission to IS and continued acceptance of its rule. Islamic law in the understanding of IS goes back to the Quran and Muhammad, but this does not necessarily mean rejection of everything that postdates the Prophet. On the contrary, IS is keen to demonstrate, on one hand, its connection and loyalty to the path and the methodology (Arabic *minhaj*) of the Prophet, and, on the other, that it cleaves to what it sees as those true and authentic parts of the Islamic tradition that developed after his death. That means, for example, that it does not reject the four major schools of law that emerged and became consolidated in the early centuries of Islam, even though these were certainly not part of the Islam of the first generation.[2] It means also that innovations, in the sense of novelties unknown to the practice of the Prophet himself, are not always to be rejected. When IS does reject customs or practices that entered the tradition after the Prophet's time, by the same token, the reason may not always lie in the date of the innovation itself as much as with other tactical or momentary needs of the movement as it struggles to accommodate itself to the reality of Islam in the world.

Fatwas

We learn a good deal about how IS works, how it governs its subjects, and how it sees the relationship between them from fatwas. The word *fatwa* has a fearsome aura, because of the famous fatwa issued by the Iranian leader Ayatollah Khomeini in 1989 against Salman Rushdie. That was a reaction to Rushdie's novel of the previous year, *The Satanic Verses*, which was judged by many to be blasphemous (in general without, it seems, actually reading it).[3] Technically, a fatwa is simply a request for a legal opinion. But because of the way Islamic law and courts in Islamic societies work, such opinions very often have the status of legal decisions—a good legal opinion tends to be adopted by those in a position to implement legal decisions. Ayatollah Khomeini's fatwa, or legal opinion, on *The Satanic Verses* was regarded, not least because of its authorship and the way it was formulated, as a sentence of death.[4]

A fatwa can usefully be compared with the ancient Roman *responsum*, or the medieval (and modern) Jewish *she'elot u-teshuvot* ("questions and answers"). Islam Online, a website created by Yusuf al-Qaradawi, a very aged (he was born in 1926) Egyptian scholar-theologian and TV personality, offers a parallel adapted to the modern world. A less august comparison might be with columns like "Dear Abby" in newspapers and, now, advice columns on the Internet. In theory all of these, from the ancient Roman *responsa* to Dear Abby, represent a request for information or help and the response to that request. In the Roman and Jewish cases, like the Islamic, the questions deal with legal matters. But because Islam, like Judaism, enters every corner of a believer's life, questions on legal matters can be about almost anything. While anyone can make a request, the answer comes naturally from someone qualified to respond, a lawyer, or a man of learning in religious matters (or, in the case of Dear Abby, someone who knows how to write a newspaper column).

Though we know who answers the questions—a scholar, a lawyer, a newspaper columnist—it is less obvious who asks them. We see the questions in the texts we have, whether they concern esoteric legal conundrums or simple requests for information or advice; and they may often also be signed, whether by a real or assumed name, or simply by "Worried, Poughkeepsie." But what if the responder, a columnist or a lawyer, does not receive those questions that he wants to answer? One solution is to write them himself. The phenomenon of the advice columnist who writes his own Dear Abby letters is well known, not least from Nathanael West's famous 1933 novel *Miss Lonelyhearts*. But what about the IS fatwas? The questions in these are not signed; nor apparently are the answers. For the questions, that need not be a problem—medieval fatwas, and many modern ones too, do not record the name of the questioner. This is because, whatever the issue that motivates the individual to ask his question, the question raises a legal problem of potentially wider relevance. So in the case of fatwas we do not have the names of the questioners. They are not of any legal significance. But we also lack the names of the responders for IS fatwas, and that is a different matter.

The response in a fatwa is an authoritative legal opinion, amounting as we have seen to a legal decision. It is an opinion on the law of Islam and is given with all the authority of Islam itself and, in these cases, of the Islamic State. In the past, when legal opinions were given by muftis—"fatwa-givers" in Arabic—their names were known. The fatwas of a particular mufti might be collected— we have large multivolume collections of fatwas by such revered scholars as Ibn Rushd, the grandfather of the famous philosopher Ibn Rushd, known in the West as Averroes; and vast collections of fatwas, covering every conceivable question, delivered by all sorts of muftis over periods of several centuries, compiled by scholars in order to make legal life and social practice easier. The collections of Ahmad al-Wansharisi, for example, of the fifteenth century, in fourteen fat volumes, or of al-Mahdi al-Wazzani, in the late nineteenth and early twentieth centuries—this one in eleven volumes—have

attained a wide circulation and great authority because of their comprehensiveness and the reputation of the scholars whose work they
contain.[5] IS fatwas are issued not by individual muftis—who might
or might not be acceptable to IS and might or might not issue rulings that comport with IS ideology or desires. Instead, reflecting a
bureaucratization of the faith that serves to consolidate religious
with political authority, they are issued by the IS Diwan al-Ifta wal-
Buhuth, the IS Department of Fatwas and Research.

IS has been running its territory for some time now, and many
questions have arisen—or been brought up by IS itself. The resulting laws, as reflected in such texts, need to be known to those who
must obey them. There is little point in having secret laws that
people can be punished for breaking even if they don't know about
them. In consequence, IS has issued numerous fatwas. A good
number of these have become available, and have been collected,
studied, and put up on the Internet, many of them in translation.[6]
They reveal a lot about how the Islamic State actually works. The
laws cover a huge variety of subjects, including obviously religious
topics but also others that appear, to Western eyes at least, less so.
Thus there are fatwas and decisions on repentance for sin, prayer
times and rules for mosques, through the administration of *zakat*
(charity tax), beards, the permissibility of Wi-Fi during prayer, and
the closing of shops during times of prayer, all the way to rules on
plunder (including the collection of an "orphans' share"), and what
are known as the *hudud* punishments, like cutting off hands for
theft and execution for blasphemy.[7]

Why Trousers Must Be Rolled

The determination to create an Islamic society, one obeying the
rules of Islam and interpreting those rules in the light of IS's own
understanding of the history of Islam, comes out in many ways,
great and small. Sometimes the difference between the two is not
easy to see.

In October 2015, the United States mounted a raid with the
intention of freeing some Kurdish peshmerga fighters from IS cap-
tivity. Somehow it went wrong, and instead of Kurdish fighters,
sixty-nine Arabs imprisoned by IS because of real or alleged con-

nections with the Iraqi government were freed. A few days later, they described how they had been treated by their jailers. One feature that stood out among the stories of harsh treatment was the insistence by IS on imposing on their captives minutely detailed behavior, in both religious and apparently nonreligious matters. Trousers were the subject of one restriction: the men were told that they had to roll the cuffs of their trousers above their ankles.[8]

Why such a rule? It had nothing to do with humiliating the men. Nor was IS worried about dirt getting onto their prisoners' clothing from the floor of their cells. Nor again was it about security—a fear that the prisoners might be hiding some weapon in the bottom of their garments. Like so much else, this restriction harks back to the earliest days of Islam. On January 18, 2015, an official IS fatwa responded to the question "Is it permissible for men to wear their garments long?" The answer was, "No. It is not permissible to wear one's garments below the ankles, whether out of arrogance or for any other reason."[9] (If the videos of IS are any guide, it appears that IS fighters do keep their trousers rolled.) Fatwas, however, are not mere arbitrary expressions of official caprice, especially not in a system that claims to represent divine order on Earth. Fatwas prescribe—technically they recommend, but, especially for IS, their recommendations have the force of law—the correct understanding of a legal issue. That understanding is grounded in the sources of legal authority. In this case the source is the behavior of the Prophet Muhammad.

Insistence on rolling one's clothing up above the ankles goes back much further than a fatwa of 2015. Here as elsewhere IS is trying to impose its vision of the Islam of the seventh century on the twenty-first. One of the traditions (hadiths) attributed to the Prophet quotes him as saying, "Don't let your clothes hang down. God does not love those who let their clothes hang down."[10] The 2015 fatwa, then, is rooted in the ancient Islamic past. In its treatment of its Arab prisoners at Hawija, IS is trying, in time-honored Islamic fashion, to follow the practice or the advice of the Prophet.

While the practice itself may appear trivial, the larger issue, of how the Prophet lived and the meaning of his actions for Muslims today, is far from trivial. The Prophet's behavior, what he did and what he recommended or rejected, offers Muslims an ideal to be aimed at, a model to be imitated, in small as in great, strictly religious and nonreligious matters alike. And at the same time it provides IS, because of its self-definition, with a way to impose its own dominance on those it controls: it allows IS to force its subjects to behave in a way that, for very many at least, appears outmoded and old-fashioned, yet that can be shown to maintain the behavior or the recommendation of the Prophet himself. What the Prophet did, how he behaved, what he said, the advice he gave—all cannot be lightly disregarded by a Muslim, and in the trousers decree as in other areas IS is able to take full advantage of the tie to authenticity that the link to the Prophet permits.

Clothing is, at least for some, a trivial matter. Time is more important.

Ramadan

When does Ramadan begin? That depends. Islam uses a lunar calendar. A month begins with the appearance of a new moon. Though the appearance of the new moon can easily be calculated astronomically well in advance—printed diaries, in the days when we still had them, used to tell us when to look out for it—Islamic religious law and tradition both require that the new month begin only when the new moon has actually been sighted. Mathematics and astronomy cannot trump the moon itself: if God in His power were to delay the new moon's appearance by a day, the new month would not begin until that next day.[11] This means that though we can calculate when the month of Ramadan should start, we cannot be certain, in the face of God's omnipotence, that it will actually begin at the time we have calculated. Official announcements are therefore couched in careful terms.[12] For instance:

> Saudi Arabia's Supreme Court has announced that the first day of the Muslim holy fasting month of Ramadan will be Thursday June 18, [2015,] Al Arabiya News Channel reported.
> The Supreme Court of Saudi Arabia has asked citizens to keep an eye out for the crescent moon on Tuesday,

which, if sighted, will mark the beginning of the month of Ramadan on Wednesday.

If the crescent is not sighted on Tuesday, fasting will begin Thursday.[13]

Astronomy thus tells us that Ramadan in 2015 was to begin on Thursday, June 18, and with it fasting too. But the Saudi Supreme Court, in telling us that, also took care to allow for the possibility of an early start, asking "citizens to keep an eye out for the crescent moon on Tuesday," which would mean starting the fasting month on Wednesday, not Thursday.

Because sighting, not mathematical calculation, determines the start of the month, and because the new moon is not always visible at the same time everywhere in the world, slight discrepancies can arise between different areas. So, too, if cloud cover obscures the new moon somewhere, or for other less easily definable reasons, this can make for difficulties in dating at a local level. The problem is not new: as long ago as 1183, when the Spanish Muslim traveler Ibn Jubayr was visiting Mecca, "the new moon rose on the night of Monday the 19th of December . . . [Nonetheless the] month's fast began on Sunday for the people of Mecca, on a claim that the new moon had been observed [on Saturday], a claim unverified but nevertheless supported by the Emir."[14]

These small differences of a day are easily ironed out with the appearance of the new moon the next month. At worst they lengthen a month by a day. In general such discrepancies do not matter, but when the month is Ramadan, it matters a great deal, because Muslims must fast from dawn till dusk every day during Ramadan, and they need to know whether the fasting month has begun, or whether they are still on the last day of the previous month, Shaban, and may still eat during daylight.

Who decides? During the Middle Ages, Muslims actually possessed the scientific knowledge needed for prediction. That knowledge came from the study of astronomy and other topics among Muslims, begun as early as the ninth century on the basis of translations from Greek. The impetus to such scientific research came from the religious need to be able to predict such events as new

moons or to work out the position of Mecca and its direction in relation to other places.[15] Despite those advances in astronomical
knowledge, from time to time we hear of witnesses testifying to
having seen the new moon of Ramadan, though as we have seen
with Ibn Jubayr, witnesses might not always be present or reliable.

The same problem arises at the end of the month. It is important to know when Ramadan ends and Shawwal, the next month,
begins: here too cloud cover could cause delay of a day in the arrival
of the new month and consequently an extra day of Ramadan, which
would mean an extra day of fasting. Witnesses are very useful, but
clouds can make them useless. Science can resolve the problem.

Occasionally scientific prediction and human observation
could get in each other's way. In 1918, the British writer and intelligence officer Harry St. John Philby, father of the famous spy Kim
Philby, was in Riyadh, the capital of the Wahhabi Saudis, for the
end of Ramadan, and reported:

> I had an uncanny feeling that my prediction (from the
> National Almanach) of the probable appearance of the
> moon was known to many of the watchers who, in spite of
> the extra day's fast involved, would be almost glad to have
> the infidel's impudence confounded by a manifestation of
> divine arbitrariness. And as luck would have it a band of
> wispy clouds lay over the moon's position throughout those
> critical moments ... As the darkness gathered about us it
> was clear that the moon was not to be seen that night, and
> disappointed figures crept down from their roofs to break
> the fast which was to be endured for another day. Yet their
> disappointment was as nothing compared to mine, for my
> "books" had failed me under a crucial test.[16]

Philby went to bed, disappointed, puzzled about his *National
Almanach* and with what looked like a ruined reputation as a Christian
Westerner with special access to arcane knowledge. He need not have
worried. At 2.00 a.m. he was awakened by a series of gunshots.

> Some *Badawin* of Dakina had come in post-haste to report
> that they had seen the crescent of the new moon and had

been sent to the chief *Shaikh*, 'Abdullah Ibn 'Abdul Wahhab, who had immediately assembled an ecclesiastical court, consisting of himself and two *Qadhis[,]* to take the evidence of the new arrivals. They had pronounced themselves entirely satisfied, and the gunshot, which had wakened me, was the first announcement to the people of Riyadh that the morrow would be celebrated as the *'Id*.

Nowadays, however, witnesses are not usually required, and the traditional legal obligation is recognized simply in the formal suggestion that if people see the new moon at a different time from that predicted by science, they should let the authorities know.

In Saudi Arabia, therefore, and, we are told, in the Gulf states and in Jordan, Ramadan in 2015 was to begin on Thursday, June 18. So too in the United Kingdom and elsewhere around the globe. In Iraq, however, matters were more complicated. In the areas controlled by the government, Ramadan began on the Thursday, like elsewhere. But in IS territory, the authorities "announced on Wednesday that Thursday is a supplementary day to the month of Shaban and that Friday (would be) the first of Ramadan."[17]

This meant that Shaban, the eighth month of the Islamic calendar, would be a day longer than expected, and that Thursday, celebrated as the first day of the fasting month of Ramadan everywhere else in the Islamic world, was to be a normal day, the last day of Shaban, in territory under IS control—including such populous cities as Mosul. For observant Muslims, which means most Muslims, this was no light matter. Should they start the fast on the Thursday, as astronomy (and possibly their own sighting) indicated and as Muslims around the world were doing, or should they adapt their behavior to a new order and wait until Friday as decreed by their new rulers?

The Calendar as an Instrument of Control

How IS came to determine that the first day of Ramadan would be a day later than everyone else thought is not clear. But they have a system that makes such decisions possible on the basis of evidence from witnesses. A letter of 26 Safar 1436 (December 18, 2014) from the Sharia Committee for the Observation of New Moons instructed governors and other senior officials to form "committees of just, trustworthy people and among them those with knowledge of observation of the new moons in your areas" in order to help make IS independent in calendrical matters.[18] Their decision illustrates IS determination to have full control of Muslims in religious as in other affairs.

Time matters. Calendars matter too. And the Islamic year is different from that used in the West. It consists of just twelve lunar months—the time between one new moon and the next. Because a lunar month lasts for about twenty-nine-and-a-half days, that means that the twelve-month Islamic year has only 354 days. This not only means that observation of the new moon can be tricky. It also means that the months of the Islamic year revolve gradually, backward, through our Western solar year. Ramadan will begin eleven days earlier next year than this. The following year it will begin twenty-two days earlier. And so on. For this reason Ramadan can occur sometimes in winter and sometimes in summer. When it happens in summer, the fasting is particularly hard in the Middle East because of the heat. As climate change brings still higher temperatures, such problems will increase.[19]

Our Western calendar, however, is not simply Western. It starts with the supposed birth of Jesus. The terms BC ("Before Christ") and AD ("Anno Domini") are reminders that, whatever the science involved in the calculations of the calendar, the starting point for our counting of years is religious, and Christian. That is why many Jews and other non-Christians, in order to avoid the use of terms that imply recognition of Jesus, prefer to say BCE ("Before the Common Era") and CE ("Common Era").

IS has now joined the party too, publishing a short treatise called "A Ruling on the Use of Christian Dates."[20] From it we learn that "the reckoning of months and days is something people need to keep track of their religious and worldly affairs, for the religious in knowing the entry and exit of the month, like the month of Ramadan." The Quran tells us (*sura* 2:189) that "They ask you about the new moons. Say: 'These are markings of time for the people.'" In other words, months are to be calculated by the appearance of the new moon. Moreover, "The Miladi [Christian, i.e.,

Western] dating that the Muslims have adopted in our time must be removed and Islamic dating must take its place." Using Christian dating gives unmerited glory to Jesus; it also glorifies the feast days of the unbelievers (that is, the Christians), including the birth date of Jesus, "despite the fact that it is not established that he was born on this date." Worst of all, using the Western calendar constitutes imitation of the unbelievers. Imitation of that sort, we are instructed, is to be avoided—Muslims should trim the mustache and let the beard grow, unlike non-Muslims; they should dye their gray hairs and "not imitate the Jews."[21] All this because "Whoever imitates a people is one of them."

The first generation of Muhammad's followers, according to the "Ruling," thought that they should use a dating system of their own, one that differentiated Muslims from others. They never thought of using the Christian dating system. (Here the authors seem unaware that what they call the Christian dating system did not come into widespread use until centuries after the time of that first generation of Muslims.) Instead those early Muslims "devised a system of dating," basing it on the tradition of the Arabs and a quranic verse: "Indeed the number of months, with God, is twelve in the Book of God the day that He created the heavens and the earth" (*sura* 9:36). Months represent lunar periods and have twenty-nine or thirty days; they do not vary in length as the "Christian" months do, between twenty-eight and thirty-one days. The twelve-month year has no leap-year additions, whether days or, as in the traditional Middle Eastern and Mediterranean lunar systems, months. The quranic verse "shows that rulings on acts of worship etc. are construed according to the months and years that the Arabs have acknowledged, not those considered by non-Arabs, the Byzantines, and Copts, even if there is no addition to the 12 months, because they have a variety of numbers of days, some higher than thirty and others shorter, while the months of the Arabs do not exceed 30 days, though some fall short."

All of this argumentation is solidly founded in texts derived not only from the Quran but also from traditions going back, via numerous medieval writers and commentators, all the way to those first generations of Muslims. It is of both religious and worldly significance. In matters of religious importance, it affects how long a woman must wait after the death of her husband before she can re-marry—the waiting period is measured in months, and the relevant months are the regular Islamic ones, not the Western months of ir-regular length. In worldly matters, it affects how one can "keep track of appointed days for work, salaries and so on." Muslims must not allow themselves to "imitate" the unbelievers in this, but must stick to the calendar authorized by God.[22]

A Birthday Present for the Prophet

Dates matter. On February 4, 2015, IS released a video showing Muadh Kasasbeh, the Jordanian pilot who fell into IS hands on Christmas Eve 2014, being burned to death in a cage. The horrific killing aroused widespread condemnation. King Abdullah of Jordan cut short a visit to the United States and returned urgently to Amman, where his government executed two jihadis, one a woman whose suicide belt had failed to explode during an attack that had killed sixty people a decade earlier. Queen Rania took part in a massive demonstration carrying a placard proclaiming "Muadh is a martyr for the truth." And Jordanian planes bombed IS targets, re-portedly killing some fifty-five IS fighters.[23]

Almost at once it emerged that negotiations for the pilot's release had been a farce. Despite the Jordanians' willingness to do a trade with IS for their pilot, Kasasbeh had apparently been killed long be-fore the video came out. An IS fatwa soon appeared justifying such "punishment." It was dated 29 Rabi I 1436, or January 20, 2015, two weeks before the release of the video.[24] And tweets by IS followers from still earlier were found referring to celebrations of the burning as just retribution for the actions of Kasasbeh and his fellows.[25]

Various sources, including Jordanian state media, then reported that Jordanian officials had worked out, or guessed, that he had been killed on January 3, or perhaps January 8, a month before the release of the video.[26] Although negotiations for a possible prisoner exchange with the Jordanians had continued for well over a month, he had been kept alive for only ten days, or at most a couple of weeks, before IS killed him.

Why did IS kill him when it did? Not only the delay in publi-cation of the video, but also the stories about IS members' jubilation show, if they show anything at all, that there was no rush about the killing—IS did not fear any U.S. or coalition attempt to rescue him. External considerations, therefore, did not affect IS in choosing to kill him on the date they did. On the contrary, they picked out a special date from the calendar. In studying what significance the date might have, however, we need to look at the right calendar. That calendar is the Islamic one. The dates in our materials— January 3 and January 8—are meaningless in this context. The Islamic dates, however, are very far from meaningless. Although it occasionally makes use of the Western calendar, generally alongside the Islamic one, IS uses the Islamic calendar exclusively when it can. The fatwa concerning the permissibility of burning the pilot bears only an Islamic date. The designs for coins put out by IS, similarly, bear only an Islamic date.[27] And very many of the IS documents that have come into Western hands bear only an Islamic date, while virtually all those that bear a Western date do so in second place, alongside an Islamic one.

This concern to use the Islamic calendar is not just a strange quirk. It reflects the very real desire of IS both to throw off Western dominance and to return Islamic society to the practices of the seventh century and the Islamic past more generally. That includes the use of the traditional calendar as reformed with the coming of Islam. In acting thus, IS is also giving practical expression to its view of time as molded by a different set of needs from those of Westerners.[28] In that sense IS prefers and wants to privilege the Islamic calendar as part of the process of rebuilding Islamic identity.

Although they were short on hard evidence, security officials in Jordan, the United Kingdom, and the United States suggested that IS's killing of the Jordanian pilot took place on either January 3 or January 8, 2015. January 3, 2015 was 12 Rabi I 1436 in the Islamic calendar; and January 8, 2015 was 17 Rabi I 1436 in the Islamic calendar.

In the history of Islam, 12 Rabi I is a special day.[29] It was on this day, a Monday, that Muhammad was born.[30] Birthdays were not very special in premodern times, nor in the desert, where births, being of people who while small are of little obvious consequence, were generally not noticed. But by the tenth or eleventh century, the

date when the Prophet was believed to have been born had acquired the status of a holiday. Not having a strictly religious function, it also became extremely popular. We hear that in the twelfth
century, one ruler in Syria celebrated the holiday by building
booths and organizing military processions and giant festivities at
which vast amounts of food were distributed. Dancing girls and
public readings of poems in honor of the Prophet, as well as
clowns and other entertainers, are also mentioned in later descriptions of the holiday.[31] In later centuries, the *mawlid*, as the holiday
is known, came to include also religious aspects, as Sufis, dervishes,
and others performed their rituals and added prayer and study to
the overall celebrations.[32]

Purists down the ages reacted very negatively to the new holiday. It was not part of the habit of the Prophet (who is generally
recorded as practicing a modest self-effacement in such matters,
and in all probability did not even know when he was actually
born). It frequently included music and dancing, both of which
were never popular among the strictly orthodox. And it looked
very like an innovation, something that is anathema to purist Islam.
Fatwas were composed on the question whether the holiday was
permitted or forbidden, reprehensible or unimportant. One very
respected scholar, al-Suyuti (of the late fifteenth century), opined
that although it was an innovation it was a good one—*bida hasana*.
In the fourteenth century, Ibn Taymiyya, much admired by the
Wahhabis and by IS, discussed it too, trying to "define permissible
reverence as against blameworthy adoration."[33] But the Wahhabis,
austere puritanical types, decided against it, and IS has inherited
their negative view.[34]

We have no sure way of knowing when Muadh Kasasbeh was
killed. Similarly, we have no sure way of knowing how those security officials determined that January 3 (or 8) was the date when he
died. And while their reports about Twitter posts may be correct, it
is just as possible that those posts reflect other events or processes
about which we are very poorly informed.

Either way, however, the desire to locate Kasasbeh's death on a
date that is the birthday of the Prophet, a major holiday for most
Muslims, is significant. If IS really did kill him on that date, this
suggests that, like their general hostility to anything that did not

form part of the practice of the Prophet himself, they wish not to honor the Prophet but rather to cause grief to regular Muslims on the day of one of their greatest celebrations. For IS, as for Wahhabis in Saudi Arabia, the birthday of the Prophet is not a holiday; the memory of the day he was born, not forming part of the practice of the Prophet himself, is not a reason for celebration. Any celebration of it is *bida*, innovation, and for that reason should be censured and forbidden.

Alternatively, if the security services who claimed that the death took place on this day actually had no sound intelligence for their very specific claim, that suggests a different motive, reflected perhaps in the slogan on Queen Rania's placard in that demonstration. According to this point of view, the security agents may well have thought that since they had to choose a date to which to assign the death, the best day to opt for was one that happened also to be the birthday of the Prophet. Choosing that day would tie his death to the birth of the Prophet; it would imply that Kasasbeh had died in defense of the faith and that his death was a martyrdom ("Muadh is a martyr for the truth"); in this way it would confirm that IS was an enemy of Islam.

Prayer

Prayer (*salat* in Arabic) has a special character in Islam. In this Islam differs from both Christianity and Judaism. In traditional churches, Christian prayer has a theatrical quality, with the congregation in the role of an audience watching the priest as he performs a ritual in front of them and on their behalf, representing them to their Creator. Even when the congregation is an active participant, the lay person has a subordinate role, kneeling in prayer, singing hymns, receiving communion, taking part in confession. The priest is more than just one participant among many. The Jewish synagogue is unlike the church. In the premodern era, it was a place of both prayer and study, and the prevailing impression there was of noise. Many descriptions by Christian visitors down the ages of synagogues at times of prayer services stress the noise and the sense of disorder, so different from the quiet and reverence expected in a Christian house of God. Even during prayer

Jews will walk around, talking to each other, gesturing, in pairs or in small groups, apparently indifferent to the prayers going on in their vicinity, creating an atmosphere almost of chaos, reminiscent more of the Shakespearean theater or an American football game than of religious respect and calm. In the modern world, while the orthodox synagogue retains much of the traditional noise and chatter, many American synagogues, Conservative or Reform, have taken on the atmosphere of the churches of the congregants' Christian neighbors.[35] The rabbi in this case is like a Christian priest—that is, not merely one participant among many.

Islamic prayer is very different. Part of the difference can be explained historically: in both Christianity and Judaism the form and content of the prayers (though not necessarily the atmosphere in the houses of prayer) are the product of a long process of development. For Jews in particular, whether on weekdays, during the Sabbath, or while celebrating the various festivals that dot the religious calendar, the prayers are a mix partly of passages from Scripture, especially the Psalms, and of other texts composed over many centuries from post-biblical times down to the Middle Ages and beyond. For this reason, some Muslim polemicists argue that Jewish prayers are not authentic, because they do not go back to the very beginning, to the earliest days of the faith: prayers composed in the Middle Ages, say, quite obviously cannot have anything to do with the practice of Abraham, Isaac, Jacob, Moses, or anyone else two thousand and more years ago. What can they have to do with the real, the original Judaism? The notion of historical development is alien to that way of thinking.

Similarly in Christianity the form and content of the liturgy have grown and developed over time, keeping pace with changes in doctrine and in social practice—language is a signal feature of this—in ways that reflect not so much the behavior of the founder, who lived and died as a practicing Jew, but rather the beliefs and rituals of different strands of Christian tradition over the last two millennia, including of course elements drawn from the Jewish tradition out of which Christianity grew. Again, whatever else they may reflect, especially for the Muslim polemicist, they do not reflect the origins.

In both of these faiths the ritual, the performance, takes place in front of the faithful: the Christian altar, or the Jewish reading desk (Hebrew *bimah*), is the scene of action, and the congregation, as audience, watches and listens to what goes on there. Even the Jewish ark where the Torah scrolls are kept except when carried in procession, which seems to be a simple cupboard, closed by doors and covered with an ornate curtain, is a site of profound importance in the ritual for the Jew: when the ark is open Jews stand in respect; they stop talking and face it. To show their backs to the open ark would be the height of disrespect. Like the Christian altar, the ark with its Torah scrolls represents a site of meaning and of action, a place to be watched and the home of religious significance.

Islam has a different prayer tradition. Unlike in the other two monotheistic faiths, the individual is the center of action. It is he— or she—who acts, performs, does, prays. While all three faiths orient their prayer houses in similar (not identical) directions, in Islam, the *mihrab*, indicating the direction of prayer in the mosque, is not a place where things happen. Things happen in relation to it, the faithful orient themselves and their prayer with it. But nothing happens in it and the faithful do not watch it or listen to anything happening there. It simply shows a direction.

Prayer itself consists of a series of movements that are richly choreographed and accompanied by the recitation of texts, mainly passages from the Quran. The prayers are a copy, an imitation of those inaugurated by the Prophet himself. Nothing has changed in their form or their content. The prayers go all the way back to the beginning of Islam itself. Movements and texts are repeated a number of times, in set patterns. The worshipper prays as one in a row of the faithful, with that row itself one of a number of rows. The pictures we see on television or in films show numberless faithful lined up, none in any special place of honor, none enjoying any preference of rank or age. Women pray separately from men and often a ruler will pray in a separate enclosure, but with those exceptions all Muslims are equal before God in worship. There is no rabbi, no priest—only an imam, which in this context means no more than a prayer leader. The imam is the one who stands "in front of" the faithful to lead them in prayer. Being an imam indicates no sacral status, no special learning: simply the ability to perform the prayer as it should be done.

The solemn gravity of Muslims at prayer, the reverent silence of the prayer hall—apart from the shuffling sound of people moving around, shoeless because their footwear has been left at the entrance—the repetition of words and of movements and shifts of parts of the body, all form part of a ritual that, not least because of its repetition several times every day over the life of the Muslim, has both a personal and a public, both an individual and a communal aspect. The individual prays alone before God, yet in the company of other faithful. Prayer is intensely personal, but it is also a public act—a repeated, individual proclamation of faith before the community. For the non-Muslim observer, the anonymity of the individual in the crowd of worshippers bespeaks the universalizing message of Islam, while the precision of the prayer itself and the individuality of the human being who performs it underscore its seriousness as an act of worship.

Prayer is an intensely personal activity because, for example during prostration, when the head and nose touch the ground and stay there for an indeterminate time, it concentrates the mind and the thought of the worshipper on God alone. The Muslim is in close, direct communion with the Creator, unmediated by any rabbi or priest. Whether on his own in a corner or among thousands of fellow Muslims, in a field or in the heart of a city, the Muslim at prayer is alone with God.

Fingers and Hands in Prayer

The Arab prisoners freed at Hawija who complained about having to roll their trousers had another complaint: they had been forced to hold their hands and fingers in a new way to perform their prayers. IS was not satisfied with the way they were praying and wanted to correct their mistakes.

Muslims pray differently from Jews or Christians. Although there is an imam, or leader, each person prays individually, and performs the prayers in a set pattern. Prayer is more than recitation or reading of words. Fingers and hands are placed and held in ritually prescribed manners, and the body is moved in specified ways over the course of the prayer. Local customs, the different legal schools, and the worldwide spread of Islam have led to slight variations in practice, but the basic patterns are universal.

Here as in other matters, IS uses religion to dominate its subjects. Even at prayer, the Muslim becomes subject to IS control. IS is invading the most private spaces of the population it rules. In correcting how people pray, IS is asserting that it alone is qualified to determine and to define the correct forms of prayer and the authentic inheritance of the Islamic past, which is the only way for the Muslim to approach God.

Tradition, as we have seen, is regarded not just as a good thing by IS. Instead, the pattern created in the distant past, the "methodology of the Prophet" himself, offers the IS Muslim the only acceptable model for behavior. Anything that departs from that model is *bida*, and so is condemned. In other words, IS preaches a purist form of Islam, one cleansed of innovations and differences from the Islam of the Prophet. Tradition, therefore, is good only if it goes back to the Prophet. As with the trousers decree, what IS sees as later changes, even if they go back to the generations just after the Prophet, even if the intentions of the faithful in adopting them are to show respect to the figure of the founder of their faith, are to be rejected.

All Work and No Play

Leisure activities, to take one example, are a problem. How should Muslims spend their free time? What is permitted and what is not? Several fatwas open a small window onto this question. Billiards and table football, or foosball, are both permitted, by analogy with chess, which Ibn Taymiyya, in the fourteenth century, allowed. But in following him, IS imposes strict conditions. Neither game should be an occasion for cursing or gambling. Cursing a fellow Muslim ("blasphemy, cursing, scorn, resentment, hatred")—which might be understandable if the game is going badly—is a heinous sin. Gambling too is strictly forbidden—even having the loser pay for the game is not allowed. Moreover, neither game should keep one from one's religious obligations. Foosball presents a special problem: the figures used in the game are of little soccer players, and have heads. But foosball "should be devoid of statues and portraits in accordance with the strong prohibition against that. And that means that the head [of the footballer figures] is cut off."[36]

The permission to play foosball is puzzling in another way. As an indoors, miniature form of soccer, it should, one might think, enjoy or suffer from the same legal regimen as the real thing, soccer. But the relationship of IS with this sport is rather more complex.[37] Reports suggested that IS planned to attack the European soccer championships in 2016. Fortunately Euro 2016 ended without an attack, after a surprise victory by Portugal. A soccer match, especially a high-profile one, offers a prime target for IS, but the game itself, among IS supporters and apparently its leaders, enjoys considerable popularity, which complicates matters. Analysis of Facebook pages of supporters of IS shows that many of them are soccer fans. One of the Brussel attackers had photographs of two legendary English soccer teams' grounds, Manchester United's Old Trafford and Aston Villa's stadium in Birmingham, on his phone, and although he is suspected of taking the pictures for IS, it remains unclear whether that was true or he had taken the photos simply as souvenirs. Games of more local interest have been the objects of IS attackers in different places around the world. IS has also killed for reasons connected to soccer: in 2015, thirteen teenagers were killed for watching on TV an Asia Cup match between Iraq and Jordan, and in the summer of 2016 four members of the disbanded soccer team in Raqqa were executed in public as spies for the Kurds. But at the start soccer was allowed, and young children, especially, were permitted to kick a ball around. A week after the Paris attacks, permission was given to show the match between FC Barcelona and Real Madrid, though this permission was withdrawn when the event began with a minute's silence in memory of the Paris victims. As with other games, IS sees soccer as basically a waste of time that should be devoted to godly pursuits, but it treads with some care because of the game's popularity.

Music, whether making it or listening to it, is also a problem. Unlike soccer, which does not have a centuries-old past, making and listening to music go back deep into human history. The Quran refers to it here and there, but its verses lend themselves to opposing interpretations, and views have always been mixed.[38] Attitudes among the religious establishment have tended to be negative, but historically the broad consensus remains undecided—the hostility of religious rigor repeatedly comes up against the imperatives of popular reality. Thus we hear frequently of famous slave-girls who were singers, even to caliphs, and we have some important studies of musical theory by Muslims in the Middle Ages.[39] Similarly, in the modern period, the first performance of Verdi's *Aïda* took place in the new Khedivial Opera House in Cairo in 1871. Although the original building burned down in 1971, it was replaced by a fine new one (built by the Japanese), where I once enjoyed a performance of *Don Giovanni*, sung in Arabic. And one of the most famous and popular of modern Arabs was the Egyptian singer Umm Kulthum, whose funeral in 1975 dwarfed even that of President Nasser a few years earlier.

IS has generally been strictly against music. An announcement of January 2014 banned music in Raqqa, including singing and stringed musical instruments. Even drums are forbidden. The reasoning is clear: "stringed instruments and song are forbidden in Islam because they detract from mention of God and the Quran, and they are a source of strife and corruption for the heart." Quran commentators and traditionists are cited in support of this position. The Prophet is quoted as predicting that there will be Muslim sinners who indulge in "fornication, silk, wine and stringed instruments." In consequence, IS forbids "the sale of songs on disks and musical instruments as well as the playing of songs of amusement in cars, coaches, shops and all places."[40] Nonetheless, numerous IS videos are accompanied by (male) singing, and the justification appears to be that the songs in question are not sung for amusement or entertainment but to extol the glory of God.

No Extra Prayers

A Muslim should not need music or football to fill his time. He can devote it to religion. Not only how but also how often a Muslim prays have aroused IS concern. An announcement from the Diwan al-Hisba, or religious police, of the IS administration for Ramadan 1436 (June–July 2015) announced the cancelation of what are known as *tarawih*, or supererogatory prayers, during the great fast of Ramadan in all the mosques of Mosul, calling them "an innovation (Arabic *bida*) and an error (*dalala*) and forbidding them completely." According to imam Saadon Nuemi of the Ninawah governorate, "Tarawih prayer is a heresy made up by clerics in Saudi Arabia and so it shouldn't be performed."[41]

Ramadan is a hard month for the believer. Fasting during the day and eating, drinking, and enjoying sex (see the Quran, *sura* 2:187) only at night make it fairly hard to work during the day, even if the fast falls during winter. At the moment, Ramadan comes around at the height of summer, when the heat is worst. One of the most popular ways of filling the days is to spend time in the mosque with fellow Muslims, in prayer. The idea is that if some prayer is good, more prayer should be even better.

Pilgrims and travelers and visitors to Islamic lands tell us about these prayers. The pious devote more time to prayer and add numerous extra prayers to the regular Ramadan schedule. It is these that are known as the *tarawih*. Ibn Jubayr, our Spanish Muslim traveler from the late twelfth century, for example, gives a detailed account of the *tarawih* prayers in Mecca in Ramadan of 1183–1184:

> The Shafi'ite imam was the most assiduous in the *tarwih* [singular of *tarawih*], in that having completed the customary *tarwih*, which is ten *taslim*, he joined in a *tawaf* with one of the groups. And when he had done the sevenfold *tawaf* and the *rak'ah*, he commenced again to recite more *tarawih*, and cracked the preacher's whip, of which we have already spoken, a crack that could be heard throughout the Mosque so loud it was, and that seemed to be a signal to return to prayers. When his group had ended two *taslim* they returned to perform again seven *tawaf*. When they had finished them, the whip was cracked again and they turned once more to the *taslim*, and then again back to the *tawaf* and so on until they had done ten *taslim* and completed twenty *rak'ah*.[42]

A year later, at the end of 1184, Ibn Jubayr was in Sicily for Ramadan on his way home from the pilgrimage. There too, though the island was by then under Norman rule, he encountered Muslims and prayed the *tarawih*:

> We passed the most pleasing and agreeable night in that mosque [in Solanto castle], and listened to the call to

prayer, which long we had not heard. We were shown high regard by the residents of the mosque, amongst whom was an imam who led them in the obligatory prayers and, in this holy month, the *tarawih*.[43]

The Englishman Edward William Lane spent several years in Cairo in the nineteenth century working on a great dictionary of classical Arabic that, even though he never finished it, retains its importance to this day. He also produced an annotated (and bowdlerized) translation of the *1001 Nights* and, more importantly, *An Account of the Manners and Customs of the Modern Egyptians*. Apart from being very readable, this work is extremely valuable, because it gives us a picture of Egyptian and Islamic society just before the tide of modernization swept over that country. Lane too observed the *tarawih*:

Immediately after the call to evening prayer, which is chanted four minutes after sunset, the master and such of his family or friends as happen to be with him drink each a glass of sherbet: they then usually say the evening prayers; and, this done, eat a few nuts, etc., and smoke their pipes. After this slight refreshment, they sit down to a plentiful meal of meat and other food, which they term their breakfast ("fatoor"). Having finished this meal, they say the night-prayers, and certain additional prayers of Ramadan, called "et-taráweeh;" or smoke again before they pray. The taráweeh prayers consist of twenty rek'ahs; and are repeated between the 'eshë prayers and the witr. Very few persons say these prayers, excepting in the mosque, where they have an Imám to take the lead; and they do little more than conform with his motions.[44]

The meritorious character of extra prayer seems obvious, as is the optional character of the *tarawih*. Their origins, as so often, are obscure, but what we know is tantalizing. *Tarawih* were not laid down by the Prophet. They seem to have been introduced as early as the Prophet's own generation, but even that does not necessarily imply prophetic authority.

A variety of traditions describe the Prophet's behavior and attitudes during Ramadan, but it is clear that they have a tendentious character.[45] Thus Aisha, the Prophet's favorite wife, is made to tell us that the Prophet offered extra prayers during the fasting month. That would seem to make imitating his practice at least permissible, possibly meritorious, and perhaps even a requirement. Yet the same tradition goes on to tell us that people would come and pray behind him but he took no notice. One morning he said to them: "Your presence was not hidden from me, but I was afraid lest the night prayer should be enjoined upon you and you might not be able to carry it on." That changes things: it now looks like a way of telling people that they need not or even should not perform such extra prayers.

Another such tradition tells us that Muhammad's friend and second successor, Umar, decided to collect people who were offering the night prayers individually so that they could perform them in groups. Then one night, seeing them do this, he remarked, "What an excellent *bida* this is." The remark provides a Janus-like cover: on one hand it suggests that the prayers are good; on the other, it tells us that they are an innovation, reminding us that innovations are not well regarded in Islam. It is argued by some that Umar's "innovation" consisted merely in determining and organizing the character of something that already existed in the practice of the Prophet, but others, for example the well-known eleventh- to twelfth-century writer al-Turtushi ("from Tortosa," in Islamic Spain), said *tarawih* were not an innovation and approved of them. In this he was following a precedent of Umayyad rulers in Islamic Spain who well over a century before his time had made the rulers of Fez undertake to perform the *tarawih*, which had been forbidden by the Shi'i Fatimids who dominated the area before the Umayyads.[46]

Tarawih thus have a mixed character. Permitted after a fashion, sometimes even encouraged by some who see prayer as good and so more prayer as better, they are forbidden by the more rigorous who see prayer as required but only in the forms and the quantity laid down, no less and no more. That explains why, for example, we hear not only of IS forbidding *tarawih* but also, more terrifyingly, of one IS commander who "stopped unarmed civilians who said

they were Muslims. He then proceeded to ask them the number of
prostrations (*rak'ahs*) in specific prayers. When they answered incorrectly, he killed them."[47]

IS and Islam

Holidays are particularly dangerous times. Because they are times
of celebration, they are liable to encourage new kinds of behavior
and lead to religious laxity of different kinds, in particular in sexual
matters. On 8 Dhu al-Hijjah of the Islamic year 1435 (October 2,
2014), IS issued a fatwa condemning several types of "innovation"
at Id al-Adha, the festival of the sacrifice, celebrated two days later.
Visiting graves was forbidden, because the festival is a time of glad-
ness and visiting the tombs of the dead makes one sad: "thus we
warn the people not to commit this condemned act." Similarly, a
good Muslim should not make the night of the Id a night of special
celebration. Despite what "some believe," there is no reason to
mark it out as different from other nights. Far more serious than
these and other transgressions, however, is the "mixing of women
with men." The fatwa reminds us of the words of the Prophet: "A
man and woman are not to be left together unless she also has her
mahrim (male relative) with her"; and similarly, a woman who puts
on perfume in order to make herself attractive when she goes out
is a whore or an adulterer. And even if a woman just shakes hands
with men this is a problem: again, the Prophet tells us that
"Whoever touches the palm of a woman and is not from her (family) is on the way to placing on his own palm the ember of the Day
of Judgment."[48]

What purpose do all these restrictions and regulations serve
for IS? On one hand, it is clear that they are about power: they
demonstrate to the people under IS rule that IS is there. IS is in
charge, IS dominates their lives, their behavior, their bodies, how
they pray, and how much they pray. On the other hand, the
changes and alterations indicate something deeper about Islam itself. IS is not simply a new regime, Islamic or secular. It aims neither to reject religion as the basis for the state, in the manner of
the secularizing Arab regimes of the middle twentieth century, nor
to use it merely as a façade for a state dominated by armies or

other elites. Nor again is IS a new version of Islam. IS sees itself as the authentic Islam of the Prophet and its practice of the faith as a true repetition of his way. Compelling people to hold their fingers in a particular way when they pray, or not to perform prayers during Ramadan that are not sanctified by divine approval, or to roll their trousers up above their ankles, reflects the way of the Prophet and as such constitutes true and correct patterns of behavior for Muslims.

While these practices differ from what many Muslims are used to, they fall, nevertheless, within the larger ambit of Islamic patterns of religious praxis. In that sense, they are not non-Islamic. In that sense, therefore, they are not automatically to be rejected by the faithful. IS policy, or strategy, in these matters is skillful and astute: it is imposing on its subjects, or offering Muslims, a version of Islam that differs very little from what they are used to. It differs only in details; those details are not innovations but in each case qualify as a return to the practice of the Prophet; the rationale or justification for them is visible and comprehensible, whether in the form of fatwas or via quasi-historical arguments; and to that degree they are even, at least for some, if not acceptable, tolerable. Thus the Islam that IS imposes wherever it can does not represent unbelief or heresy; it is not anti-Islamic. It is not, in fact, all that easy to oppose. Like the more general message of IS, it has a slippery aspect to it. If the message is Islam, so the feeling goes, why is it necessary to oppose it?

CHAPTER FIVE

Women, and Children Too

IN THE IMMEDIATE AFTERMATH of the attacks in Paris in mid-November 2015 the police tracked a couple of the terrorists to an apartment in the modest neighborhood of Saint Denis. As the siege began, a young woman appeared in a window, shouting "Help me!" The appeal was a ruse: the young woman was a cousin and accomplice of the leader of the Paris attackers. When the siege was over, some five thousand bullets and multiple explosions later, she was dead, with, according to one report, "part of [her] spine landing on a police car."[1]

News stories painted a picture of a young woman with a difficult but not spectacularly hard or very unusual background. Her immigrant parents split up when she was young; the preceding July her father had returned to Morocco, once a French protectorate, after forty-two years in France. She had been involved with drugs and perhaps done some drug peddling on a small scale; she had set up a contracting business that failed after less than a year; she had taken dance lessons as a young girl, drunk alcohol, and even gone clubbing. She also, until recently, had had little or no interest in religion ("I never saw her open a Quran," said her brother).

But recently she had changed. In June, six months before the terror attack, she had taken to covering her face outside and behaving more "respectfully." A picture that surfaced online showed her wearing a striped zipper jacket over a long dress. A veil covers her head and hangs down below the chin, concealing her face above the eyebrows and below the lips: she may be smiling as she makes two "V" for victory signs with her hands, a ring on the middle finger of her right hand. A second photo purporting to show her lounging in a bubble bath was later identified as a picture of someone else, but it went well with the larger image that was gradually emerging in the Western media, of terror as fun, the terrorist as party girl, and, no less importantly, the party girl as a full participant in that fun. Bonnie, perhaps, to her cousin's Clyde.

The young woman's death may have been an accidental by-product of the Paris attacks. She was not directly involved in them; her intended role was apparently limited to providing a safe house for the surviving attackers. After making the mistake of placing a call on her cellphone that brought the police onto their tracks, she was caught up in the ensuing mêlée. But what happened at the apartment in Saint Denis, her attempt to lure the police into a trap, the wide circulation of the pictures, and her biography all contributed to the creation of another martyr story for IS, another example of the selfless and devoted sacrifice of those fighting against the corrupt Christian West in the path of Allah.[2]

Hasna Aitboulahcen—her name points to a Berber background—represents one type of the IS ideal of femininity. She is not alone. The activist supporter of the cause can be a terrorist, or an aide to other terrorists. But she can also be a doctor or an educator. She can serve in other ways, too, as a mother or a homemaker. Above all, she serves best, we are told, when she worships Allah and keeps to her family and home. An IS version of the old German role model for women expressed in the words *Kinder Kirche Küche* ("Children, church, kitchen"), this outlook actually represents an extremist form of a deeply conservative social ideal that became fused many centuries ago with religion.[3]

Tourists for Terror

Another type of IS women is seen in some fuzzy photographs captured by cameras at Gatwick Airport near London on February 17, 2015. These show Khadiza Sultana, age sixteen, and two fifteen-year-old friends, Amira Abase and Shamima Begum, as they made their journey from London's Bethnal Green, home to many British Muslims of Bangladeshi background, to Turkey, on their way to join IS. The pictures show them modestly dressed and looking down demurely as they pass through security devices, not apparently different from thousands of other young female Muslims. Good students, though apparently less good in the time immediately before their flight, they were models to their fellow schoolgirls, and fairly typical in their behavior: they read novels, wore cosmetics, debated with their friends, Muslim and non-Muslim. The pictures showing them arriving in Raqqa, just off the bus from Turkey, could show three young female tourists getting off a bus in Torremolinos or Malta or a skiing resort in Switzerland. The only real difference is that they are apparently wearing hair coverings.[4]

These three schoolgirls are not terrorists, nor aides to terrorists. Given their ages, it may not be clear, even to them, why they abandoned their homes and went to Syria. But it is also likely that they were attracted by aspects of IS ideology that are readily available to them via modern social media.[5] The posts and tweets of Amira Abase bring out the sheer ordinariness of these schoolgirls. In them she chats about clothing and high-school exams and even soccer (her favorite club was Chelsea). Their radicalization appears to have taken the form of a rapidly deepening conservatism—in late December 2014, Abase posted pictures of her newly bought lingerie from Victoria's Secret while at the same time asking whether it is forbidden (*haram*) to get her nose pierced. A little after that, she expressed concern for Syrian refugees and asked about Arabic language courses. Later on, but still only in mid-February of 2015, she wrote "PRAY ALLAH GRANTS ME THE HIGHEST RANKS IN JANNAH" (Arabic for Paradise). Less than a week after that, she and her friends got on the plane for Turkey. Abase's father, it turned out, had taken part in an extremist Islamist rally outside the U.S. embassy in London in 2012. For these girls, as for Aitboulahcen, the leap from a secular lifestyle, if one inflected through conservative surroundings, to radicalization does not appear to have been difficult or too much of a stretch. It also did not take very long, less than a couple of months.

The Bethnal Green trio do not seem to have become IS fighters, but they have turned up in recruiting pictures for the movement and were married off almost at once to IS fighters. Their story also recalls the cases of two Austrian Muslims of Bosnian background, Samra Kesinovic and Sabina Selimovic, who flew to Turkey and joined IS in Syria from there. Not unlike the Bethnal Green schoolgirls, these two joined the ranks of IS, and were married to IS fighters. Unlike them, they became fighters themselves, and one of them, Kesinovic, was either killed in action or beaten to death while trying to escape. The other was later reported to be trying to make good a return to her home.[6] The Bethnal Green contingent also apparently had second thoughts about their hosts and tried to go back home.

Local Girls

Female fighters and volunteers for the cause are in fact not all that rare. As many as 10 percent of the Western recruits to IS may be women.[7] Local female volunteers are also not uncommon. When the Sinai Province of IS carried out an attack on the Swiss Inn Resort hotel in El-Arish, in northern Sinai, in mid-November 2015, it claimed that it was retaliating against the Egyptian government because it would not release some female IS fighters whom it was holding.[8]

The three cases are of course different: in the first, a foreign woman has been drawn in, apparently by a cousin, and used in a major attack. In the second, some schoolgirls have been attracted, apparently via computer-based media, to join IS ranks. And the last showcases locally based women members or sympathizers of the movement who have been caught and imprisoned by Muslims hostile to IS. The first represents an Islamic version of Batgirl or of Jennifer Lawrence as Katniss Everdeen—the ordinary girl as superhero. The second plays this pattern for a more general, maybe also a more conservative audience, at a lower level of involvement and action, while the third advertises IS concern not only for its fighters but also for Muslim women in general and their right to be treated in a special way, unlike men. In all three cases, however, and in others like them, IS is demonstrating its ability to attract women to its ranks, to wield its ideology as a weapon to appeal specifically to women, and to use women differently from men in its campaign.

Our understanding of IS and women is dominated, even shaped, by these images. They are frightening in their own way. But they are not the only images we have. They are one part of a larger picture of the relationship of the sexes in the Islamic State: a picture that is more varied and rather more nuanced than the spectacles they offer us may suggest. Apart from anything else, we also have reports, brought alive by videos and interviews, showing women of the Yazidi community who have been caught by IS, imprisoned, sold as slaves, worked as sex slaves, raped, forcibly married to IS fighters, even burned alive.[9] These show a different view of women, or of non-Muslim women, and so a different way of categorizing the world.

Most Women's Experience of IS

Hasna Aitboulahcen, Shamima Begum, and the rest are stand-outs. Most women of the Islamic State are more normal. Half the population is female and virtually none are Islamic superheroes or volunteers for IS. The territory ruled by the IS at the end of 2015 was larger than the United Kingdom and had some eight to ten million inhabitants. How do the millions of women under IS rule live? What is their real status and what does IS rule mean for them? How does the Islam in "Islamic State" affect them?

Not just in the infidel countries of the West but in Islamic countries too the position of women has changed and been transformed in many ways over the past century. In most countries the veil has been increasingly abandoned (in Turkey, the secularizing ban on the headscarf is an on-again off-again battle). Women dress as they wish, though not with quite the same freedom as in some Western countries. Women, and girls, now receive education on a par with and often physically alongside men and boys. Health facilities do not distinguish between the sexes or segregate them as they once did. Women take part in the workforce.[10] In most Islamic countries, if to varying degrees, men and women are no longer kept separate, whether in employment or in the street, in cafés or in shops and offices, or on the screen. Egyptian television and cinema dominate the Middle East, and Bollywood too, from outside the Islamic world, enjoys massive penetration in, for example, Nigeria.[11] Several Islamic countries have had women prime ministers or presidents—Turkey, Bangladesh, Pakistan, and Indonesia—though strikingly no Arab country.

From the end of World War II, oil revenues, especially in Iraq, and secularizing ideology in both that country and Syria meant that women's rates of literacy went up, education improved, health indices rose, and women began to engage in the work economy outside the home, even to take part in politics.[12] Much of this implied the abandonment of the veil and the knocking down of the fences that separated men and women. The fall of Saddam Hussein in Iraq and the outbreak of the civil war in Syria have undone these successes: in both countries rates of literacy have declined, especially among women; educational institutions and standards have suffered disproportionately from the strife; and hospitals and medical treatment have been devastated.[13]

IS rule has exacerbated all of these trends, but it has done so as part of a larger strategy. For most women, IS rule means subjection to a hugely broad and intrusive set of norms and rules that deliberately remove or cancel the advances that women have enjoyed over the last half century. IS aims to return, on one hand, to the strict separation of sexes that once characterized those societies and, on the other, arising from that, to a strict hierarchization of the sexes, with males on top. The first forms a central element of the religious propaganda of the movement; the second lurks barely out of sight behind an Islamist rhetoric of service to Allah and obedience to His will expressed in terms of female empowerment.

Fatwas on Women's Life

Fatwa no. 44, dated December 17, 2014, of the IS Department of Fatwas and Research, was one of a number released that day on issues related to women.[14] The question that was asked (or at least that IS wanted to answer) concerned important issues: What are the characteristics of women's proper covering (*hijab*, literally "veiling")? What are the characteristics of improper showing (*tabarruj*—

the word means literally "playing up her charms, making herself pretty," from a root that means simply something "apparent," "visible")? The authoritative response was extremely detailed:

> Proper covering includes: (1) having the entire body and hands concealed, (2) being thick, not thin, (3) being unadorned, (4) being loose-fitting, not tight-fitting, (5) being unperfumed, (6) not resembling men's clothing, and (7) not resembling infidel women's clothing. Improper showing includes: (1) showing anything of the body before unfamiliar men, (2) showing any part of the clothing beneath the veil, (3) suggestive ambling in front of men, (4) leg slapping, which is highly arousing, (5) coy and flirtatious talking, and (6) mixing with men, touching their bodies, shaking their hands, and crowding together with them in cramped vehicles.[15]

This is not just about dress. Nor is it only about behavior, or comportment. It is about keeping women in their place. Women must cover their entire bodies—including, according to another fatwa, their eyes, which must be concealed "even if only with something thin," to permit them to see, through a gauze, darkly, without being seen.[16] Any resemblance to what men or "infidel" women wear is forbidden. The covering must be effectively shapeless and so thick and loose as to make them, their bodies, and thus also their personalities, invisible. Adornment and perfume are prohibited. (Women are permitted, however, to bleach their eyebrows, as those giving the fatwas were unaware of any text that explicitly forbids this—but they stress that it is still preferable for them not to do so.)[17] Women may not be seen and even when they are present nothing about them should make their presence felt. The womanhood of the Islamic woman is to be expressed entirely in negatives.

What is the point of all this? That is answered by the second part of the response: no unrelated man is to see any part of a woman's body, nor even any clothing underneath the full body veil. More than that, men are not to be tempted by "suggestive ambling" or "coy and flirtatious talking," while "leg slapping" is seen as "highly arousing" and coming into contact with them, especially in crowded vehicles, is out of the question. Another fatwa says that even wearing a weapon over the full body veil is legally troubling: it may not be done if doing so shows the outline of the body underneath. Kalashnikovs, however, may be a partial exception.[18]

As has often been pointed out, this is about men, not women. This is about protecting men from women's wiles, dressed up as protecting women from strange men. Thus another fatwa, dated 20 Rabi II 1436 (February 9, 2015), prohibits the keeping of pigeons on people's roofs, in order to "put a stop to the greater criminal act of harming one's Muslim and Muslim women neighbors" by staring at them through open windows.[19] The memory of Bathsheba and King David lives on. The fatwa is also about preserving the rights that men enjoy over women, under the guise of giving women protection. Women may travel only with the permission and in the company of a male relative.[20] Otherwise, however, men and women are to be strictly segregated. Educational institutions have to keep the sexes separate, so too hospitals, and medical personnel of one sex may not treat people of the other unless others are present.[21]

All this is policed by special detachments of women's morality police (not dissimilar to those that operate in Saudi Arabia).[22] They operate under the medieval-sounding title of Hisba, and they check up also on such matters as women's behavior in shops. Forbidden types of clothing may not be sold. The Hisba officials in Mosul supervise the display of women's clothes in shops, in addition to keeping an eye on women in the shops and moving around the city without full legal dress. Another announcement forbids women wearing adornment to enter the shops, or to take off their *niqabs* (full body veils) while there, and instructs the sales staff not to talk to them about anything except their purchases. Naturally, a woman may not go into a shop alone, but must be accompanied by a male relative, a young son, or a group of other women.[23]

The fatwas that detail all of this also offer information on the justification for these restrictions and prohibitions. Like so much else, they do not spring from the heads of IS itself. They reproduce the practices of the Prophet and of early Islam, as these are recorded for us in the ancient literature of Islam and interpreted by the legal authorities of IS. And they reflect also the traditional status and rights of women in the Middle East, which fed into Islamic notions of correct behavior for women over many centuries. In dragging Muslims, and Muslim women in particular, back to the attitudes and behavior of an earlier age, IS is trying to replicate what it sees as the behavior of the Prophet and the society of his time. But it is not unaware of the modern world and understands too that it cannot simply expect its dictates, even if they are supported by the force of tradition and the texts of the past, to sway everyone.

Women Writing about Women

We know relatively little about the day-to-day lives of individual women under IS rule, and much of what we hear may be too specific or sensationalized to be truly informative. For the great majority, the rules and regulations of IS offer a fairly reliable guide. But there are also women who live in IS by choice, and while their lives may be just as regimented as those of the rest, they are more likely to reveal something of them and of why they have chosen to live there. They are also more likely to have the opportunity and the desire to do so.

Autobiographical accounts by individual IS women are rare, and suffer from all the problems inherent in the autobiographical genre in general—in presenting an account of the self, are they trying to paint a true picture or one that conforms to the expectations of others? Who is the intended audience? Are they self-justifications or apologias? Do they conceal more than they reveal? Are they publicity for an individual or propaganda for a cause? Do they tell the truth, and if so, what kind of truth?[24]

Most of what we know of such women comes, though, not in such self-consciously literary form. The Internet and social media, from email via Twitter and Facebook, Instagram and Snapchat, to electronic publications of many other types, have enabled IS women to express themselves and to speak in both a public voice and the semi-private mode that characterizes communication in the twenty-first century. The female volunteers for IS have thus "a discursive presence that has no historical precedent"—one that gives them direct access to audiences of both sexes.[25]

Property in Paradise

Marriage is not what it is all about for these women. Jihadi brides are not the story. Women who make their way to IS territory and marry jihadis are not going there for that purpose. Popular explanations that stress sexual or marital ambitions in this way miss the point. What the women themselves tell us is that they go to IS territory in order to live lives of freedom, as God wishes them to, serving Allah and preparing for *aakhirah*, the world to come.

Yet, on the way to that world, marriage beckons. A woman on her own has real problems in the Islamic State. Just getting around outside the house is next door to impossible, as one young woman found out, without a *mahram*, a male guardian. *Deen*, religion, recommends marriage as the proper state for a woman; according to this view, marriage creates the proper framework for life. Virtually all the young IS women whom we can track are married or getting married, generally to jihadis (and often becoming widowed too). Matchmaking, however, is not always easy. While some marriages are arranged through friends and family, as is common in the Islamic world, men and women cannot meet in the Western way. So IS has set up a marriage bureau, in the province of Aleppo, for single women and widows who wish to marry jihad fighters. It even arranges honeymoon trips for the newlyweds: bus tours of the caliphate.[26]

The bewitching charm of a true Islamic marriage overcomes all barriers. One young woman, Zaynab, an immigrant to Raqqa from Australia with her father and siblings, was married at the age of fourteen to a fellow Australian. The man is a friend of her father who is well known for appearing in Australian media in photographs that show him holding amputated heads and for offering Yezidi women for sale ("don't worry brothers, she won't disappoint you").[27]

Another woman, Shams ("sun" in Arabic), a twenty-six-year-old doctor who made her way to IS territory without her parents' knowledge and was married to an IS fighter, had no common language with her new groom—he spoke fluent Arabic and French, but she was from Malaysia, presumably spoke Malay, apparently knew some Hindi and Urdu (her parents were from the subcontinent), and had moderate English. Yet at their first meeting, after a few minutes of silence, "I flipped my Niqab," their eyes met, "I had palpitation that is faster than the speed of light," and "he asked a question that I shall never forget for the rest of my life: 'Can we get married today?'" Shams agreed and, following a telephone call to get permission from her parents (the mother screams for joy in the background), they married. Not only do they not speak a common language; they also do not share a cuisine: "I told him that I don't know how to cook Moroccan or Western food. He laughed and said that he don't mind." They downloaded dictionary apps on their mobile phones: "It helped and it was so much fun Al Hamdulillah" (Arabic for Praise be to God). "What does actually matter is—Heart. When you love someone for the sake of Allah, He will 'tie' a knot between our hearts and make the attachment strong, regardless the differences between two of you."[28]

Shams maintained a blog, *Diary of a Muhajirah*, using the pseudonym Bird of Paradise. Though her account was frequently shut down, she kept on reopening it in order to detail her life in the Islamic State. It shows her joy at being in the land of the caliphate, at living the real life of a Muslim. That life includes other, harder aspects of the reality of marriage. The true IS woman is married to a fighter for IS who never knows if he will come back from a mission. Shams's husband went off to fight almost immediately after their marriage. She told him, "I am not a strong woman. So please make *du'aa* [Arabic for prayer] so Allah [will] grant me strength to overcome the hardship." "He hold my fingers and said" (presumably with the help of the dictionary apps), "'Indeed you're not a strong woman. You're a superwoman . . . Because I am a superman and you're my wife.'" Indeed she is. "After breakfast I prepared his bag and hand his kalash" (Kalashnikov). Not everyone returns: visiting a friend, Shams finds her celebrating—her husband has just been killed in combat—and she is greeted warmly: "My husband is a Shaheed" (Arabic for martyr). "He is In sha Allah in the garden of Jannah, married to Hoor-al Ayn" (Arabic for the women of paradise, whose eyes have a sharp contrast of black and white; see Quran, *sura* 56:22. Our word *houri* comes from this). "Today is the day of celebration. Today is the day of joy. No one shall cry!" The widow is comforted. Her mother has told her that the dead man "has bought a house in paradise and [is] waiting for them."

Pride and Prejudice in the Islamic State

Beyond the excitement of battle and celebrating death, being a woman in IS territory is difficult: childbirth is hard, and mother-hood under the threat of imminent widowhood harder. Shams rec-ommends that potential *muhajirat* bring books with them and download others. Reading keeps the mind occupied. She is currently reading Ibn Qayyim al-Jawziyya, a prolific early fourteenth-century Syrian theologian who was very devoted to his principal teacher, Ibn Taymiyya, a fiercely dogmatic and controversial writer whose work still has much influence both among the Wahhabis and for IS. She has also brought *Pride and Prejudice*. After Ibn Qayyim, who wrote such books as "Aid for the Yearning One in Resisting the Devil," Jane Austen promises escapism—in the paradise of the Islamic State, the courtship of Elizabeth Bennet and Mr. Darcy is spicy reading.

Dreams of Victory

Muhajirat, women who have made the *hijra*, migration, to IS lands, arrive there not only from the West but also from other Islamic countries in order to help build the IS paradise. Such women often feel exalted and exhilarated by their experience. They go there with a purpose and they find different paths to fulfilment of that purpose: simply living a life of piety according to IS rules; working as a teacher or a nurse; marriage to an IS fighter, especially if he dies as a martyr; even cooking for the fighters. Their faith confirms the value and the dignity of their work and provides the justifica-tion for their move to the lands of the caliphate.[29]

One IS woman who has written about herself at some length, Ahlam al-Nasr (a pseudonym meaning "Dreams of Victory"), is the author of not only a blog but also two prose texts about her move to the Islamic State territory, and, on top of all that, a volume of poetry.[30] A Syrian woman with a mother and a grandfather who are professors of Islamic religious subjects (her father is a pharmacist and is well known for his skill at memorizing the Quran), Ahlam al-Nasr became enthusiastic about IS at what seems to have been a very young age and decided to make her way there from Saudi Arabia, where her parents were living. As she describes it:

The Islamic Caliphate was the dream of my life since the dawn of my childhood, but my only share of it were social media accounts that were closed down from time to time ... The situation of the one who is far from the Caliphate and impatient for it is like the situation of the fish hanging by the tail just above the surface of the sea, seeing it but unable to reach it.

As a variation on the suffering of Tantalus, the image does not quite work (the fish would die from lack of water), but the point is clear. Excessive despair and hope combined to drive her to go. (Simplistic psychologizing might see this as teenage angst, but a surprising number of such volunteers for the cause are very young, and often, like Hasna Aitboulahcen and the Bethnal Green trio, have been living at the meeting point of two very different worlds.) Her mother, apparently the dominant parent, soon followed her, along with the rest of the family, realizing, as she wrote, that "I was a Daeshite in thought and method. I was a Daeshite before Daesh was there. I have known for a long time that the only solution for Muslims is jihad."[31]

For Ahlam al-Nasr, arrival in IS territory meant arrival in Paradise. "Life is beautiful [here] my sisters, full of Godly blessings and gifts ... We can achieve all of this when we rule according to Islam. In the land of the Caliphate I saw [female] modesty and piety, and people who close down their shop for prayer. Likewise I saw vibrant commerce and abundant goods, a variety of fresh vegetables." The veil is not forbidden there, nor is growing a beard a crime.[32]

Her poetry conforms to classical Arabic patterns. It possesses the two qualities that define poetry in Arabic: it is rhymed and it is in meter, following a fixed pattern for the distribution of long and short syllables in every line. One poem, which IS publicity describes as by "the poet of the Islamic State," begins:

At last our Lord has granted me His generosity, and I have touched weaponry, my friend.

I have experienced the caliphate and the sublime, and felt happiness and relaxation.

The State of Islam will endure for ever, by the grace of
God it will snatch success.[33]

Ahlam al-Nasr is enchanted by her new life. "I was allowed to
cook for the mujahidin. I was almost flying out of joy. I was literally
obsessed with making sure that everything was clean and good. I
started repeating 'This food will be eaten by the mujahidin; this
silverware will be used by the mujahidin. I am now among the mujahidin . . . Is that real, or is it a dream?'"

The Khansa Brigade

Against this background, we are fortunate to have an IS document devoted entirely to women. Produced by the Khansa Brigade (in Arabic
sariyyat al-Khansa), which seems to be a kind of moral police force
composed of women and concerned with enforcing women's morals
in the Islamic State, it lays out clearly something of the ideological
underpinnings of IS attitudes to women and treatment of them.[34]

The name al-Khansa highlights the central aspect of IS notions
about women. The original al-Khansa (whose name means "snub-
nosed," or "gazelle") was a famous poet in the late sixth and early
seventh centuries. Two of her brothers were killed in battle—
though battle is a grand name for what cannot have been, in the
circumstances of the time, much more than very small, local skir-
mishes—and she wrote elegies about them. The poems celebrate
the brothers' martial qualities, and it is for this reason, more than
on account of her real qualities as a poet, that al-Khansa's name is
used here.[35] The image of a woman as a backup support, and ad-
mirer of the fighters, those who do the heavy lifting, not only
serves to provide women with a role, it also fits a widespread tradition in many cultures. Beyond that, by describing women as cele-
brators of the prowess and achievements of men, such writings tie
the two sexes together, cementing them as a single body of fighters,
albeit differentiated by sex, struggling for a common aim. But all
the while that image makes clear which is the top sex, and which is
the one with the secondary rank and role.

If al-Khansa represents an ideal Muslim woman, however, she
is not a typical one. The pamphlet goes on to make very clear its

authors' idea of the typical Muslim woman. It is cast in suitably Islamic style. On the cover we see the bismillah ("In the name of God the Compassionate, the Merciful"), that begins every IS document and very many Islamic texts of all periods. We do not, however, see any insignia of IS or even its name: this is as it should be, for the female authors stress that this is not an official IS paper, nor does it even lay out IS policy or ideology. Such matters are the responsibility of men. Rather, they tell us that the document simply offers their own modest contribution to illuminating the role of women in the movement and in Islamic society in general. We are to understand that the two are basically the same thing.

Instead of the formality of IS markings, we see, at the bottom, the title of the pamphlet, "Woman in the Islamic State," with, below it, a secondary title, "Woman in the State of the Caliphate." On the right is a photo of a woman. Because she represents the IS female ideal, she is totally invisible, enveloped in a full body covering—even her eyes seem to be hidden, with only a thin, transparent gauze to permit her to see. On the left, facing her, is an upturned M-16. Is the apparent irony of a U.S.-manufactured weapon being used both against the West and in this IS design deliberate, or should we see the weapon merely as representing a stand-in for any heavy gun?[36] Between the two versions of the title is a logo showing what looks like a partial globe, in purple, bearing the name of the issuing department—the Khansa Information Brigade—topped by a black IS banner with the ubiquitous slogan of IS: There is no god but Allah, Muhammad is the Messenger of Allah. IS branding is becoming more prominent in this sort of literature. On the left, cutting the globe more or less in half, is another upturned gun, surmounted by what seems to be a turban.

Aside from questions of authenticity, which arise here as with anything linked to IS, we can be fairly confident that this pamphlet constitutes a semi-official publication of the IS movement. Coming from an official organ of the IS as a state—its control on women's morals—and laying out that organ's view of women's status and roles in Islamic society, it cannot have been published without formal internal approval and must reflect at least in its general lines the attitudes of the leadership. Those attitudes in their turn are founded on their interpretation of Islamic religious tradition and legal requirements.

The text aims at a double target: first, it seeks to criticize the treatment of women in Saudi Arabia, which it says has a "deceptive Islamic model"; and secondly, it propounds what it presents as a sound model for the Islamic woman: "If men were men," it says, "then women would be women."[37] Men, we understand, are not permitting women to fulfill their potential. Women are entitled to an education, and indeed they should be educated, but "the only true knowledge" is sharia, not studying "the brain cells of crows, grains of sand, and the arteries of fish." As we have seen, physical concealment is demanded. But concealment is presented as a virtue, with the writers recommending that women "remain hidden and veiled, to maintain society from behind this veil." At the same time, a rhetorical trick transforms this concealment into female empowerment: "This, which is always the most difficult role, is akin to that of a director, the most important person in a media production, who is behind the scenes organising."

The analogy is striking, summoning as it does the image of film, which not only reminds readers of the most modern technology and the social media used so effectively by IS, but also constantly and repeatedly presents the human figure. But it is remarkable in another way too: the director is indeed often, as this manifesto says, "the most important person in a media production," and that because he (or she) is "behind the scenes organising." But "important" is a slippery term. While the director of a movie is in every sense the boss, seen or not, behind the scenes and anywhere else, and it is he who makes the decisions, he is not necessarily the most important person there. Importance in the making of a film varies depending on who is judging and what they base their judgments on. The director may be the most important, but so may the star, even props or costume or location.

The woman as presented here in the IS scenario is in no sense the most important person in the Islamic State. If the IS women who wrote this thought (or wanted us to think) most immediately of media and the film director, though, another comparison comes even more forcefully to mind. This is of the women who, far from being oppressed, worked behind the scenes in pre-modern Islamic societies. These women, we are so often told, exercised soft power, quietly and delicately, influencing their menfolk out of sight in the harem while "remaining hidden and veiled," to borrow the manifesto's phrasing. Some harem women certainly did exercise a great deal of influence, but they were exceptions to the more general rule of exclusion and powerlessness.[38]

The manifesto does much to exploit the notion of women's empowerment. It claims that the "soldiers of Iblis" (a name for Satan in Arabic) are keeping women from Paradise. They are not allowed to stay at home but are compelled to go out to work, acquiring worldly knowledge to the exclusion of religious learning, and tricked into wasting their time on clothing that does not cover them and plastic surgery that deforms them. The Muslim woman, by contrast, is not confined to her home—though "We say, stay in your houses." She may leave it, for the right purposes, such as jihad (if the imam permits it), to study the sciences of religion, and for medical reasons.

"Islam has never been a friend of ignorance," according to this document. But "much of the worldly sciences have no use for Muslims." The Muslim woman should learn, but what she needs to know she can acquire between the ages of seven and fifteen. The manifesto offers a modest, "quick, simple proposal, not something in depth, just to give an idea." Until she is nine, she should learn *fiqh* (essentially religious law) and religion, quranic Arabic, and science, by which IS means accounting and natural science. From the ages of ten to twelve, more of the first two subjects should be learned, together with rules about marriage and divorce, as well as knitting and basic cooking. The needs of the jihadis must be met. And the last couple of years should be devoted to more sharia (Islamic law) and skills needed in raising children, in addition to Islamic history and the life of the Prophet and his followers. This should suffice for a woman, since "it is considered legitimate for a girl to be married at the age of nine. Most pure girls will be married by sixteen or seventeen, while they are still young and active."[39] According to this view, the Western mantra of equality with men only gives women "thorns." The ideal is instead exemplified by Maryam, the daughter of Imran (that is, Miriam, the sister of Moses), who is praised in the Quran for her obedience, piety, and chastity (*sura* 66:12).

Much has changed since the advent of the Islamic State. An investigative team from the Khansa Brigade visited Raqqa and Mosul to check on "the happy situation that Muslim women face and their return to what was there at the dawn of Islam and the black robes that enrage the hypocrites and their friends." Among the things they investigated was *hijab*, proper covering: "Now, women are able to travel to their people in Raqqa without having to show their face to the eyes of even one inspector. Respect for their bodies has returned ... Causes of their humiliation are prevented ... Muslims, with the permission of God, were cleansed." Not only are women properly covered up; justice is available to them in proper Islamic courts, dispensed by incorruptible judges who fear God. Even Christian women benefit: "If Christian women come to the state courts to declare their conversion to Islam, then they enjoy full protection from any harm or abuse." More broadly, in daily life IS is "expending all efforts to eradicate ... poverty and realise social justice."[40] Electricity and medical treatment, water and food supplies, schools and other public facilities are no longer neglected or ruined by corruption. Mixing of the sexes has been done away with.

The women of the Khansa Brigade offer four conclusions: first, the caliph and his soldiers hold their state dear. "Women have been raised aloft ... Their rights are protected. Second, fear God, bring up your children so that your sons know true *tawhid* [Arabic for monotheism] and your daughters know chastity and decency. Know that you are the hope of the Ummah. The guardians of the faith and protectors of the land will emerge from you." Third, the ummah of Muhammad "would not rise without your help." And fourth, "women have been returned to their Rightful *jilbabs* [Arabic for women's clothing] and sedentary lifestyle. Throw the sputum of your culture, your civilization and your thinking into the sea."

The language throughout the text is a mixture of command, telling women what they should do and how they should behave, and empowerment: acting in the right way is a privilege that is given only to them; their rights are protected by the IS leadership and manpower and hence by the community and by society. They are the true sources and guarantors of the future success of Islam. The attractions of a Western lifestyle and of Western civilization are traps to take Muslim women away from the right path of service and obedience. Exercising a free choice to follow the commands of God is the true empowerment.

A Hidden Battle of the Sexes

Living a traditional, secluded lifestyle offers one way of fulfilling the IS female dream. Another way in which women are empowered by IS and at the same time fill an important, almost vital, service role for the movement is recruitment. Women not only constitute an ideal additional source of recruits; they also, as we saw in the case of Ahlam al-Nasr, work in other ways. Cooking is only one task they can take joy in doing for the menfolk: they can also encourage others to join the mission.[41] One rather obscure study has looked intensively, by manual means rather than using computer algorithms, at those involved in "extreme networks." It sought to see how important women are to the connectivity of users in those networks. While men terrorists far outnumber women, the authors sought to find out whether men were also more important in networking and encouraging others to take part. To answer this question, they used a factor that they called BC, or "betweenness centrality," to measure how effective networkers of each sex were at receiving and sending along messages within the network. Heavy on jargon and mathematical formulas, and with a rich array of tables and diagrams, the study nevertheless comes up with easily understood conclusions: women "tend to be key players in both high-profile online and offline settings." More strikingly, while men tend to dominate numerically, they found that "women emerge with superior network connectivity at the collective level that is associated with benefits for system robustness and survival."[42] In other words, it is women, not men, who are doing the bulk of the Internet communications that can lead some to join the movement. This does not mean, obviously, that women are communicating only with women, but it does mean that women are doing more communicating on the Internet than men, and more effectively—that is, they are doing more to spread the word. In an IS world that confines women to their homes, proselytizing on the Internet may not only offer a way out of the domestic sphere, but also represent a more useful and at the same time more enjoyable form of electronic activity than reading, whether Jane Austen or even Ibn Qayyim.

In the end, though, the proper way for a Muslim woman to be a woman is to understand that "the purpose of her existence is the Divine duty of motherhood."[43] She is there to bear children to ensure the future of Islam, and with it, the future of IS.

Suffer the Little Children

The images are haunting. They show little children—only boys; girls are apparently spared. They look no older than eight or nine. All are slight of build; dark-skinned, they look out at the camera through big eyes. They could be children anywhere. They wear blackish, skirt-like robes over long trousers that somehow accentuate their youth, and they each put on a brown balaclava before beginning. Then, one by one, in a grotesque game of hide and seek, they hunt down a trussed up Syrian prisoner in some ruins and shoot him to death. The last, the sixth child shown, slits his victim's throat. Each victim states his name, his date of birth, and his role in the security forces before he is killed. The victims are virtually numb. They know their fate. There is no escape, no hope of salvation. A last humiliation, butchery by a child, is heaped onto everything else that they have suffered.[44]

The boys are also taught hand-to-hand combat. The universally popular sport suits eight-year-olds. Like other educational programs, this one includes study too, alongside fighting. The boys are shown sitting obediently at little desks learning the Quran. The combination—of religious study, hand-to-hand combat, and killing—forms a unity. Religion, ceremonial play, and ritualized execution together tell the boys that they are full members of the faith, that they are learning their duties and fulfilling their roles already as young menfolk and as Muslims.[45]

Adulthood comes early in the IS. The early experience of murder dulls believers' inner resistance as it renders the fakery of *Miami Vice* or Hollywood tomato juice not only possible but also real and everyday. Blurring the line between reality and the screen, not least by releasing videos of such scenes, IS takes the new snuff out of the

X-rating into the living room, or the adolescent bedroom. Slaughter—shooting or slitting the throat of a helpless prisoner— functions as an extension of the excitement of the play-acting involved in the hand-to-hand combat, and the fighting and the killing are given their sanction in the texts of the Quran that they study.

Children in combat situations are not new. Some of the most affecting of war photographs show children. Child soldiers too are not new. Conflicts the world over have used them. Sierra Leone, Uganda, and South Sudan in the most recent generation have given us horrifying examples. In this area, as in others, however, IS has made its mark. Its video messages are clear: defeat is inevitable, the punishment for losing horrific. On July 4, 2014, a row of twenty-five Syrian soldiers were shot in the head by a string of anonymous little boys against the magnificent backdrop of the ruins of Palmyra, just 134 miles from Damascus. In December 2015, a video showed large-eyed eight-year-olds shooting and beheading their victims. And in early January 2016, a boy who may have been no more than five warned Britain of atrocities to come, possibly before himself shooting a prisoner.[46]

The Evil That Men Do

But the videos of little boys killing grown men go further. In taking the children and using them in this way, IS is also working very deliberately to form a future generation. There can be no certainty that the attractions of the caliphate will continue to draw recruits from within or from the outside world to the ranks of the movement. Restrictions on travel to the territory controlled by IS will inevitably become heavier and more effective. The children whom we see in the videos are not the only ones: according to one report, IS has as many as 1,100 child recruits.[47] Some of these may be the children of other members or supporters of IS; others are likely orphans taken from families in the territory under IS control; still others are probably children kidnapped from their parents.

All of these children are very young. All of them have been brought up by the movement and have acquired an exclusive loyalty to it. They learn only what the movement wants them to know. They understand that the enemies of IS are their enemies. Those enemies are also, as they learn from their study of the Quran, the enemies of Islam. And all of this they learn as they approach adolescence and prepare for adulthood. By the time they reach manhood, if they ever do, this will be all they know. At the same time, many of those who have brought them up and educated them and taught them to kill will be dead. The children will then form the replacement generation, the successors to those who are gone.

A Reusable Past

In a narrow sense, a comparison can be made here with a major phenomenon of the Islamic past. Slave soldiers, mamluks, ruled Islamic states for many centuries during the Middle Ages, right down to the start of the nineteenth century. Mamluks of this sort were often purchased as slaves from outside the world of Islam when they were extremely young; brought to their new homes, in Cairo for example; kept apart from other young people; and raised together, acquiring a strong esprit de corps and mutual loyalty in the absence of any external ties, as well as deep bonds to their owners. The theory was that this approach should make the mamluks a solid body of support for their leaders, because they had no temptation to offer their loyalty elsewhere. Brought up as Muslims, they had no religious affiliations outside the particular form of Islam in which they were educated. Bought or acquired very young, they had no links to their former homes or families. Knowing only the military world for which they were prepared, they had no way of leaving it or of adopting any other activity.[48] If theory did not always work out perfectly in practice, it worked often enough, and there was little else on offer.

The children of IS are in very similar case. As with the child soldiers of the Lord's Resistance Army in Uganda or other such groups, when they are captured or otherwise freed from IS domination, it will be extremely hard to de-program them. In fact, for children brought up as IS fighters, the de-programing may be even more difficult, because of the ways in which Islam, a major world faith with an age-old culture, has been built in to their training as a central defining element, and the young age at which they receive their indoctrination. The identification that they have been taught to see between their training and the classical civilization and greatness of Islam (regardless of IS methods of dealing with the remnants of that past) will make it all the harder to teach them the distinction once IS is no more.

The Sword and the Pen

Medieval Islam knew a division in society between those who work with the sword, soldiers, and those who operate with the pen—clerks, administrators, and so on. IS is similar. The little boys who slaughter grown men tied up like chickens so that they cannot resist are a tiny minority of the children under IS rule. As with women, so too most children in the Islamic State are not fighters, nor are they in the ranks of those being prepared to die or to serve in some frontline role.

IS has a two-pronged strategy. On one hand it aims at the apocalypse and judgment day; on the other, it recognizes that the way there may be long. In the meantime, a state must be administered, and its population provided with services that are calibrated to the ideals of IS. That means, among other things, education. IS has internalized the famous saying attributed to the founder of the Jesuits, "Give me a child until he is seven and I will give you the man." Numerous documents emanating from IS territory deal with different aspects of education. All of them breathe not only an eerily familiar air of bureaucratic normality, but also a sense of purpose that extends far beyond mere rote learning of the Arabic ABC and the need to know mathematical formulas or how to use a computer. Acceptance of the value of Western scientific learning, in IS as in a number of other non-Western countries over the last half century, does not compel adoption of Western models in other spheres. Like administrative instruction everywhere, the IS documents describe timetables and examination schedules. As before the IS takeover, different subjects are to be taught at certain times; examinations will take place on particular dates—only now the IS logo appears at the top of the page. Other matters are different too. As we have seen before, sexes are to be separated, with girls not taught subjects reserved for boys; and certain subjects formerly taught have been eliminated from the syllabus of the IS child.

Other subjects are included or given greater attention than in the past. Quran studies are encouraged. Indeed, there are even prizes for memorization of the holy book.[49]

Schools are not the only path to formation of the whole person. Even in the Islamic State, children need extracurricular activities, and scouting offers another means to improvement along desirable IS lines. A circular of May 2015 announced the opening of "the second session of the Cub Scouts of the Caliphate Institute" in Raqqa province. Aimed at boys ten to fifteen years old with an ability to read and write, the session provided education in "Sharia sciences, arts of fighting, military sciences." We are instantly reminded of the scenes of those children killing soldiers and going off to hand-to-hand combat and Quran study sessions. A second such announcement was more specific: quoting the Quran (*sura* 8:60) and it seems unconsciously echoing Sir Robert Baden-Powell's famous scout motto, the announcement declares, "And prepare for them whatever force and strings of horses you can, to terrify thereby the enemy of God and your enemy." "Here there will be preparation of the cub scouts in faith through . . . the Sharia sciences, preparing them in the material world and teaching them the arts of fighting that they may be capable of taking over the banner of jihad." A couple of telephone numbers make registration simple and easy.[50] Run through the IS ministry of education and under the supervision of the IS *wali*, or governor, this cub scouts organization has a peculiar status. Syria is, and Iraq as an original founder member is potentially, a member of the World Scout Movement, but scouting in IS territory, despite that echo of Baden-Powell, has different aims from the international movement.

The Keys to Paradise

Women and children are central to IS, more than to other terror movements. They represent tomorrow in a way that today's recruitment efforts, those videos and social media networking and sermons by the caliph, cannot do. Without women there will be no more children, and without children there will not be a guaranteed stream of young jihadis into the future. If Armageddon, in the form of the final battle at Dabiq, somehow fails to arrive in the very near future—and there can be no certainty about when it will come—future generations will be necessary.

Building the IS ideal of a seventh-century world here on Earth means having women as well as men, and keeping these women, as the Khansa Brigade tells us, in the home doing what women do. IS is a man's world but men are not alone in it. Women complete that world.

Women and their children thus fill important roles in the IS worldview. They are not equal to men. All are codependent. The women and children need the men of IS to protect them, to fight for the movement, and to bring about the apocalypse. The men of IS need the women to offer home comforts, in every sense, but they also depend on them to provide for future generations and to guarantee that what they are doing has a future. Those who go off to die, not least on suicide missions for the movement, need to know not only that in dying they will find their reward in that house in paradise, but also that they are contributing to building the antechamber of paradise here on Earth.

CHAPTER SIX

Christians and Jews and . . .

THE PICTURE SAYS IT all: atop what looks like the entrance to a monastery or a church, an IS fighter with a rifle over his back carries a black banner of IS flaunting the IS slogan "La ilaha illa Allah, Muhammad rasul Allah" (There is no god but God, Muhammad is the Messenger of God), as he works intently to topple a large cross. Its tilt testifies to the success of his efforts and the imminence of collapse. The flag flutters higher, just a little higher, than the topmost point of the falling cross. The photo is weirdly reminiscent of those sculpted representations in medieval churches showing the church and the synagogue as two maidens. The church stands erect, eyes to the front, wearing a crown and carrying a staff with a cross on top; the church triumphant. The synagogue is motionless, often blindfolded, her head bent to one side, carrying a broken lance to remind us of the lance that pierced the Christ's side. The symbolism is clear—Christ has won, the old dispensation of the synagogue has been defeated. In the present case, the imagery is just as clear: the cross is coming down as the banner of Allah rises on high. Islam has won, Christianity has lost.[1]

Mosul

It is not clear what institution the cross and arch belong to. The news stories that carry the picture, from July 2014, refer generally to a church in Mosul. The media tell us routinely, and apparently basing themselves on a single source, of forty-five Christian institutions in that city (churches, monasteries, cemeteries, and so on) belonging to various ancient and, to Western ears, exotic Christian sects taken over, destroyed or converted to IS purposes—a church turned into an arms depot, or a cemetery whose graves have been defiled and its tombs overturned.[2] The fall of Mosul to IS forces in the summer of 2014 unleashed an assault on Christianity in northern Iraq wide in scope and damaging to the very existence of Christianity there. In the words of Justin Welby, the archbishop of Canterbury, "because of [IS] the Christians face elimination in the very region in which Christian faith began."[3]

Mosul has had a Christian community since early times. Christianity spread east as well as west from the Holy Land, reaching the town of Nineveh, close to the site of what became Mosul, by the second century. A shrine of Jonah adorned the city, recalling his visit there and his prediction that Nineveh would be overthrown; and Saint George, he of the dragon, and the patron saint of England, is said to be buried here too. The choice of location for his grave points to the city's importance in Christian tradition. Later on, in the ninth century—long after the Islamic conquest—the area was still home to Christian writers of importance such as Ishodad of Merv and Moses bar Kepha, both of whom wrote extensive biblical commentaries in Syriac.[4]

By modern times, Islam had sunk deep roots in the region. As long ago as 1184, when Ibn Jubayr, from Islamic Spain, visited the city, he found a mosque over the grave of Saint George and an Islamic poorhouse at the shrine of Jonah.[5] But although it was displaced from these sacred spots, Christianity hung on, with Mosul remaining one of the largest centers of Christianity in northern Iraq until the arrival of the Islamic State. Since then, not only have many Christian institutions and buildings been appropriated or destroyed, but the Christian population has also shrunk dramatically, as Christians have been killed, forced to convert to Islam, or driven to flee in the face of oppressive and discriminatory new taxation. Few if any Christians remain in the city today.[6] Regions occupied by IS may soon be empty of Christians for the first time in nineteen centuries.

What is IS aiming at in its treatment of Christians in Mosul and elsewhere? Is its behavior driven simply by bloodlust and greed, or can we discern something else? Butchery and booty appear to be the main motives for IS. Christians have been killed and much of their property, both personal and communal, has been seized or ruined. But there may be other ways to understand the behavior of IS leaders and fighters.

According to the report just mentioned from the end of July 2014, IS forces took Mosul on June 10 that year. Confiscations and destruction of Christian properties occurred during that initial period, immediately following the victory. In those first weeks, it appears that IS was following a traditional Islamic view that conquerors can do much as they please to the defeated. Confiscations and destruction, in that light, simply reflect a form of pillaging at the state level.

By mid-July, however, conditions in Mosul had become more stable, and IS sought to institute new arrangements for the conquered population. Before IS, Mosul had been a major center of Christian life in northern Iraq. Figures are impossible to ascertain, since both local Christians and Muslims had been much on the move since the period following the fall of Saddam Hussein, but what is sure is that Christian numbers in the region have been falling heavily in the last couple of decades, as the Sunni-Shi'i struggle has not spared local Christians. Many have become internally displaced, while others have left the country for new homes in the West.

IS has given the process of decline new impetus, both by its conquest and by the consequences of that conquest. The takeovers of Christian property, as well as the punishing treatment meted out to local Christians, have done much to ravage Christian life and terrorize believers. There are reports that as Christians emigrate from IS territory—the very word emigrate is a hideous misnomer for the manner of their exile from the place that has been their home for more than two thousand years, since centuries before the arrival of Islam—their money and any gold or jewelry that they have is taken from them, even ripped off their arms.[7]

That harshness is part of a larger policy. On July 17, 2014, the Justice Ministry of IS issued an ultimatum to the Christians of Mosul.[8] This document begins with a frightening quotation from the Quran (*sura* 7:164): "And when a community of them said, 'Why do you warn a people whom God is going to destroy or punish severely?' they said, 'To be absolved before your Lord and perhaps they will beware of Him.'" It is clear what message this is intended to convey. The Christians are being warned: God, as represented by IS, is going to destroy them or punish them severely and if they do not take advantage of the warning they will suffer, with IS feeling "absolved before [their] Lord" for their destruction or severe punishment.

The quranic context from which this short passage is taken shows that the original reference here is to Jews, both believing, obedient Jews and disobedient ones. In the present document, however, the passage is applied explicitly to the Christians of Mosul. For those who know the Bible it also recalls strongly the famous complaint uttered by Jonah.

God has sent Jonah to warn the people of Nineveh about God's intention to destroy their city. Unlike others to whom such warnings are sent, the king understands the gravity of his situation and immediately orders his subjects to repent, to fast, and to put on sackcloth. Their good behavior works: God "repented of the evil which he said he would do unto them; and he did it not" (Jonah 3:10). But then Jonah becomes angry—why has he wasted his time, first fleeing from God on the ship and being swallowed by a big fish, and then, under pressure, going to Nineveh and delivering his warning of total destruction: "Yet forty days and Nineveh shall be overthrown" (Jonah 3:4)? Now he sees that it was all for naught; nothing is going to happen to the people of Nineveh. He asks God, Why did you give them that warning? Why did you promise to destroy them? You knew that you would change your mind and forgive them. Didn't I tell you so? "I knew that you are a gracious God, and full of compassion, slow to anger and plenteous in mercy, and repent of the evil" (Jonah 4:1).[9]

The quranic passage recalls that moment from Jonah, but it serves a different purpose. As the ending shows, it begins with the record of a warning, but instead of showing a merciful God it ends with a merciless group of men.[10] In effect, if not in words, God offered Nineveh a choice: repent or be destroyed. The site of ancient Nineveh is next to modern Mosul. Now IS offers the Christians of Mosul a choice too. The document tells us that the leaders of the Christians in Mosul have been summoned to a meeting by the IS ministry of justice (Diwan al-Qada). They have failed to keep the appointment—did they fail to come out of fear? Would the consequences have been any different if they had turned up?—and as a result are now offered a plain choice: they may convert to Islam; they may opt to remain as Christians and pay the *jizya*, the special tax imposed on non-Muslims; or "if they refuse that, only the sword for them."[11]

The Christians of Mosul face a terrible dilemma: they can give up their age-old beliefs and accept the religion of their new rulers; they can agree to pay a special tax in order to retain their faith and live under the rule of Islam as practiced by IS; or they can be killed. The choice echoes to some degree that which many Christians faced at the dawn of their faith, when numerous believers died as martyrs. But IS is not wholly lacking in mercy: "the Commander of the Faithful—Caliph Ibrahim—may God make him mighty—has given them the blessing of allowing them to get themselves out of the borders of the state of the Caliphate at the latest by Saturday 21 Ramadan 1435 (July 19, 2015) at noon. After this, there is only the sword."[12]

Raqqa

Far away, across the old international frontier, erased by IS, in Raqqa, the IS capital in Syria, the arrival and installation of IS rule had similar effects for local Christians. Raqqa was taken by IS earlier than Mosul, between late 2013 and early 2014. Some newspaper reports at the time spoke of destruction and seizure of Christian communal buildings, churches, and monasteries, as in Mosul. And by late February of 2014 IS issued a "first document of protection" (*awwal aqd dhimma* in Arabic) for the Christians of al-Raqqa.[13]

This is a much more formal document than the one we have seen from Mosul. That was quite literally an ultimatum, in the form of an announcement by IS authorities, giving the Christians in that city just two days to make up their minds whether to stay, as subject Christians or as converts to Islam, or to go, finding a refuge elsewhere, somewhere outside the Islamic State. Here, in the very heart of the Islamic State, we have a long, formal document giving official recognition to a Christian presence in the IS capital and laying out the conditions of Christian existence there in considerable detail. It is cast in rather odd form, as a contract between two parties, IS itself and a group of Christian "representatives," including even a clause providing for Christian failure to live up to the terms of the contract. But the document is more complex than that suggests.

Prehistory

The document is entitled "First Contract of Protection in Syria between the Islamic State and the Christians of the Province (Arabic *wilaya*) of al-Raqqa." But it is actually two documents in one. The first of these offers an account of how the second one came to be. Introduced by the formula In the Name of God the Merciful the Compassionate, it immediately sets the tone for what is to come: if this is an agreement between two parties, those parties are emphatically not equals. In the Name of God the Compassionate the Merciful is an explicitly and typically Islamic formula; this is an Islamic document. What follows makes this even clearer. It prepares us for the contract to come by telling us that "a number of Christians of the province of al-Raqqa have applied to the emirate of the Islamic State following the State's announcement of the rule of Islamic sharia law in this province where God has given His monotheistic servants power in perfect form." The response by IS? The same options as those given to Christians in Mosul: they may convert to Islam, "abandoning the polytheism (Arabic *shirk*) they practiced formerly"; they may remain Christians and pay the *jizya*, submitting to sharia law; or they can refuse either option, in which case they "are people of war and between them and the Islamic State there is nothing but the sword."

The Christian delegates asked for time, we are told, to discuss their options and make their decision. They returned on 20 Rabi

II 1435 (February 20, 2014). What they "chose was to pay the *jizya* . . . after they were offered the detailed rules organized in the contract of dhimma." A final "Note" tells us that "the names of the signatories to the contract have been erased at the request of those making the compact and with the agreement of the representative of the Islamic State." This initial document closes with the exclamation "God is the greatest" and a quotation from the Quran: "And to God belongs glory, and to His Messenger and to the believers, but the hypocrites do not know" (*sura* 63:8).

Everything about this text bespeaks the power of Islam. The introductory formula is emphatically Islamic, leaving no space for non-Islamic, Christian beliefs. The disparity in power between the participants in the meetings could not be clearer. Their meeting was very carefully arranged: "close to twenty" representatives of the Christians appeared, but only one representative of the Islamic State: many supplicants in the presence of a single, faceless bureaucrat. The document itself offers non-Muslim subjects of the Islamic State a status as subjects of Islam or worse. The reference to the religion of the Christians as *shirk*—polytheism in Arabic—which reflects a traditional Islamic understanding of the Trinity as representing three divinities in Christian eyes—demeans and insults the Christians involved in this accord. "At the request of those making the compact, and with the agreement of the representative of the Islamic State," the Christians' very names—their identities—are erased, possibly as a means of stressing their desire for self-protection via anonymity at a moment of the deepest humiliation, of betrayal of their Savior.[14] And the document closes with not only the standard assertion of the power of God (God is the Greatest, Allah al-Akbar), but a quranic affirmation of that power in the face of the "hypocrites" who do not know God's power.

If all of this demonstrates the power of God and of his Muslim followers, it also raises other questions. Why does IS need or wish to make a contract with the Christians whom it has conquered? Why does a contract between IS and a group of Christians, one freely entered into (as freely as was possible for the Christians), need an introductory text? What need is fulfilled by a preface of this sort? Does it perhaps have a further tale to tell?

A Pact of *Dhimma*

Part of the answer comes in the second text in the document. Like the first one, it begins with a proud declaration of Islam: the shahada, There is no god but God, Muhammad is the Messenger of God, followed by the standard introductory formula, In the Name of God the Compassionate the Merciful. A string of paragraphs follow, again stressing the Islamic character of the document: these include quotations from the Quran, prayerful affirmations of faith in God and His power and in Muhammad as His messenger, and an emphatic declaration denying that Jesus is anything but a mortal: "And we bear witness that Jesus the son of Mary is a servant of God and His Messenger and His word that He cast into Mary, and a spirit from Him," and quoting from the Quran in support of this: "the Masih [a name for Jesus in Arabic, derived from the Hebrew form of the word Messiah] will not disdain to be servant to God" (*sura* 4:172).

Only after all this do we get to the actual text of the legal document that IS grants to the Christians of al-Raqqa. It is worth looking at in detail.

> This is what the servant of God Abu Bakr al-Baghdadi the Commander of the Faithful gave the Christians of al-Raqqa by way of security: he gave them a safe-conduct for themselves and their property and their churches and the rest of their offspring [*sic*] in the province of al-Raqqa; their churches will not be destroyed, nor will any of them be taken away, nor any of their landed property, nor any of their wealth. Nor will they be treated badly on account of their faith, nor will any of them be harmed.

> And he laid the following conditions upon them:

> 1. They shall not renew in their city or in its surroundings any monastery or church or hermitage, nor shall they restore any of them that has become dilapidated.
> 2. They shall not display a cross or any of their books in any of the streets or markets of the Muslims, nor shall they use loudspeakers when they perform their prayers and other religious rites.

3. They shall not let the Muslims hear the recital of their books and the sounds of their bells and they shall strike them (only) inside their churches.

4. They shall not engage in any hostile acts towards the Islamic State, such as sheltering spies and those sought for judicial reasons by the Islamic State, or any Christian or others whose hostility has been confirmed, or helping them to hide or to get away or do anything else; and if they know of the existence of a conspiracy against the Muslims then they are bound to inform (us) about that.

5. They shall undertake not to display any of their religious rites outside the churches.

6. They shall not prevent any Christian from embracing Islam if he wishes to do so.

7. They shall respect Islam and the Muslims and they shall not speak evil of anything to do with their religion.

8. The Christians undertake to pay the *jizya* for every adult male among them. Its rate is 4 dinars of gold (by "dinar" here is meant the gold dinar that was used in business because that is of fixed standard, and it weighs a mithqal of pure gold or what equals 4.25 grams of gold) for the rich, and half of that for those of medium standing, and half of that for the poor among them, on condition that they hide nothing of their wealth from us, and they have to pay it twice a year.

9. They are not permitted to own arms.

10. They shall not trade in pigs or alcoholic drinks [Arabic *Khumur*] with the Muslims or in their markets and they shall not drink them in public—i.e., in public places.

11. They shall have cemeteries of their own, as is usual.

12. They shall obey the restrictions laid upon them by the Islamic State, such as modesty in dress, concerning buying and selling, etc.

And if they fulfil the conditions they have been given then they shall have the protection of Allah and the *dhimma* of Muhammad the Messenger of God, may God bless him and give him peace, for themselves and their properties and their wealth, and none of their rights nor their faith shall be changed, nor shall any of his [*sic*] bishops be changed, nor any of his [*sic*] monks, nor shall they pay a tithe on their wealth unless they bring money for trade from outside the frontiers of the Islamic State. And if any of them makes a claim against a Muslim or anyone else then the judgment between them is that of Islam, no one behaving unjustly or being treated unjustly, nor will any of them be seized for the crime of another.

And they have the protection of God and the *dhimma* of Muhammad the Prophet, the Messenger of God, may God bless him and give him peace, until God comes with His command as long as they stick to the conditions given in this document.

And if they change anything of what is in this document then they have no *dhimma*, and the Islamic State in Iraq and Syria can treat them as it treats people of war and hostility.[15]

At the end is a signature, partly erased, for the Amir al-Muminin, the Commander of the Faithful, the caliph Abu Bakr al-Baghdadi, the name of the Islamic State in Iraq and Syria, together with a stamp showing a logo of the IS and the Islamic date, 22 Rabi II 1435 (February 22, 2014). (This is just two days after the date in the introductory document, recalling the two-day period given to the Christians of Mosul to think things over.)[16] And below all that a number of signatures, none of them legible and many of them erased. We recall the "request" made by many of the Christians that their names be erased from the document.

The pact with the Christians of al-Raqqa is a strange and extraordinary document. Though it is signed by the Amir al-Muminin Abu Bakr al-Baghdadi in the name of the Islamic State, it is not a law. Nor does it affect an entire population or the total area of the caliphate. It applies only to Christians, and only in the province of al-Raqqa. It is cast in the form of an agreement, though as an agreement it is extraordinarily one-sided. Though it was signed by as many as seventeen Christian leaders, their signatures have been carefully erased "at the request of those making the compact and with the agreement of the representative of the Islamic State." It begins with the Islamic statement of faith, the shahada, and follows that with a series of quranic quotations and statements of Islamic religious belief, among which at least two make it clear, in accordance with Islamic teaching, that Jesus is a "servant of God."

The contents of the document regulate relations between government (in the form of IS) and a part of the population under its control. It defines membership of that community by religion—which in this case need have nothing to do with belief or with self-description or how a person sees himself or herself but is simply a function of birth. It regulates behavior of individuals based on their religion. It does all this by means of a contract between the state and the "leaders" of that community, though without giving any indication of who these are or of how they are selected, as leaders or as representatives, or what qualifies them for such a role. And more importantly, it also sets out consequences for the breaking or the non-observance of the "contract." Those consequences apply not to the individual who might not observe the conditions thus imposed but to the entire community. Each individual Christian is thus responsible for the behavior of all Christians. All Christians are thus responsible for the behavior of each Christian.

If this all looks somewhat medieval, that is because it is. In tone, language, content, structure, and form this document, or pair of documents, resembles closely another document, or pair of documents, over a thousand years old, allegedly issued to other Christians in Syria by conquering Muslims. That document, the so-called Pact of Umar, is certainly not as old as it pretends to be, but it formulated in writing a set of arrangements that had evolved over the preceding decades, or possibly as long as two centuries, for the Christians—and later, by extension, the Jews—of the early Islamic empire. In some areas, such as Yemen, the conditions laid down and the larger situation that they described survived into the twentieth century. Now they have been revived, in Syria, in the twenty-first.

Every single clause in our modern document has its parallel in the old Pact of Umar. Even in terms of language we can trace the influence of that document—for example, the loose, back-and-forth use of singular and plural possessives in the final paragraphs, where it describes the conditions "they" have been given, but then goes on to speak of any of "his" bishops or "his" monks, before saying that "they" shall not pay a tithe. The only signal difference that marks this text as not completely medieval occurs in the second condition.[17] The corresponding section of the medieval text refers to Christians praying loudly, while this one, in a single, isolated note of recognition of modern technology, cautions them not to use loudspeakers.[18]

The Pact of Umar

One of the proud boasts of medieval Islam is that, unlike medieval Christianity, by and large it tolerated those of other faiths— Christians (and Jews too). In general, medieval Christian Europe did not have Muslims (at least outside Islamic Spain), but during the Middle Ages Christians are found, aplenty, all over the Islamic, especially the Arab, world. They were there as the result of conquests that occurred mainly in the seventh and eighth centuries. When the Muslims arrived, they found that almost everyone in the former Byzantine territories was Christian. So were many people in the former Persian lands. Their presence confronted the conquerors with a problem: how were they to organize their conquests and their new subjects?

Until very recently it was thought that the so-called Pact of Umar was the answer to this question. Neither a pact, in a strict sense, as we have seen, nor, almost certainly, a document associated with either of the two early caliphs called Umar (Umar I, ibn al-Khattab, who reigned 634–644, and Umar II, who reigned 717–719), what we know as the Pact of Umar presents itself as a product of a request from the inhabitants of an unnamed locality in Syria to the conquering caliph. Like our present compact, it comes together with an introductory text:

> Abd al-Rahman ibn Ghanm related: When Umar ibn al-Khattab, may God be pleased with him, made peace with the Christian inhabitants of Syria, we wrote for him as follows: In the name of God the Compassionate the Merciful. This is a letter to the servant of God, Umar, the Commander of the Faithful, from the Christians of such-and-such a city.

When you came against us, we asked you for a guarantee of
protection for ourselves, our offspring.

The letter, if it is that, continues with the requests, separated into
(unnumbered) clauses, that we are acquainted with already in our
present-day text in the form of conditions. And they are followed
by the medieval equivalent of the ruler's signature and statement
that this is "approved." The text survives in a number of versions,
and though our modern text does not copy any of them word for
word, the contents are the same as what we have seen.[19]

How old is the Pact of Umar? Does it date back to either of
the caliphs of that name? For a long time it was thought this was
indeed the case, though some elements in different versions of it,
as well as the very existence of those different versions themselves,
hinted at a later date and another type of background. Nowadays it
is thought that the Pact gathers up and puts together a number of
rules and regulations, reflecting more general practices and attitudes, that had grown up during a longish period after the arrival
of Islam in the seventh century. Far from being a generous ruler's
response to a plea from those whom he has conquered, it is a literary invention made in all probability long after the alleged event
with quite other interests and concerns in mind.

In that sense, the old Pact of Umar is a valuable document. If it
is not as old as it pretends to be, if it is not a genuine record of actual events at the moment of the Islamic conquest, if it does not
tell us how relations between Muslims and their new subjects, between Christians and their new rulers, were formalized, it does
nevertheless offer us a window into how the status and rights, as
well as the obligations and duties, of Christians in the new dispensation developed over time.

Those rights and obligations are not those of religious minorities in the modern Western world. It would be naïve to expect
them to be. But they are also, perhaps more surprisingly, not the
invention of Islam or the Muslims. The long tradition of which
they are part, the history of so-called *dhimmis*, those who enjoy
the protection (*dhimma*) of Islam, has led many to assume that
Islamic acceptance of Christians (and Jews), with Muslims broadly
tolerating their cult in return for submission to Islamic rule and

law and payment of a special tax, represents an Islamic innovation. The comparison with ancient and medieval Christian intolerance of those of other faiths, and even of other sects within Christianity, lies always at the back of Westerners' minds for comparison. In fact, however—and it has taken until now for this to be recognized—Muslim conquerors, newly arrived in the territories of two great empires, both filled with members of religious minorities, did what most conquerors do. Wanting and needing to ensure that their conquests remained peaceful, that their new subjects paid their taxes, and that life more generally carried on without interruption or disturbance to themselves, they simply adapted and adopted many of the legal arrangements of their predecessors in the region. A very recent close study, the first of its kind, of "non-Muslims in the early Islamic empire" has as its subtitle "From Surrender to Coexistence," reflecting what actually happened. In the confused and heady circumstances of the conquests, whose speed and comprehensiveness must have taken the conquerors as much as the conquered totally by surprise, simply taking over existing arrangements offered the easiest and most efficient answer to pressing immediate problems. The Pact of Umar, which is to be dated very much later, offers a formalization and a codification, in Islamic terms, of what happened.[20]

Copying the Past

The similarities between the pact of al-Raqqa and the Pact of Umar are not mere coincidence. The parallels of shape and structure between the two documents are so great that we can be sure that the modern text must be modeled after the older. Those who composed the Raqqa document must have had that earlier document in mind. Not only are the conditions and restrictions imposed on Christians the same in both documents, but also both have that curious introductory passage explaining how the text came into existence and laying the responsibility for that on the Christians themselves. If there were nothing else to alert us to a link, that (especially in the context of everything that we know of IS practice toward others) would be sufficient indication of a source or a model.

Identifying a source and a model, however, is one thing. That does not provide an explanation. Why has IS taken up this ancient, and rather strange, document as a template for its treatment of Christians in Syria? For although it is convenient that the old document has an apparent link with Syria ("such-and-such a city in Syria"), the similarities between the two documents extend far beyond this commonality.

Over the years several ways of explaining the purpose of the Pact of Umar have been suggested. It has been seen as aimed at humiliating the Christians, even while granting them a limited degree of toleration. It has been portrayed as intended merely to create and maintain a sort of fence separating the Christians from the Muslims, in order perhaps to protect the new Muslim rulers from the dangers of contamination from an alien faith, but with no other aims such as degradation or humiliation, far less conversion. And it has been understood as having a larger ambition, the conversion of Christians to the faith of their rulers: the idea is that the restrictions on Christians' practice of their religious rites as well as the heavy poll tax would have made conversion appear an easy and attractive way out.

Conversion to Islam, in particular, whether or not it was the aim, looks good as an explanation because over the last fourteen centuries Christian numbers all over what has become the Arab world have been in decline. We can even probably suggest that it became the Arab world at least in part through the process of mass conversion to Islam, an Arabian religion. Even if the correlation doesn't prove causation, conversion to Islam does look like the most obvious way to explain that decline. Conversion to Islam is a one-way street: regret, back-sliding, apostasy, or conversion from Islam to another faith is not allowed. Though we find examples of apostasy over the huge expanse of Islamic history, it is rare, and death often follows, so that the attractions of other faiths tend to fade. With change of faith going only in one direction, the consequence, Christian decline and Islamic expansion, is easy to understand. In a practical sense, therefore, while it is easy to sympathize with the fear expressed at Christmas 2015 by Archbishop Welby, that we may be witnessing the final emptying out of Christianity in the lands of its earliest history and growth, it may also be excessive to lay too much of the blame for this shift on IS. The number of

Christians in this region has been declining for many centuries, in fits and starts, ever since the arrival of Islam in the seventh century.

Christians have converted for all sorts of reasons, sometimes under the pressure of heavy taxation; occasionally under heavier and more direct, individual pressure; often too for genuinely felt reasons of faith. Reasons for conversion are rarely as easy to identify and define as we might imagine, and when we are considering the transformation over many centuries of the religious identity of entire population groups, or, in the case of the Middle East, almost entire population groups, real knowledge is unavailable and generalizations are unreliable.

The pressure exerted here by IS, both in Mosul and in Raqqa, is balanced to a degree by the availability of exile for those who find conversion unacceptable. Remaining under Islamic rule, with a minority status, can carry its own attractions—exile is usually not an attractive option—but in the end that approach can encourage a kind of creeping conversion.[21]

This is not to say that IS rule is gentle or welcome. Rather, its effect on the survival of Christian communities in Iraq and Syria may be aimed less directly at destroying Christian life than at maintaining a traditional pattern of Islamic-Christian relations in the region. That pattern, based on the formulas encoded in the Pact of Umar and similar documents, and regardless of the intentions of those who set them in motion, led more or less inevitably to Christian decline over the long term. For that reason IS rule in the region now is probably just hastening the completion of a process that is already approaching its end.

This interpretation is confirmed by what we know of IS rule beyond these texts. One of the regulations imposed by IS in Raqqa and Mosul required the payment of *jizya*, the poll tax on members of permitted religious minorities. Among the documents made available by Ayman al-Tamimi is receipt no. 1391, issued by the Islamic court in Raqqa on December 8, 2014, acknowledging acceptance of 27,000 Syrian pounds (at that time about $155) as "payment of jizya."[22] The implication seems to be that the payment was made in court or in an office. And it seems also that, despite what the pact says, the payment was made in local currency, not in gold.

The pact calls for a payment of four dinars, of 4.25 grams of gold each—payable in two installments per annum.[23] So the payment here should have been two dinars, equivalent to 8.5 grams of gold. In December 2014, when the payment was made, the price of gold was just under $1,200 per ounce. With 8.5 grams amounting to just under a third of an ounce (one ounce equals 28.35 grams), the sum due should have been around $350 to $375. But the payment was only $155, less than half that sum. The explanation is in the pact: it provides that the full payment of four dinars is for the rich, but the tax is only "half of that for those of medium standing." The taxpayer was probably not very rich.

We know nothing further about how the payment was effected. In medieval times, in accordance with the quranic injunction that *dhimmis* should make the payment "out of hand," *an yadin* in Arabic, personal delivery was generally required. A rich man or a person of high status could not avoid handing the tax over in person by sending a servant to make the payment for him. And sometimes humiliation came to be part of the ceremony too, as an understandable extension of the requirement for payment in person.[24]

We do not, yet, hear about Christians converting to Islam as a way out of their current difficulties in the Islamic State. Forced conversion seems to have occurred, though it is unclear what this has meant for the individuals involved.[25] And we saw that the Khansa Brigade boasts that Christian women who come to the court to convert enjoy full protection.[26] But emigration, flight, is well documented. So too are other means of discouraging Christianity: in February 2015, IS forces carried off "scores" of Assyrian Christians from villages in northern Syria. The actual number of men, women, and children taken remained unknown, with estimates ranging to well above one hundred. The seizure followed IS demands that crosses be removed from churches. Possibly this should be seen as connected with the clause in the pact requiring Christians not to make their faith public in sight of Muslims. Some nineteen of the Christians were released in early March. According to one local Christian, the release followed payment of a ransom, which was possibly seen as a *jizya* payment.[27] He said that in a similar, earlier incident, the preceding November, as much as $1,700 was paid for each released Assyrian Christian, or enough, given our previous calculations, for the *jizya* for four individuals.[28]

Special taxes; kidnapping, whether for ransom or taxation; forced emigration; and encouragement to conversion are not all that the Christian communities under IS rule endure. Far away from their core territory of Syria-Iraq, in regions of Libya controlled by IS, executions, even random killings, of Christians occur too. In April 2015, IS released a video showing the killing of "dozens" of Ethiopian Christians by beheading or shooting. Earlier, some Egyptian Christians working in Libya were similarly seized and beheaded. One of the executioners, masked and speaking with an American accent, told the camera, "You will not have safety, even in your dreams, until you accept Islam. To the nation of the cross: we are back again."[29]

Christian Martyrdom

The address to "the nation of the cross" shows that this is not about Christians living under IS rule with the protection of a pact of some sort. What is at issue here specifically is IS hostility to the nations of the West, loosely subsumed under the heading of Christians, "the nation of the cross," and the Christians are in each case visitors, immigrants, and guest workers, not locals. Convert or die, the traditional Western image of what is offered by Islam, is accompanied by the possibility of living under Islamic rule and paying the *jizya*, the poll tax. The video stresses the attractions of life under such conditions, even as it also illustrates what happens to those who refuse to convert or pay the tax.

In a crudely literal analysis, the Christians killed in the video are killed less for their faith itself (and for sticking to it) than simply in order to make a point about that faith: we cannot know anything about the thoughts of the Christians who are thus murdered, or for that matter about the truth of the claims made in the video, but IS wants us to understand that death is what awaits, following the inevitable conquest that is to come, if we do not accept Islam.

Christians and others in the West are, very properly, horrified by the murders. The Western media describe and condemn them, though without always fully apprehending the distinctions that IS makes.[30] For Christian churches and their believers the killings seem especially cruel—and at the same time offer an opportunity. For them, the dead are more than mere victims of savagery. Killed for their faith, they are seen, and presented, as martyrs. Thus one report in October of 2015 recounted the execution of eleven "indigenous Christian workers" near Aleppo. They had been given "the option to leave the area and live." "The 12-year-old son of a ministry team leader also could have saved his life by denying Christ." The person who had trained the workers had begged them to leave, but they "chose to stay in order to provide aid in the name of Christ to survivors." We hear of more entreaties that they should leave while they still can, and of their refusals to abandon their charge. Then, in early August of 2015, IS militants captured them "in a village whose name is withheld for security reasons. On Aug. 28, the militants asked if they had renounced Islam for Christianity. When the Christians said that they had, the rebels asked if they wanted to return to Islam. The Christians said they would never renounce Christ." What follows is predictably gruesome. The fingertips of the little boy are cut off and he is severely beaten; the father is told that the torture will stop if he returns to his old faith. The father refuses; he and two other Christians are beaten in their turn. And finally all are crucified, their bodies left on the crosses for two days, next to signs identifying them as "infidels."

The story does not end here. Eight others, two of them women, were asked the same questions. The women said that they were "only sharing the peace and love of Christ and asked what they had done wrong to deserve the abuse." They were then raped in public, praying as they suffered. After that all eight were beheaded. "Villagers said some were praying in the name of Jesus, others said some were praying the Lord's prayer, and others said some of them lifted up their heads to commend their spirits to Jesus." The ministry director said. "One of the women looked up and seemed to be almost smiling as she said, 'Jesus!'"[31]

Another account, from a year earlier, tells of the martyrdom of a five-year-old boy in the Christian town of Qaraqosh, not far from Mosul. According to the report, from the Anglican Communion News Service, IS fighters "cut the boy in half during an attack."

Canon Andrew White of Saint George's Anglican church in Baghdad was "almost in tears" as he told the story, not least because "the little boy, they named him after me—he was called Andrew."[32]

Such stories could easily be multiplied. A search on Google turns up many more. Occasionally we find warnings that some of the atrocities may have been staged for propaganda purposes or that certain images may have been taken from other contexts. The warnings ring true: although we find atrocities documented also in the mainstream press and media, stories of Christian martyrdoms like these seem to be confined to Christian outlets. These outlets are also often the location of appeals for money, to support Christian missionary endeavors and provide aid to local Christians.

How, then, should these stories be regarded? As true records of actual events, or as pious inventions designed to elicit sympathy and support for the victims? Certainly the Christians under IS rule appear to be suffering, but the martyrdom stories wear a well-known appearance. Young women who pray as they are raped in public and die smiling with Jesus on their lips recall ancient tales of early Christian martyrs; they also strain credulity. Even against the background of other IS horrors, the story of the five-year-old boy beggars the imagination. Yet it also reminds us of the fate of a great biblical prophet, Isaiah. The Bible tells us of a twelve-year-old child, Manasseh, who inherited the throne of Judah. Falling under the influence of evil advisers, he abandoned the worship of the true God and offered sacrifices to false idols. Although Isaiah is not mentioned in the Bible in connection with this ruler, he is said in later sources to have fallen victim to him. A text known as the *Martyrdom of Isaiah*, composed probably in the first century, tells us that the prophet fled from the king, and was found hiding in a tree. In order to kill him, they sawed the tree, with Isaiah still inside it, in half. The New Testament Epistle to the Hebrews (11:37) offers a model for this particular martyrdom: it refers to faithful people who were "stoned, they were sawn in two, they were killed with the sword."

In this context, the Ethiopian Christians killed in Libya are a puzzle, because Ethiopia has long enjoyed a special relationship with Islam. At the start of his ministry, facing persecution in his home town of Mecca, the Prophet Muhammad sent a number of his early followers across the sea to seek temporary refuge in Ethiopia. Tradition tells us that they found a generous and tolerant welcome at the court of the then Negus, or king, of Ethiopia. That tradition has helped over many centuries since then to infuse Islamic writings with an unusually friendly attitude toward Ethiopia and its Christians. The IS killings of Ethiopian Christians, then, like the martyrdoms of other Christians in Iraq, point to a deliberate decision to spurn historical tradition in these cases in favor of a broader attitude toward Christians that does not permit exceptions that belong to a distant past.[33] The re-creation of a pact of protection for Christians as a community in IS-controlled territories all over Syria and Iraq, too, is less about tolerance and far more about a desire by IS to re-create the conditions of the seventh century, when Islam was all-conquering, all powerful, and when Christians begged for merciful treatment.

And Jews?

The IS video in which child recruits to IS are shown killing six members of government-aligned Syrian security forces is entitled, bizarrely, "To the Sons of Jews."[34] It begins with a shot of Israeli prime minister Benjamin Netanyahu, but seems to have no other reference to Jews or Israel. Any link with Jews seems forced at best. What is IS trying to tell its audience here? Why the awkwardly placed concern with Jews?

In principle, we should expect IS attitudes and behavior toward Jews to be very similar to those toward Christians. Both are so-called People of the Book, because they each possess scriptures that are recognized by Islam as coming from God, though in Islamic terms these texts are corrupted and imperfect in the forms they have today. Both Christians and Jews, in theory at least, are covered by the conditions of the *dhimma* that we have just examined. Both survived, in different ways and with very different fortunes, during the Middle Ages and the modern period under the rule of Islam.[35] Unlike Christianity, Islam in its high period remained largely free of the poison of anti-Semitism, though we should not misinterpret this to mean that Jews were not despised in the Islamic world.[36] Neither Jews nor Christians enjoyed equality with Muslims before the law or in other areas, but unlike in medieval Christian Europe, where Muslims and heretical Christians were not tolerated, medieval Islam was open, with limitations, to members of these two groups.

IS and the Jews

Like al-Qaida, IS has faced the question of Jews and Jewry. Like al-Qaida again, IS seems to have evolved a reaction dictated more by pragmatic considerations than theory. In IS eyes, Jews are bad, as the Quran and Islamic tradition more generally indicate; this means that Zionism is bad too, not least because it represents Jews holding power over Muslims, something that is unacceptable. This is worse even than Christians doing so, in that Christians at least had states of their own throughout the history of Islam, whereas Jews, until the founding of Israel, were always a despised minority in the region.

At the same time, two facts make the question of IS and Jews different. First, there are no Jews in the Islamic State. Jews lived in what became the Islamic world in the seventh century, but only a very few live there now—a few dozen in Yemen, a handful who appear from time to time in Afghanistan.[37] Otherwise, remaining Jews are clustered in Morocco, Turkey, and Iran (where, in an echo of the communitarian approach to minorities codified in the Pact of Umar, they have a reserved seat in the Majlis, or Parliament).[38] Iraq, where Jews had lived since at least the sixth century BCE, now has none, and only a handful are said to remain in Damascus from where they trickle slowly out. Now, the lands where IS rules are free of Jews.

The experience of individual Jews who happen to fall into IS hands is different. These are principally aid workers or journalists, such as Steven Sotloff, who was kidnapped in Aleppo in 2013 and transferred later to IS, who killed him in September 2014. They have suffered dreadfully, but apparently not on account of being Jews per se, but rather because they are seen as Westerners and as agents of the West, therefore as enemies of IS. Their Jewishness as such does not seem to be an issue for IS.

Secondly, in the tradition of widespread Islamic hostility to Israel and to Zionism, we might have expected IS to be fiercely opposed to Israel and to be organizing attacks on the Jewish state—but this has not happened. IS has not ignored Israel or Zionism. But it has done little to give serious expression to hostility to Israel, beyond mouthing a handful of fairly standard anti-Zionist slogans. Like many others, IS leaders and fighters take little trouble to distinguish clearly between Jews and Zionists, either in their language or in their thinking, but what they say, like what they do, appears to be largely formulaic in character. Thus they speak of marching toward the liberation of Palestine and of freeing Jerusalem from Jewish hands. In a Christmas message for December 2015, the IS caliph is reported to have said, "Jews, soon you shall hear from us in Palestine which will become your grave. The Jews thought we forgot Palestine and that they had distracted us from it. Not at all, Jews. We did not forget Palestine for a moment. With the help of Allah, we will not forget it . . . We are getting closer every day."[39] But they have done little—even, so far, from the Syrian theater just next door, where they are literally on Israel's doorstep in the Golan Heights—to realize such dreams. More than this, they appear not to have been able to arouse "lone wolf" attacks inside Israel or the Palestinian territories, and it is striking that recruits for IS from the territories or from within Israel itself are few in number.[40] From Israel it is estimated that some forty have gone to join IS, and lower numbers still have gone from the Palestinian territories. By comparison with the numbers joining the fight from other countries, both Western and Islamic, these are very low. (The Muslim populations of Israel and the Palestinian territories are of course relatively low too, but the absolute numbers seem to be the issue here.) It is tempting to explain this disparity in terms of the struggle at home, against Israel, but there are similar struggles elsewhere today and these do not appear to be holding recruits back. Al-Qaida too, of which IS is originally a splinter, seems to have preferred to concentrate its efforts, like its ideological claims, elsewhere.

Another explanation lies in IS itself. IS sees its principal opponents as other Muslims, not Jews or Israelis. This does not prevent IS from conflating the two, however. Thus it has launched attacks, more verbal than military, on the Hamas leaders of Gaza for being insufficiently assiduous in applying Islamic law and hinting that they are allied to the Israelis. "We will uproot the state of the Jews and you and Fatah and all of the secularists are nothing and you will be overrun by our creeping multitudes," they said in one video at a time of truce between Hamas and Israel.[41] There have also been a variety of reports of IS advances in the Golan, on the front line with Israel, as the forces of both Bashar al-Asad and the opposition to his regime falter. Such developments increase the danger or the likelihood of direct conflict between IS and Israel.

The Quran speaks about Christians and Jews in a variety of voices, sometimes friendly sometimes hostile, but later attitudes, in part dependent on the Quran, tended to the disdainful. What stands out in the approach adopted by IS is that it differs from the policies that IS has adopted in other areas. In those other areas, IS has attempted very explicitly to return to and re-create the society of the seventh century, of the time of the Prophet. That represents the best of times, and the behavior of the Prophet is assumed to reflect also the will of God. In the case of the Christians, and with them the Jews, however, IS seems to have changed tack: as we have seen, the foundation that it has taken for its treatment of these minorities under its rule is the Pact of Umar. Whatever that document is, it is not of the seventh century, nor has it anything to do with any caliph called Umar. More importantly it has nothing to do with the Prophet. It very clearly postdates his life and career, belonging to the period of the conquests at the earliest.

In that sense, IS behavior here is uncharacteristically errant: it avoids the model of the Prophet's life and deliberately follows a later pattern. Why is this? The answer probably lies in the need that gave rise originally to the Pact of Umar, or to the situation that it reflects: the life and career of the Prophet did not produce a usable model in this area, because in Arabia he converted most of the Christians and either converted or killed all the Jews. It was only when the Muslims moved out and made their first massive conquests outside the Arabian Peninsula that they encountered the need for a legal model that would take care of the huge numbers of Christians whom they now found themselves ruling. That model is what we find reflected in the Pact of Umar.

Yet if that explains the background to the pact of Raqqa, it still leaves us with an oddity in IS behavior. Their ideology pulls them backward to the early seventh century and to the patterns of the Prophet's life. Where Christians are concerned they find themselves unable to use that source, and have to adopt a later model, one well known to history and tradition, but without real roots in the earliest days of the faith. Their recourse to this approach suggests something of how they operate in general. It does not indicate, as some have suggested, that they are merely cynical opportunists. Instead it seems that in seeking to apply what they understand to be an Islamic model based on the life and times of the Prophet, they have been compelled by circumstances to be somewhat elastic in their definition of the period of the Prophet.

Treatment of Other Religious Groups

The experience of other groups confirms that a mix of attitudes influences IS approaches to those it sees as different. The Middle East is a hodge-podge of different ethnic and religious groups. Some are fairly large, in the millions, like the Kurds, who are spread over four different countries; others are tiny, like the Samaritans. Originally a Jewish sect, having split off from the mainstream possibly as early as the fifth or sixth century BCE, and known today principally because of the role of one of them in a parable of Jesus (Luke 10:25–37), the Samaritans declined dramatically in numbers over the centuries and today number no more than a few hundred, in suburbs of Nablus in the West Bank and Tel Aviv in Israel.

Many of these groups are offshoots of the great faiths of Christianity and Islam. Others are remnants of ancient Jewish, Christian, or medieval Islamic sects, on the Samaritan pattern. Others again represent religious formations derived from a mingling of people and ideas between and among these and other faiths that have somehow, against the odds, survived into the twenty-first century. Some are ethnic groups with a standard religious definition but occasionally heterodox beliefs or practices.

In many parts of the world such variety is normal and irrelevant. In central and eastern Europe, for example, as under Ottoman rule, such groups were once scattered over the territories of large empires. Until the end of World War I, precise definition—of ethnic identity, of religious affiliation, occasionally even language—

was difficult, and did not mean much because it did not matter. After 1918, everything changed. Numerous nation-states came into being, claiming the rights of nations and corralling smaller groups, or sections of them, inside their frontiers. This called for definitions both of nations and of minorities, whose rights needed to be protected in the new states. Soon communism arrived, then fascism, then communism again. All imposed definition, for better—and often for worse—on the inhabitants of vast regions. Until then, many people would not even have known what labels to apply to themselves.[42]

In Iraq and Syria, too, many minorities of different types have somehow survived the buffetings of history into the twenty-first century, to find themselves now in the arms of IS. Kurds have suffered—though IS seems occasionally to make efforts to safeguard them as fellow Sunnis. Shi'i Muslims suffer too, as do other smaller groups like the Yezidis and Shabaks and Kaka'is, whose very names were unknown to outsiders until the present conflict. All of these fall variously under IS definitions of heresy and all have been made to realize the implications of such categorization.

Kurds

Kurds present a different problem from Christians or smaller minorities. They are Sunnis; they are very numerous; a lot of IS territory, in northern Iraq in particular, is inhabited or claimed by Kurds; in some areas that land also lies along the Turkish border through which IS needs or needed to receive supplies and sell oil; and they are armed and dangerous. For all these reasons IS treats the Kurds with much more care than other groups or tribes. A small series of IS documents attest to how IS has tried to combine fierce military attacks on Kurdish-held territory, especially in the so-called Rojava, the semi-independent Kurdish lands across the north of Syria and Iraq along the Turkish border, with gentler treatment of Kurds under their direct control.

The documents begin with a false rumor. "Enemies of Islam continue to harm this young state, and defame the image of the Islamic Caliphate." In the province of Ninaweh, in Iraq, where Mosul is situated, reports were circulating in Ramadan of 1435

(July 2014) to the effect that IS was "forcibly displacing Kurds from Wilayat Ninawa."[43] Nothing could be further from the truth. IS was at pains to correct this calumny. It insisted that there was "no truth to this tendentious rumor." Further, "the Sunni Kurds are our brothers in God. What is for them is for us, and what is upon them is upon us." This is to remind us, and them, that Kurds are Sunnis. The Islamic State "will not allow any one of them to be harmed"—at least "so long as they remain on the principle of Islam and do not clothe themselves in anything that contradicts it."

The condition is clear: Kurds and IS Muslims are brothers and from the IS point of view must behave as brothers. So long as the Kurds do that, in IS judgment, they will be kept safe. If they step out of line, however, they join the ranks of the enemy.

IS conquered Raqqa, in Syria, in January 2014. The Kurds there were for some time exempt from its savagery. IS was keen to promote calm among the Kurds and decided, toward that end, to encourage the Kurds to acquire a greater knowledge of religion. A year and a half later, in early June of 2015, IS arranged for special sessions on sharia, following afternoon prayers, over a period of ten days.[44] Attendance was encouraged by the promise of certificates at the end for those who performed successfully, as well as "valuable prizes." Moreover, the sessions were to be held in the Kurdish language. Despite the general IS preference for Arabic, as the language of the Prophet, it recognized the usefulness of employing a language that the Kurds might understand and appreciate. The Kurdish language is little recognized otherwise, and in this way IS might kill two birds with a single stone.

It seems that, despite IS gentleness in Mosul, and regardless of those "valuable prizes," some Kurds in Raqqa did step out of line, since our next piece of evidence reveals an expulsion. An undated document—it must be from mid-June 2015—tells the Kurds of Raqqa that, with regret, IS has to expel them: Kurdish parties have allied themselves with the "Crusader" war on IS, it says, and "in your midst are those who have cooperated with the Crusader alliance," and so, in order to avoid "confrontation between us and you on account of some of the foolish ones among you, we ask you to leave Wilayat al-Raqqa within 72 hours."[45] This is not hostility, it is stressed, and the departing Kurds are invited to register their real estate as they leave so that they can get it back later.

The cynic will scoff at this. It is clear that IS is simply using this as a convenient and easy way to find out what the Kurds own so that they can confiscate it. But on 10 Ramadan 1436 (June 26, 2015) a directive addressed to IS soldiers instructed:

> We have given a pledge to the Kurds of Raqqa city who went out of Raqqa city for Tadmur city that we will not use their homes, and as you know the believers adhere to their conditions, thus one may not enter or use the homes of the Kurds in Raqqa city, and whoever is shown to have violated this order will be referred to the judiciary.[46]

Even with the best of intentions and the strictest of discipline, however, sometimes soldiers will not do as they are told. By July 5, some soldiers had apparently attacked Kurdish property. A proclamation of that date denounced such behavior (it is "absolutely forbidden," "under any justification or pretext") and promised condign retribution for the offenders—the damage must be repaired, and a punishment would be meted out, ranging from three days' imprisonment for a first offense to thirty lashes a day every day for a week for a second offense, rising to expulsion from the province a third time.

IS efforts to woo the Kurds under their rule have not met with much success. The Kurds of the region are more interested in striving for independence than in seeking accommodation with their neighbors, especially violent ones. A common religious identity does little to compensate for the acceptance of yet another in a long line of alien rulers.

Shi'is

Shi'is are the principal victims of IS fury. Two reasons explain this. First, like sectarians in other faiths, Sunnis—IS is aggressively Sunni—and Shi'is tend to see each other as the worst of heretics and the most dangerous of enemies. If for no other reason, this is because sectarians see in each other people of a correct faith who have gone wrong. And because their brothers have gone wrong, they stick to their guns, insisting on the truth or the rightness of their theological or religious position. That is, unlike people of different faiths, who are excused for not knowing and recognizing the truth, members of a different sect of one's own faith are viewed as knowing the truth, but insisting on their own, wrong, version of it. This is why intra-religious quarrels are so often much fiercer than quarrels between different faiths. No one hears of religion-based quarrels between Christians and Buddhists, or Jews and Hindus— their faiths are more fully separated ideologically (and often geographically).

The second reason is that, unlike the Christians and the Jews and other little groupings of ethnic or religious types in Iraq and Syria, Shi'is actually matter: in Iraq the fall of Saddam Hussein unleashed a long-suppressed Shi'i majority that seized power and ever since has done little to pacify or to reconcile with the Sunni minority that dominated the country for so long. The roots of IS lie in part in the U.S. invasion that deposed Saddam and destroyed the country's political infrastructure, creating a vacuum that the Shi'is were quick to fill. IS is in a sense an Iraqi Sunni reaction to the Shi'i realization of its own potential within Iraq. IS was able to exploit that to deepen the Sunni-Shi'i divide in that country and to transform a sectarian political divide there into what is now a religious holy war in the region and elsewhere between the soldiers of truth, IS, and the rest, in first place the Shi'is of Iraq and their allies. These are on the one hand the Iranians, who are also Shi'is, and on the other the Alawi-dominated regime of the Asad family in Syria. Alawis, also known as Nusayris, are an offshoot of a branch of Shi'ism. It is for this reason that IS refers always with contempt to the Syrian government as Nusayris.

Shi'is, as a group, meet with the worst treatment of all at the hands of IS. Their soldiers captured by IS are shot in the hundreds, their bodies thrown into anonymous mass graves or dumped in the river to float down to Baghdad and horrify the populace. Seen as apostates because of their religious deviance from the Sunnism of IS, they are entitled to no toleration from IS and repentance for that deviation or conversion to Sunnism are not options.

Yezidis

Yezidis, like Shi'is, have borne the shocking brunt of IS hostility to those unlike themselves. Yezidis are not Christians, nor are they Muslims, Sunni or Shi'i, nor are they Zoroastrians. Followers of an ancient monotheistic faith, with many accretions from other religions, that has somehow survived in the north of Iraq, they are not numerous, with a total population in the region and in the diaspora of probably less than half a million. They lack protectors, local or external, and like many minorities historically they are at the mercy of those who rule them. Concentrated in particular near Mount Sinjar, they became famous recently when IS forces attacked them there in the summer of 2014, killing many and taking many others, both men and women, captive. IS tried to force them to convert to Islam, and raped and sold many of the women as slaves.[47] A UN report described genocide, killing and kidnapping, forced conversion, and young children taken away and trained as IS fighters.[48] In the end, it was Kurdish peshmerga soldiers who were able to offer them some relief and evacuate many to Kurdish-controlled areas in northern Iraq.

The IS approach here, as with Christians and Kurds and others, is not random, nor is it that local commanders allow their foot soldiers simply to give free rein to their bloodlust. While it is certainly true that IS fighters enslave, rape, and even kill women, they do it in accordance with their understanding of ancient rules. Conquered people, especially non-Muslims, have no rights. Christians and Jews are theoretically tolerated, and Kurds as Sunnis enjoy more or less full rights. But Yezidis, as followers of a religion that has no recognition in the Quran, who are occasionally described as devil-worshippers, and with rites and ideas that look suspiciously like borrowings from a variety of other faiths, enjoy no such protection.

Shabaks and Kaka'is

Along with Shi'is and Yezidis, two other smaller minorities have suffered. Shabaks and Kaka'is, each with fewer than half a million believers following syncretistic religions that meld elements drawn from Islam and other faiths, are scattered in the province of Mosul, near Mount Sinjar.[49] They fell under IS rule as the movement swept across the region and, like the Yezidis, received the treatment IS reserves for infidels: destruction of their villages, murder, kidnappings of children, forced conversions, enslavement, and forced marriage of the women.

IS and Others

IS treatment of those it deems others is not random, nor is it meaningless. It offers IS a means to reward its fighters in ways known throughout history, and opens a path for IS to demonstrate, as the pact with the Christians demonstrates, that they are cleaving to patterns of behavior inherited from the purest and best periods of their past as well as to rules laid down by the founder of their faith and his followers at the beginning of Islamic time. For IS it is important to be able to show that it is not merely a terrorist gang, or a group without Islamist credentials. The brutal treatment of others confirms that IS, in its own eyes at least, is a group that follows time-honored rules governing relations between Muslims and non-Muslims—rules that have the sanction, thanks to their creation by the founder of their faith, of heavenly approval.

At the same time, such behavior confirms that IS is aware of realities on the ground in the territory it dominates. IS is generally unafraid to break taboos and, apparently, to disregard the imperatives of strategy, tactics, and even logic, but how it looks at and deals with the different groups in its surroundings demonstrates that it takes very careful account of military and social facts before it unleashes its forces in any region.

CHAPTER SEVEN

Apocalypse Now

D ABIQ IS IN SYRIA, close to the border with Turkey. Its history goes back to the time of the ancient Assyrians, in the ninth century before Christ, when it was known as Dabigu. More recently, in the seventh and eighth Christian centuries, it lay on the northern border of the early Islamic empire, a little to the north of Aleppo, between Manbij in the east and Antakya close to the Mediterranean coast. As a glance at the area on Google Earth confirms, it is "a green and pleasant land," in the words of one of our medieval sources.¹ When the Umayyads, the great first dynasty of Islam, sent their armies to raid the Byzantines, in what is now Turkey, Marj Dabiq, the plain, or meadow, of Dabiq, was their last resting point before they entered Byzantine territory.² The seventh Umayyad caliph, Sulayman ibn Abd al-Malik, actually died here, in the year 717, which was the year 99 of the Islamic calendar. He had gone there after leading the *hajj*, the pilgrimage, to Mecca, and at the time of his death was preparing for another raid against the Christians, aiming first at nearby al-Masisa and, more distantly, at Constantinople.³

Sulayman was buried in Dabiq. But when the Umayyads were overthrown by another Muslim dynasty, the Abbasids, in 750, the new rulers set about eliminating not only living Umayyads but even the graves of their dead caliphs. Their aim was both to desecrate the graves and dishonor the corpses of their enemies, and to wipe out all visible remains or tangible memory of the earlier dynasty.[4] Umar ibn Hani tells us that, under the first Abbasid caliph, al-Saffah, "The Killer," he was sent out with a party commanded by one Abdallah ibn Ali to destroy the graves of the Umayyad caliphs, "and we dug Sulayman ibn Abd al-Malik up out of the soil in Dabiq, but we found only his spine, his ribs and his skull, so we burnt them. And we did the same thing to other members of that family." The Abbasids evinced a real hatred for the Umayyads: when the grave of another early Umayyad caliph, Hisham, turned up nothing but "the tip of his nose," Abdallah ibn Ali took that and gave it eighty lashes before burning it.[5]

Hundreds of years later, in 1516, the plain of Dabiq acquired significance again as the site of the decisive battle that put an end to the domination of the Mamluks, who had ruled Egypt and, more intermittently, Syria and Palestine, since the middle of the thirteenth century. The victorious Ottomans, commanded in that battle by Selim I, the Grim, would control the region for four centuries, until World War I.[6]

Why should any of this matter? Why should it be of interest or importance to us now, in the twenty-first century? The answer lies in the Islamic State's exploitation of ancient traditions about Dabiq. Dabiq has more than dry historical importance: the same writer who tells us about the desecration of the grave of Sulayman in the distant past also tells us, in a very matter-of-fact way, something about the future. According to him, "the Rum" (from a word meaning Romans, referring to the Byzantines, and hence a name for Christians) "will descend on Dabiq or al-Amaq." This is a reference to a hadith, or account, of the Prophet Muhammad, in the great ninth-century collection of Muslim ibn al-Hajjaj, in which he tells us that the Final Hour will come only when the Rum come to Dabiq or a nearby place, al-Amaq.[7]

The Last Battle

Dabiq is thus to be the scene of the Muslim version of Armageddon. We possess a highly detailed account of what will happen. It is very unlike the Christian Armageddon, described for us in the Book of Revelation (where the name itself appears at 16:16). Instead in the hadith we learn, fairly straightforwardly, almost prosaically, about a battle:

> Abu Hurayra reported Allah's Messenger (peace be upon him) as saying: The Last Hour will not come until the Romans land at al-Amaq or in Dabiq. An army consisting of the best [soldiers] of the people of the earth at that time will come from Medina [to counteract them]. When they arrange themselves in ranks, the Romans will say: Do not stand between us and those [Muslims] who took prisoners from amongst us. Let us fight with them; and the Muslims will say: No, by Allah, we will never get aside from you and from our brethren that you may fight them. They will then fight and one third of the army will run away, whom Allah will never forgive. Another third [of the army] which will be constituted of excellent martyrs in Allah's eye, will be killed and the [final] third who will never be put to trial will win and will be conquerors of Constantinople. And as they are busy in distributing the spoils of war [amongst themselves], after hanging their swords by the olive trees, Satan will cry: The Dajjal [the Antichrist] has taken your place among your family. They will then come out, but it will be of no avail. And when they come to Syria, he will come out while they are still preparing themselves for battle drawing up the ranks. Certainly, the time of prayer shall come and then Jesus (peace be upon him) son of Mary will descend and lead them in prayer. When the enemy of Allah sees him, it will [disappear] just as salt dissolves itself in water and if he [Jesus] were not to confront them at all, even then it would dissolve completely, but Allah will kill them by his hand and will show them their blood on his lance [the lance of Jesus Christ].[8]

This tradition, or hadith, is very detailed. Not everything in it is crystal clear, partly because of the way in which classical Arabic often uses words like "he" and "him," "they" and "them" and "it," without always making sufficiently clear what or whom it is referring to.

Nonetheless, with all the obscurity that that leaves us, a picture emerges: a Christian army (the "Rum") will be met at Dabiq by an army of Muslims from Medina ("the best [soldiers] of the people of the earth"); the "Romans," prudently or out of cowardice, try to avoid a battle with them and to fight only against those Muslims who have taken Christian prisoners, in order to try to win their freedom; and the Medinan fighters reject that possibility—they will not abandon their brothers, nor will they avoid a battle with the Christians. A battle ensues. But this is not a regular battle, with gains and losses and irregular results. This is a fateful battle for the true faith and the results are patterned in religious terms: one third of the Muslims are put to flight, their cravenness earning undying unforgiveness from Allah. Another third of the Muslim army earns the crown of martyrdom, dying in the battle. And the final third not only wins the battle but goes on to conquer Constantinople, the heart of the Christian world. That should be the end of the story, but it is not: while they are resting from their victory and sharing out the spoils, Satan will attempt to destroy them by means of the Antichrist, the Dajjal in Arabic. The text becomes somewhat obscure at this point, but it appears that they confront him, with little success. Then they return to Syria and Jesus comes down from heaven to lead them in prayer. This is their salvation, for his appearance causes the Dajjal and his forces to disappear, "just as salt dissolves itself in water."

The Power of Hadiths

How old is this tradition? As we have seen, the account of this battle comes in a hadith. Hadiths are part of the ancient lore of Islam. Like the Quran, they are associated with the figure of the founder, Muhammad. The Quran was delivered, according to Islamic tradition, directly from God to the Prophet by the angel Gabriel and represents the speech of God Himself. Hadiths are different. They represent speech of the Prophet or anecdotes about him (the word hadith comes from a root that carries both the meanings "to talk" and "to happen"). Within a couple of centuries of the Prophet's death in 632, vast numbers of hadiths were circulating among Muslims. Not all of them can be shown to have a real connection to the Prophet. Many were invented, often for pious reasons, occa-sionally not, to explain or justify religious practices, political ac-tions, or attitudes among early Muslims. Attribution to the Prophet, if accepted as correct, conferred on hadiths a final authority.

Muslims in the Middle Ages recognized the difficulty inherent in blindly accepting everything that was ascribed to Muhammad, and developed a variety of ways to examine and filter the materials they had. Hundreds, possibly thousands of fake hadiths were iden-tified and expelled from collections and from pious circulation. Does this mean that all those that remain in the great collections are genuine? Dogma tells us yes. But scholars are more cautious, and there may be good reason to doubt some of the hadiths still in circulation today.

Does this hadith come from Muhammad? Answering a ques-tion of this sort takes us deep into the study of hadith and of hadith transmission, a field important to medieval scholars in the Islamic world and one that, with its necessary chase after tiny details across centuries of source materials in Arabic, appeals to the detective in most of us. It is a little like starting to assemble a vast jigsaw puzzle without a picture on the lid and with many of the pieces missing, broken, or bent. And the underlying picture is in effect the whole of the early history of Islam.

In one sense it is impossible to know how old this hadith about Dabiq is: its text comes assorted with a list of transmitters who carry it all the way back to the Prophet. Each transmitter appar-ently received it orally from the one before him and passed it on to the next, with the chain extending from the Prophet to the time of the hadith-collector Muslim ibn al-Hajjaj in the ninth century. If each transmitter really knew the ones before and after him in the chain, and if they were all truthful, and if each of them did in fact pass it on from his predecessor to his successor in the chain, then there would be good grounds to accept it as genuine.

Asking and answering such questions is part of how hadiths were tested in the Middle Ages. Entire books—biographical dic-tionaries—are devoted to identifying people who transmitted ha-diths; to giving us the dates of their lives, information about their careers and studies, and whom they heard hadiths from and who heard hadiths from them; and to recording whether they are regarded as faithful transmitters, less than reliable, or, even worse, known to invent hadiths and attribute them to the Prophet of Islam.

In the case of the Dabiq hadith, there were five transmitters. We know that the transmitters did overlap chronologically. Each man could easily have studied, as our hadith's chain of transmitters tells us, with his predecessor on the list. But "could have studied" does not need to mean "did study." And as to the rest all we have is the word of the man who wrote the tradition down in his collection. Piety may well have made him an honest man, but we have no definitive means of weighing the honesty of each of the links in the chain of transmitters, or of authenticating the hadith as a whole.

The Geography of Armageddon

If we turn from the external shape to the content of this hadith, the situation does not improve much. The reference to Dabiq is more than a little worrying: could the Prophet, who spent most of his life far away in the deserts of Arabia, have known the name of this place? (A faithful Muslim will have no difficulty in believing that God, Allah, may have let Muhammad know this; but for non-Muslims this path to knowledge is unavailable.) Why, quite apart from this, should Dabiq be a place of such significance? And why should Constantinople matter for the end times?

For Muhammad Constantinople was a Christian place of real importance, the distant capital of the Byzantine empire, eastern Rome, and it continued to represent the Great Satan for Muslims in religious and political terms all the way down to the time of our hadith-collector Muslim ibn al-Hajjaj in the ninth century and for a long time thereafter. But it had lost most of its real significance by the time of the Crusades, and it ceased to be a Christian city with the Islamic conquest of 1453 when it effectively lost its very name, Constantinople, becoming Istanbul for most purposes from that time onward.[9] For four centuries after that it was the heart of a great empire, but that empire, of the Ottomans, was Islamic, not Christian. Why should it play a Christian role in the end times for Islam? Or is modern Turkey what is meant here? But even then, regardless of the importance of Constantinople—which was after

all, as Istanbul still is, a major city—what about Dabiq? Are we to
suppose that a Christian army of some sort will find its way
through Turkey and into Syria, two large modern Islamic states, to
the plain of Dabiq for this final battle between the two faiths? Or
does the picture that is drawn here, whether it goes back to the
Prophet himself or to someone else before the hadith was written
down in the ninth century, offer us simply a faithful Muslim's idea
of how the end times will turn out?

End Times

For many outsiders, Americans and Western Europeans in particular, it may look as though IS has other aims, most spectacularly the
establishment of a state ruled by Islamic law, sharia. When we find
Americans and others opposing, by legal and occasionally by extra-
legal means, the building of mosques in their local communities
and trying to pass legislation to prevent the imposition of sharia
law in their states, it is clear that they see IS as a tool for the spread
of the Islamic faith to all corners of the world. And indeed, IS itself
proclaims that that is among its aims. But the spread of Islam is
only a way station along the path to a more far-reaching aim, the
apocalypse.

For Muslims, Christians, and Jews alike an apocalypse is one of
the signs, one of the events, of the end times. It heralds the final
judgment and the eternal fate of the believer. But for most
Muslims, as for most Christians and Jews, the scriptural imminence
of the end time has been deferred under the pressure of this-
worldly, quotidian reality. For Christians, the Second Coming was
promised in the gospels as coming in the lifetime of those hearing
the promise: Jesus himself said, in the gospels (Mark 13:30; also
Matthew 24:34), "Verily I say unto you, that this generation shall
not pass, till all these things be done." Similarly Matthew 16:28
(see also Mark 9:1; Luke 9:27): "Verily I say unto you, There be
some standing here, which shall not taste of death, till they see the
Son of man coming in his kingdom." And, from a different point of
view, the first epistle of John (2:18) tells us: "Little children, it is
the last time; and as you have heard, that Antichrist shall come,
even now are there many Antichrists, whereby we know that it is

the last time." That Second Coming did not materialize quite so immediately, and its fulfillment has been put off by most Christians to an indefinite future.

Scripture itself does not specify such an imminent salvation for Jews. That was a notion that entered Judaism after the closing of the biblical canon. Nevertheless, Jews "believe with perfect faith," as Maimonides put it elegantly in the twelfth century, "in the coming of the Messiah; and though he tarry we wait daily for his coming," similarly recognizing that imminence need not mean putting off daily tasks.[10]

So too Muslims: the Quran communicates in the manner of a hell-fire preacher, warning its hearers—for the Quran is a record of God's speech delivered by Muhammad to his fellow Arabs—not only of the joys of paradise but also of the torments of hell. And those torments may come at any time. The final day is not coming at some vague, infinitely far-off time in the future: the language of the Quran makes it clear that every human being faces an urgent need to prepare for it, through correct belief and behavior. But, like Christians and Jews, most Muslims do not think or behave as though they believe that the final day, the Hour, is just around the corner, next week, or tomorrow, or this afternoon. Some Muslims, like some Jews and Christians, spend their lives repenting and weeping while contemplating the horrors of hell, but they are generally the ones whom all rational thought must see as having little to worry about. The other members of all these faiths who hold to the notion of an imminent apocalypse tend to be those who also want to try to bring it forward. Thus some Christians see the occurrence of four "blood moons" as a sign of the end times, and a few Jews used to call for "Moshiach Now" ("Messiah Now"), as if to compel God to do His work at their urging rather than in His own good time.[11]

When will the end time occur? The Prophet, or those who ascribed this hadith to him, did not vouchsafe such a pedestrian piece of information to us. While what is to happen is described in impressive detail, no date is given. God, Allah, will make it happen when He wishes. But not everyone is content to wait. IS seeks to make Dabiq the scene of the final battle and hence the beginning of the end time, and it aims to make that end time now.

Anticipating the Apocalypse

The continuing strength of religious belief among Muslims nourishes IS and the ideology it propounds. Ideologically IS shares much with other Islamist movements. Like them it wishes to expand the reach of Islam and to create a more Islamic society; and like them it exploits the religious belief of Muslims to promote those ends. But IS is unique among Islamist movements of reform and renewal in having a messianic ambition. It promises an imminent apocalypse.

This is not simply a minor doctrinal detail, such as we might see differentiating members of one Christian church from those congregants on the next corner. Messianism, millenarianism, the apocalypse, whatever label we use for it, has a long history in Islam, and is found everywhere from east to extreme west. It is not the most widespread of Islamic attitudes or doctrines, nor for good reasons the most successful. However successful it may be in the short term, acting "in the expectation of a future that never happen[s]" tends not to win success in the long term.[12] It is obvious why. Nevertheless, the imminence of an end time remains a real prospect for many Muslims, more so than for most Christians. Belief in the imminent return of Jesus (Isa in Arabic), to initiate the end times, and in the impending coming of the Mahdi, also as part of that process, is extremely widespread: half or more Muslims in most countries outside the ex-communist world expect to see them arrive in their lifetimes.[13]

Discussions and publications on the subject of apocalyptic speculation are frequent in the Islamic world. David Cook, who published a learned account of early Islamic apocalypticism in 2002, followed that up just three years later with another lengthy study, this time devoted entirely to modern ideas and discussions on the subject.[14] He was able not only to show the longevity and rootedness of such ideas in both learned Islamic thinking and popular belief over the past fourteen centuries, but also to confirm the intimate relationship between Islamic apocalypticism and extremist political action. In that sense IS does not represent a major new departure.

Modern apocalypticists in Islam, like their peers in Christianity, see and draw parallels between features of the textual roots of their respective traditions—the Quran or the Bible—and modern events. Thus the United States is interpreted as the great adversary of Islam, a stand-in for the enemy of true faith in the Quran known as Ad, and fated, like Ad, to disappear into oblivion in disgrace. The modern state of Israel, for its part, is seen, naturally, as having inherited the evil character of the Jews in the Quran, described especially in *sura* 17:

> And We conveyed to the Children of Israel in the Scripture that, You will surely cause corruption on the earth twice, and you will surely reach [a degree of] great haughtiness . . . Then when the final promise came, [We sent your enemies] to sadden your faces and to enter the temple in Jerusalem, as they entered it the first time, and to destroy what they had taken over with [total] destruction.[15]

For similar reasons, the Six Day War of 1967 was seen as initiating the end times.

The particular apocalypse for which IS is preparing is what it itself, in its online magazine *Dabiq*, labels the Islamic Armageddon, borrowing that label from the New Testament vision of the Book of Revelation. That is to be the final battle between the forces of good and those of evil, understood as those of IS and those of "Rum," Christendom and its allies. This battle is to take place at Dabiq, in Syria, and while its date is unknown IS is doing all in its power to make it happen as soon as possible.

The notion of an apocalyptic final battle combines a terrestrial drama typical of revolutionary political movements with the heavenly promise of a messianic sect. Over these it spreads the contemporary lure of the extreme violence of video games. France had the fall of the Bastille, Cuba the attack on the Moncada barracks; Russian communism had the October Revolution, China the Long March. IS aims at Dabiq. Its siting of its capital at Raqqa, not far from Dabiq, is clearly deliberate. The intention is to draw the United States and others into a major battle there, so that when the chips are down, whenever the final battle occurs, IS can use the location, and its meaning for Islamic messianism in its IS form, as a rallying point for support.

Will IS win that battle? For IS it is inevitable that the "Christians" must lose, condemned by fate as expressed in the ideology of IS and the prophecy upon which that ideology is built. But there is another sense in which victory at Dabiq is irrelevant: as we have seen, the battle at Dabiq has no military significance in earthly terms. The battle there is to occur as part of a longer and more complex choreography. Its significance, in terrestrial terms, lies merely in its being a prelude to something much larger, the end of the world and the final judgment. The formalistic division of the Muslim fighters into three groups—some to die in battle as martyrs, others who "will never be forgiven" by Allah for turning tail and fleeing, and a final third that will enjoy the fruits of victory—has little to do with real combat. Thus a military defeat at Dabiq, should it occur, need not be seen as a disappointment or a failure.

Why Dabiq?

Why Dabiq at all? It's a nowhere place. It is the name of the IS magazine, but that simply poses the question again—why use that name for the magazine of a movement like IS? It is because of the hadith, but why does the name occur in that hadith? And why has IS chosen to make use of the tradition about Dabiq, rather than any number of other traditions about the Islamic Final Hour? What is it about this tradition that makes it particularly useful or attractive to IS? One superficially simple reason, apart from its association with the Prophet, which it shares with so many other such predictions, is its geographical specificity. Dabiq is located very conveniently in territory that quickly and easily came under Islamic control in the seventh century; it lies very close to Raqqa, a fact that helps to explain the choice of that city as the IS capital and center of operations; battles around Raqqa can thus, if necessary, be presented as preparations for the major battle that is to signal the end of the world; and it lies in territory that was part of the larger world in which the Prophet lived and had his career.

The Dabiq tradition is not, however, the only hadith associated with end-of-the-world ideas in Islam. Other traditions place messianic events and apocalyptic struggles in all sorts of places.

Khorasan, in what is now roughly northeastern Iran, was a popular location for such predictions in the eighth and ninth centuries, because that was where the Abbasids, who successfully seized power in the Islamic world empire in 750, drew much of their support. Placing apocalyptic predictions that benefited them in regions they controlled and painting their movement as messianic served to legitimize their revolution and to give them greater status in the eyes of their subjects. The scholar Wilferd Madelung labels these "propagandistic apocalyptic" traditions because they help to drum up support for the cause that is predicted to bring salvation.[16] Similarly, late twentieth-century writings that portrayed the jihadists of Afghanistan as anticipating and helping to bring closer the Islamic end times took advantage of the strengths and successes of the anticommunist uprising in that country to identify the Taliban and their associates as the harbingers of salvation for Islam more generally.

But Dabiq has more on its side than either Afghanistan or Khorasan. Its appeal goes right back to very early Islamic times, to well before even the Abbasids were thought of. The hadith about Dabiq ignores Afghanistan and the Taliban to concentrate Muslims' attention on a place, in a territory, that was important in the history of Islam as long ago as the eighth century and may even have been known to Muhammad himself. This hadith has a very sound-looking *isnad*, or chain of transmitters, taking it all the way back to the Prophet; and all historical characters involved in it can, as any good end-time prediction demands, be identified with participants in events of today. Dabiq thus belongs to the past as well as the present, and on that basis can lay plausible claim to the future.

For the faithful Muslim, the inclusion of this hadith in the ninth-century collection of Muslim ibn al-Hajjaj validates it as coming from the Prophet Muhammad, in the first part of the seventh century, and hence as offering a definite and credible prediction of the future and more specifically, in this case, the coming end of time. The non-Muslim and the historian see hadiths in different terms. For them a hadith is a document of the past with a definite background and context. They may not be easy to identify, and may not make the hadith itself credible, but they can teach us a great deal about the meaning and role of the hadith as a document in history.

To see prophetic hadiths as not necessarily authentic predictions of the future is not to attack Islam, nor is it to suggest that texts like these should be dismissed. Quite the contrary, as this case shows, they have real importance for those who accept them, and for that reason need to be treated with respect and taken seriously, even if not quite in the way that they appear to demand. Seen in those terms, this hadith, like others, seems to have its origins not in the first three decades of the seventh century, but in the early eighth. That is when Dabiq actually mattered, when it had its Andy Warhol–style fifteen minutes on the world stage. Dabiq never mattered at other times, except in 1516 when the Ottomans defeated the Mamluks—at a place that coincided with the eighth-century location largely for reasons connected to geography and the logistics of warfare between two states with a shared boundary in what is now the borderland of Syria and Turkey.

At that original, eighth-century moment in Islamic history Dabiq possessed great symbolic significance: it appeared to mark a key point, in geographical terms, on the path to the capture of Constantinople. Conquest of Constantinople—the capital of the eastern Roman empire, Islam's only serious remaining rival, and the richest and most important city in the known world—would be a major step toward completing the conquests of Islam. It would help to bring about the millennium.

Dabiq, we are told, was where Muslim armies rested in Islamic territory immediately before crossing the border to fight the armies of Byzantium. That otherwise incidental fact of geography marks a birth date for the hadith: this tradition, ascribed to the Prophet, has meaning only when Dabiq itself has meaning. In the time of the Prophet himself, in the early seventh century, Dabiq would have been meaningless; it was simply a plain somewhere in Byzantine territory. Muhammad may or may not have been aware of it: we have no way of judging. By the middle of the eighth century, attempts to conquer the Byzantine capital had sputtered and died down. Not until the Ottomans, many centuries later, would Muslims renew attempts to take the great city.[17] The only time at which the hadith could have been created, with a reference to Dabiq that made sense to people hearing it, is the brief period when Dabiq actually mattered, that short period in the early eighth century when, following the conquest of northern Syria by Islam, we witness Umayyad attempts to take the Byzantine capital, using Dabiq as a jumping-off point for entry into Byzantine territory. And that time, as we have seen, coincides neatly with a date that, in Islamic terms, happens to look or could be made to look potentially significant: the end of the first century of the *hijra*, that is, the completion of a hundred years since the start of the Islamic calendrical era, a time that to many looked like a possible date for the End, to be brought by the reigning caliph, Sulayman.

Sulayman

Why Sulayman? What makes this caliph different from others? What is his relevance for IS and for us in the second decade of the twenty-first century? A minor Umayyad, Sulayman ruled for only a couple of years, dying on his way to an attack on Byzantium that failed because of his death. Like other rulers before and after him, he tried to pass the caliphal succession on to his own offspring and like others he failed in that attempt. The force of a tradition hostile to automatic inheritance by a son was too strong, and in any case the son in question died too early.[18] Instead, Sulayman was succeeded by a cousin, Umar ibn Abd al-Aziz. Umar lucked out in this process partly because he was well known as a man of great piety and probity and, although like Sulayman he too ruled for only a couple of years, he alone among the Umayyads left a good reputation even among his enemies. As we have seen, when the Abbasids tried to efface the memory of all things Umayyad, Umar was the one member of that dynasty for whom they made an exception.

Sulayman had an unpleasant character, even by the standards of absolute rulers of the past.[19] He is represented as a glutton and a cruel voluptuary. A strange story that is presented in several versions in our sources has him preening in front of a mirror in a green robe and boasting about his youthful figure. Green is the color associated with the Prophet, and the story was probably told either in a positive sense, to elevate the messianic character associated with him or, perhaps more likely, negatively, to show him as comparing himself impiously to the Prophet. (The story goes on to tell us that Sulayman died shortly thereafter.) We also have a particularly gruesome account of him and some cronies cutting the heads off four hundred Byzantine prisoners, in some cases using blunt swords. While the cruelty involved here will certainly have looked different to medieval people—this was another time and another place—the story was just as certainly designed, regardless of its truth, to portray him in this way. It also recalls accounts of IS butchery of large groups of prisoners today.

But other features of his rule paint a different picture: as a young man Sulayman had led the *hajj*, the great annual pilgrimage, to Mecca, and he did it again as caliph, in 716. He also invested great resources in piping water through the desert to the town of Mecca, where water was a prized scarcity, often brackish when available—hence the frequent quranic emphasis on running water as a feature of Paradise. With numerous pilgrims arriving every year, increasing the pressure on the existing supply, this was an essential improvement.

Sulayman also appears to have chosen Jerusalem as the center of his rule, unlike the rest of his dynasty who ruled from Damascus. Before modern times, Jerusalem never served as a political or administrative center for the Muslims in Palestine. The move had undoubted religious meaning, partly because its role in both Jewish and Christian messianic history gave Jerusalem great significance in Islam as well, and since, as governor of Palestine before he became caliph, Sulayman had been involved in developing Ramla, near Lod, as the new provincial capital. In addition, Sulayman engaged in a massive campaign against Byzantium, both by land and by sea, that placed the capital, Constantinople, under siege for a full year, from 717 to 718 (the Muslims were able to sow crops and eat the resulting harvest a year later). As the only significant opponent of Islam, Byzantium represented a major challenge, not only in political and military terms but also, as a great Christian empire, in religious terms.

Two processes came together in the reign of Sulayman. First, the long series of immense conquests of Islam in its first century reached what was more or less its conclusion. In this initial wave of expansion, the frontiers of the Islamic empire attained what became their first settled limits, and growth became less a matter of extending physical borders and more one of consolidation and of increasing the number of Muslims via conversion. Secondly, this happened, along with the reign of Sulayman, just as the first century of the existence of Islam approached its end, and because he was only in his mid-forties it looked very likely that he would still be caliph in the year 100.

A Digression about Calendars

This requires a calendrical digression. Sulayman was caliph between 715 and 717. The Prophet Muhammad died in 632. But he went on his famous *hijra*, or "migration," from Mecca to Medina a decade earlier, in 622, and it was from that year that Muslims began their new calendar. A new calendar is striking: Christians, Westerners, the whole world today uses a calendar that starts, notionally at least, with the birth of Jesus, which led to the start of Christianity, a little over two thousand years ago. But the calculations on which that depends were made many centuries after the fact, and use of the Western calendar, Anno Domini, actually began only in about the ninth century.[20]

The most important feature of the Islamic calendar is that, like the Christian one, it has a universal aspect. Other calendars tended to have a local or a very specific character: we hear of dating by the years of different consuls, at Rome; by regnal dates, based on the beginning of a ruler's reign; or, for some ancient cities, by years from the date of their foundation. British Acts of Parliament were until 1962 dated not only by regular years, but also by years since the sovereign ascended the throne. Thus the Penalties for Drunkenness Act is formally dated "1962 10 and 11 ELIZ 2," referring to the fact that 1962 represented the end of the tenth and the beginning of the eleventh year since the Queen's accession. Similarly, the 1994 constitution of the Dominican Republic is dated "fourteenth of the month of August of the year 1994, 151 years of Independence and 131 of the restoration," referring to the country's independence as a separate state from Haiti in 1844 and to the restoration of sovereignty following a Spanish attempt at renewing imperial rule in the 1860s. Such expressions carry real meaning for those who use them, but obviously they are all in their different ways very local. The Islamic calendar, by contrast, like the Christian, is universal.

Another important feature of the Islamic calendar is that it has no leap years. It is based on a year of twelve months, all beginning with a new moon. As the Quran explains:

> Indeed, the number of months with Allah is twelve [lunar] months in the register of Allah [from] the day He created the heavens and the earth; of these, four are sacred. That is the correct religion, so do not wrong yourselves during them. And fight against the disbelievers collectively as they fight against you collectively. And know that Allah is with the righteous [who fear Him]. Indeed, the postponing [of restriction within sacred months] is an increase in disbelief by which those who have disbelieved are led [further] astray. They make it lawful one year and unlawful another year to correspond to the number made unlawful by Allah and [thus] make lawful what Allah has made unlawful. Made pleasing to them is the evil of their deeds; and Allah does not guide the disbelieving people.[21]

This is understood to be a prohibition of the ancient practice of what is known as intercalation.[22] Unlike the solar year, which has slightly over 365 days, a twelve-month calendar based on the moon has only some 354 days—twelve times twenty-nine-and-a-half days, the time between one new moon and the next. So every lunar year is eleven days shorter than a Western, solar year.[23] Before Islam, adding an extra month every two or three years, intercalation, solved the problem by keeping the two systems in sync with each other—and also kept the lunar calendar in sync with the seasons. Islam forbade the practice, however, and the result is that months now circle through the seasons—Ramadan, the month-long fast, can fall in any season of the year, making for difficulties if it falls during the hot summer as it has done in recent years.

All this means that the hundredth year of the *hijra* is not 722, as we might have expected, but 718–719. Sulayman was caliph from February 715 to September 717, which in the Islamic calendar was mid-96 to early 99.

The Death of Sulayman

Sulayman's death in the year 99 was a surprise to everyone. It had looked as though the end of that first century of Islam might be crowned by the conquest of the great city and the fall of the old Roman empire to the new world of Islam. Poems magnified Sulayman as the expected Mahdi.[24] A story that is more than mere flattery reports that "when Sulayman became caliph, he was informed by some learned men that the name of the caliph who would take Constantinople would be the name of a prophet" (Sulayman is simply the Arabic form of the name Solomon, and the biblical king Solomon is a prophet in Islam); "now none of the Umayyads was called by the name of a prophet except for him. And he was very keen on achieving this and made preparations for it, never doubting that it was he who would do it."[25]

Traditions and predictions tied the caliph Sulayman and his great campaign against the Christian enemy to his projected final encampment at Dabiq, where the expected arrival of huge Byzantine armies would announce the final Hour, in the chiliastic Islamic year 100.[26] It was not to be: Sulayman died, the attack on Constantinople was abandoned, then Umar came to power and brought the center of the empire back to Damascus, before dying himself after a mere two years or so on the caliphal throne.

The link between Dabiq and Sulayman is tighter than it might at first appear. We saw earlier that Dabiq is described as the place where Umayyad armies rested before crossing into Byzantine territory to try and conquer Constantinople. Umayyad attacks on Constantinople took varied forms, however. The principal attacks were made by sea. Dabiq scarcely appears in our sources as a way station for Umayyad armies on land. It appears in fact only in the time of Sulayman, in reference to the famous campaign during which he died. Later references to it in Arabic texts as being a place where armies rested on the way to attack Byzantium magnified a single occurrence into a regular military habit. The significance of Dabiq, as a place heralding the conquest of Constantinople and consequently the Final Hour, therefore, appears to be tied not to Islamic armies in general, or to Umayyad ones more particularly, but specifically and exclusively to the reign of Sulayman, and with the date 100 of the Islamic era in mind.

The death of Sulayman meant the end of the great campaign intended to topple Byzantium as a great power. It meant also the end of the millennial, messianic expectations associated with that event, with Sulayman, and with the year 100. His successor Umar lacked the militaristic ambitions of Sulayman, and no such predictions were made about him. Umar, like Sulayman, died after only a couple of years on the throne, and anticipations and predictions of the conquest of Byzantium faded. All was not, however, forgotten. Millennial hopes and messianic expectations do not always disappear simply because of a minor obstacle—nonfulfillment at a particular time or in a particular person. The memory of the expectations linked to Sulayman did not disappear. The poems and what "learned men" had predicted were not forgotten, though what they said came to be seen as little more than the normal exaggerations of panegyric for a ruler. With the year 100 long past and the implications of that date forgotten or deliberately ignored, Sulayman himself was consigned to a generalized historical oblivion, submerged in the anti-Umayyad propaganda of the Abbasids, and the tie between him, the year 100, and Dabiq as anticipation of the conquest of Constantinople and the Final Hour was obscured and neglected.

The larger predictions, about Dabiq and what it meant for Islam and the end of the world, however, survived and became absorbed into the larger mass of traditions carrying the authority of the Prophet. They were postponed, reserved to an immeasurably distant future. If the year 100 and the caliph Sulayman were not to mark the beginning of the conquest of Constantinople at Dabiq, then that place, in a reliable prediction ascribed to the Prophet himself, will still be the site of the start of the final apocalypse; but that can happen only if the right conditions are prepared.

Using the tools of modern scholarship, it is easy to deconstruct the cluster of ideas and bits of information underlying this particular explicit and detailed prediction. We can observe it developing out of the circumstances of a specific historical moment, only to see that moment pass without delivering on its promise. As a consequence, and in order to retain at least a kernel of that promise, it was shorn of the details that tied it to that moment and instead became a much vaguer, looser prophecy of a distant, millennial future. But religion is not scholarship and messianic movements have little interest in analyzing the roots of their claims. It is that vague, loose remnant of a larger prophetic bundle that IS aims to realize.

Conclusion

THE ISLAMIC STATE REPRESENTS a major challenge to the world today. An obvious comparison is with the Iranian revolution of 1978–1979; yet IS is more threatening. Far more than the Iranians of 1978–1979, IS enjoys the advantages conferred by modern media and instantaneous communications. IS is completely unafraid about being brutal and about being seen as uncivilized in its methods. IS is successful beyond borders—extending over two countries today and active much farther, in other countries and continents nearly worldwide. Only Latin America seems to have escaped its attentions, at least so far.[1] IS employs terror on a wide scale, something that Iran has done in essence only against Israel. IS attracts large numbers of recruits from outside, both from the Islamic world and from the West. IS attacks, in Islamic countries and in the West, seem indifferent to the efforts of law enforcement and to military responses. IS attempts to obtain nuclear material, even for a so-called "dirty bomb," if successful would be much more, and far more immediately, dangerous than the Iranian activities that the West has spent so much effort blocking over the last two or three decades.[2] Above all, IS preaches an ideology that has a much more broadly Islamic appeal than that of the Iranian Revolution: it is Sunni and not Shi'i, hence identifiable with the great majority of the world's Muslims; again unlike the Iranians, it makes genuinely universal claims; it proffers an institution, the caliphate, with appeal and historical claims right across the spectrum of Islam; and, in this too unlike the Iranians, it not only promises an imminent apocalypse but also is attempting to follow through by engaging in extreme forms of violence aimed at hastening that end.

In all these respects and others, IS defies both the West and, as importantly, the world of Islam. For the West, IS represents at base a military and security problem, one that it will eventually succeed in facing down, even in the form of IS operatives inside Western states. Ideology matters too, but the special character of the problems that IS presents means that it needs to be tackled differently, with greater understanding and sophistication and over a longer term. Victory depends both on defeating IS militarily and on convincing Muslims to reject its ideology.

Whatever its passing attractions among disaffected Muslim youth in Europe and North America as an ideology, IS thought represents no serious challenge to Western ideas or thinking. For Islam, by contrast, the challenge is deeper, more immediate, and more complex. Security and political and social stability are real problems everywhere in the world of Islam, even without IS, but in addition to setting up problems on those levels, IS presents a more disturbing and significant challenge to Islamic societies and states. That challenge is ideological and religious.[3]

The Islamic State is brutal, ugly, and unpleasant, but its message is worryingly attractive to Muslims, precisely because it comes from inside Islam and appears to rebuke them in Islamic terms for not being good Muslims. It seeks to galvanize them to action in order to improve them as Muslims, offering both a theoretical basis and a series of practical models for action. Its message cannot simply be ignored or brushed aside. Muslims will have to confront it and, in some way, respond to it. In the twenty-first century, all Islamic societies and states, not only those that see and describe themselves in terms of Islam but all those that have a Muslim majority, have somehow to defend and to justify their understanding and their versions of Islam as the basis for their polities—indeed even for their very existence. This is as true for states like Saudi Arabia and the (Shi'i) Islamic Republic of Iran, and for movements like the Taliban or al-Qaida, with all their own hang-ups about the modern world and inclinations toward a return to medieval practices, as it is for relatively Westernized, secularized states like Turkey or Tunisia. It is as true of those Islamic places that adhere to Sunni as to Shi'i Islam. IS repudiation of Shi'i Islam in favor of an austere Sunni version of the faith does not exempt Shi'is, as Muslims, from the need to react to IS in ideological terms. The larger challenge, however, is not just to these but to all Islamic states, all states with Muslim majorities, all places where Muslims find themselves, and even the rest of the world, non-Islamic as well as Islamic.

As we have seen, and as Paris and Brussels and a host of other Western targets confirm, all states sit in the crosshairs of IS's strategy and ambition, but Islamic states face a peculiar challenge. As Islamic states, states with majority Muslim populations, they occupy a middle position. Western, non-Islamic states are the enemy, to be fought without quarter and worn down to defeat, whether at Dabiq or on the way there. Islamic states and their people, by contrast, are called upon to join the fight, to give up their deviation from the true path and hostility to IS and rejoin the path of struggle in the way of God, *fi sabil Allah* in Arabic, to help bring about the Islamic apocalypse as understood by IS.

One way of measuring the depth of IS success is to look at its recruitment. Thousands of Westerners and probably tens of thousands of Muslims from Islamic countries have joined the ranks. What explains the attraction of IS? Economic distress, social exclusion, poverty, lack of jobs, as well as older motivations like anti-Western and anti-capitalist feelings, to say nothing of sheer adventurism, do not go very far in helping us understand. Whatever truth they contain leaves unexplained the failure of such motives to draw into IS the far larger numbers of Muslims who suffer equally from these problems but remain immune to the pull of IS. The message of IS is not, however, primarily political but religious, nor is it cast in political but in religious terms, so it is in religion and the religious message of IS that we should seek a more comprehensive explanation for IS's success.

All this is to say that Muslims and Islamic states face in IS a different kind of dilemma from that confronting the West. IS presents itself, especially to audiences in more traditional Islamic societies, not just as an alternative to the neocolonial imperatives of the globalizing West, but also as a more authentically Islamic version of the beliefs and lifestyles that people in those societies already have. Those who claim that IS is a response to the regular bogeymen of the anti- and post-colonial struggle are at best no more than half right. When Western commentators and analysts ignore the real meaning and significance of religion in such movements as IS, and in its congeners like the Taliban and al-Qaida, they are committing more than an error of categorization—that is, defining a problem and its solution in the wrong terms. They are perpetuating a form of deliberate self-deception that pretends that the observer has somehow advanced beyond the pre-Enlightenment simplicities of the injunction to obey God's will and fear His anger and by that token that IS has too. IS is there to tell us that God, as the mirror of the faithful, is alive and well and IS is His messenger.

Unlike Westerners, non-Muslims, Christians, and others, Muslims in the Islamic world and elsewhere are not being asked by IS to give up their beliefs and adopt new ones. IS stands for no innovation: instead it holds out the familiar. Its audiences are being instructed to return to the behavior that is consistent, logically and in a sense legally, with the beliefs they already hold. IS tells its listeners that it stands for Islam. To an important degree, IS has successfully taken over and made Islam its own, thereby excluding the majority of Muslims and in the process pushing aside the great bulk of mainstream Islamic leadership and traditional teaching. It has worked at the level of sloganizing and symbolism, taking over the central identification of a Muslim and making it that of a follower of IS. But it has gone much further than that, creating a special language and a reading of history that enfold Muslims in a self-view that at once isolates them from non-Muslims by presenting them as victims of enmity and persecution and offers them the compensation of victory in a coming apocalypse followed by eternity in Paradise.

The very name of IS tells us this. Previously it was the Islamic State in Iraq and Syria. Now it is simply the Islamic State. A starker assertion of identity can scarcely be imagined. It is no accident that the United States, in its principal officers and representatives, from the President on down, and followed obediently by the media, insists on referring to IS as ISIL or on attaching the words "self-proclaimed" or "so-called" to terms like IS or caliphate whenever it refers to them. The use of "ISIL," with its antique usage of Levant, as distinct from Syria, and "so-called" with its seeming rejection of the caliphal assertions of IS, actively denies IS even at that elementary level any claim to reality or legitimacy.

Countering the Islamic State

What does IS represent to the greater Muslim community? What does mainstream Islam have to counter the message of IS? How do most Muslims view IS? How do Muslim leaders, social and religious as well as political and military, see IS? One way, perhaps the best way, to find out is to see how these groups are reacting to IS—and in particular, how they are attempting to contain and counter, or to restrain and destroy, the effects of IS propaganda and terror in their own societies.

IS has the rare distinction of having a wall-to-wall coalition of opponents. It has managed to unite virtually everyone against it: Muslims and non-Muslims; Sunnis and Shi'is; the West and "the rest"; Russia and the United States; Muslims in Western countries like the United States and France as well as Muslims in Indonesia and Egypt; moderate Muslims everywhere alongside other radical Islamic movements such as al-Qaida and the Taliban.[4] It seems not only to relish standing alone but actively to seek out that role. In part, that is a necessary product of its ideology: a caliph, as we have seen, by definition demands universal jurisdiction and obedience. But in adopting a stance of whoever is not with us is against us IS has also taken on the risk of alienating too many potential supporters. While success on the battlefield may lead to greater support, that support is unlikely to outlast any military success. Moreover, another aspect of its ideology—the stress on hastening the Day of Judgment—may well turn further backing away entirely. Even among believers, eagerness for that Day is not unanimous.

Reaction to IS by Muslims and Islamic countries—expressed both in practical, military action and in ideological form—has varied. Several Islamic countries have contributed to fighting IS on the ground, but such action has been hesitant, slight, and largely ineffective. At Mosul, indiscipline and lack of motivation, inadequate training, and possibly sheer terror at the prospect of contact with IS combined to sweep away the advantages conferred on the Iraqi army by their up-to-date equipment, massive firepower, external support, a defensible position, and vast numerical superiority (30,000 Iraqi government troops as against 1,500 IS fighters): the Iraqi army broke and ran in the face of a few hundred IS fighters on Toyotas. The terror was understandable: the horrific death of a Jordanian pilot who fell into IS hands indicates something of the risks involved.

In March 2015, the secretary-general of the Arab League, Nabil Elaraby, recognizing the magnitude of the challenge, called for "the formation of a multi-purpose common Arab military force" to counter IS.[5] The call was boosted by General Sisi of Egypt, and shared aims with a number of other countries that have fought against IS or have suffered from its attacks; but with Elaraby stressing that participation must be voluntary, such a unified force has not materialized, and political divisions and rivalries are likely to keep it from being formed. The character of IS, as a military force and organization, with territorial domination in large areas of Syria and Iraq and reach far beyond—in Arab countries, other non-Arab Islamic countries, and still other countries in the West—means that military action aimed at degrading IS can only be one part of a much larger enterprise.[6]

Reactions

In February 2015, at the National Prayer Breakfast, President Obama reminded his audience how faith could be "twisted and misused in the name of evil" and referred to "those who seek to hijack religions for their own murderous ends."[7] The *New York Times* noted, however, in reporting on the event, that the President, not for the first time, refrained from labeling such attacks as those on *Charlie Hebdo* or the shootings in Paris "Islamic extremism," and that the speech "was Mr. Obama's latest effort to avoid branding recent violence by the Islamic State or those professing common cause with it as 'Islamic' extremism. His team said that doing so would play into the hands of the terrorist group and other terrorist organizations, legitimizing their message."[8] While none of that prevented the matter from becoming a minor election issue, the example of an earlier president who had used the word "crusade" unthinkingly was certainly on the minds of President Obama's speechwriters.[9] Earlier, he had expressed himself more trenchantly, if less accurately: "ISIL is not 'Islamic.'"[10]

The problem of identifying and defining the enemy is not simple. Are IS terrorists Islamic? Or are they merely using religion "for their own murderous ends"?[11] On May 11, 2016, when British police carried out a simulation of a terror attack in Manchester, the fake terrorist shouted the words Allahu Akbar, "Allah is great," several times. When the public took offense, the police apologized for using a phrase that "so vocally linked the exercise with Islam," even though, as they said, "The scenario for this exercise is based on a suicide attack by an extremist Daesh [ISIS] style organisation and the scenario writers have centred the circumstances around previous similar attacks of this nature, mirroring details of past events to make the situation as real life as possible for all those involved."[12]

Other leaders proffer sharper views. Sadiq Khan, elected as the first Muslim mayor of London in May 2016, said, referring very directly to Islamist terrorism: "I believe that British Muslims have a special role to play in tackling extremism. A special role not because we are more responsible than others—as some have wrongly claimed. But because we can be more effective at tackling extremism than anyone else. Our role must be to challenge extremist views wherever we encounter them."[13] As a parent, he is concerned, he says, about his teenage daughters. As a political rather than a religious leader, however, Khan could do no more than suggest that extremism of the IS variety needs to be confronted and resisted.

The strategies adopted by the British and French governments in the wake of IS attacks amount to little more than throwing money at the security agencies and urging private citizens, especially Muslims, to report extremist propaganda to the authorities.[14] And sometimes the money is not even new: in Britain, when Prime Minister David Cameron announced plans to spend 20 million pounds ($29 million) teaching immigrant Muslim women English to help them integrate into British society, a Green Party politician tweeted that he was just restoring funding that had been taken away in an earlier round of cuts.[15] More ambitiously, if with scarcely more generous funding, France announced a 40 million euro ($45 million) investment in a plan of action against jihadist radicalization in May 2016.[16] That project aimed to detect the early signs of radicalization, to improve the care given to victims of terrorism, and to encourage study of the problem—and in particular it envisaged the creation of special centers in every region of the country for the "reinsertion" into French society of youth who have been radicalized or who are in danger of becoming so. The first such center was to be in operation as early as the summer of 2016, taking care of penitents "of whose sincerity and will for reinsertion for the long term we are certain." The fifty new measures of the plan include funds for university research, with scholarships for studies on radicalization and terrorism, along with a permanent commission that will try to coordinate the links between such research and antiterrorism efforts by the government.[17]

The reality is that all such investment will be meaningless unless it is accompanied by internal Islamic counterattacks on IS.[18] Those are not lacking. They are also far from the kneejerk Uncle Tom–like rejections demanded of Muslims by so many non-Muslim rabble-rousers after every attack by IS. The counterattacks have been numerous, they have come from all over the world, they have been energetic and detailed and varied, they have stressed the unrepresentative character of IS and its actions, and they have confronted the problem head-on. In India in August 2014, for example, in the state of Kerala, a senior Muslim cleric, Sheikh Abu Bakr Ahmed Kanthapuram, the venerable general secretary of the All-India Sunni Jamiyyathul-Ulama, condemned IS and other such groups in unequivocal terms: "The militant groups among Muslims are causing harm to Islam in the false garb of Islamists. Any support or endorsement to the extremist and terrorist organizations goes completely against the Islamic sharia ... They are not just anti-Islamic but are enemies of humanity." He concluded, "I urge all the Muslims to condemn their activities and to pray for the people who suffer from their merciless activities."[19]

A year later, over one thousand leading Muslims from all over India (which has a Muslim population of more than 172 million, or roughly 10 percent of the world's Muslims) issued a collective condemnation in similar terms. The initiative brought together an immensely wide variety of representative Indian Islamic organizations and scholars. According to one report in the newspaper *The Hindu*, this was not a single fatwa but a collection of individual fatwas filling fifteen volumes, copies of which were sent to the secretary-general of the United Nations and to other world leaders. Unfortunately, all that seems to be known of the contents of this collection, and of the identities of those participating in it, is in the newspaper reports that say much the same as those of the Kerala fatwa published a year earlier.[20]

A ninety-minute film from Indonesia, which has the world's largest Muslim population—more than 200 million followers—takes a different tack. Aimed at a younger audience, and adopting some of the cinematic methods and skills of IS itself, it proffered a "relentless religious repudiation" of IS and marked the start of a campaign by Indonesian Muslims, under the leadership of the Nahdlatul Ulama, a vast organization of Muslims in that country, to combat IS ideology and propaganda.[21]

India and Indonesia, whose populations together represent one-fifth of the world's Muslims, have like many other countries been sources of recruitment to IS. But it is striking that the numbers who have gone to IS are very small: perhaps as many as seven hundred fighters from Indonesia have reached the Middle East (though not all of these have joined IS), while from India the current estimate seems to be a mere twenty-three.[22] The numbers are small to tiny, both absolutely and in terms of their relation to the total numbers of Muslims in the different countries. It is tempting to associate their size with the impact of local condemnation of the movement.

Britain offers a different picture, at least in statistical terms: in late 2014, six imams there issued a fatwa condemning both IS and the Asad regime in Syria and forbidding British Muslims to go to Syria to fight for either side, and stressing that "It is a moral obligation upon British Muslims to help the Syrian and Iraqi people without betraying their own societies." Like so many such documents, this one too condemns the barbarity of IS and its betrayal of Islamic teachings and past practice, and it too is buttressed by quotations from the Quran. Yet the number of fighters who have joined IS from Britain is said to be about 750, not dissimilar to the numbers and proportions coming from France and Germany.[23] Britain is not a Muslim-majority country and does not have a long Islamic history. Perhaps in India, with its long history of Islam and its vast Muslim population, and in Indonesia as a Muslim-majority country, local condemnation of IS means more in the eyes of potential recruits.

Two other reactions command attention here. They are significant because, like the great Indian fatwa initiative, they boast a large group of sponsors and, unlike the Indian initiative, these sponsors comprise an international group of leading Islamic scholars and institutions. Both attempt to give a united Islamic response not only to the challenge of IS but also to wider problems facing Islam in the modern world.

The first is the so-called Marrakesh Declaration. In January 2016 a number of Christian religious websites, followed soon afterward by the *New York Times*, publicized the release of a document calling for Islamic countries to protect their Christian minorities.[24] Though it does not mention IS by name, the Marrakesh Declaration is clearly a response to the excesses of IS in the area of inter-religious relations. It describes the "use of violence . . . as a tool for . . . imposing one's point of view"; and explains how the current situation has "enabled criminal groups to issue edicts attributed to Islam, but which, in fact, alarmingly distort its fundamental principles and goals in ways that have seriously harmed the population as a whole."

The effort being made here is instructive. It shows, first of all, in case that needed demonstration, that leading figures in religious and broadly intellectual circles in the Islamic world recognize a need for interfaith respect and seek ways to promote it. Secondly, it confirms that the barbaric treatment dealt out by IS to non-Muslims is rejected as non-Islamic by Muslims who are in different ways representative of their faith. The list of signatories to the declaration is long and includes people from all over the Islamic world, virtually all of them involved with legal and religious institutions whose authority gives added force to what they say here.

The Open Letter to al-Baghdadi

The weightiest and most sustained written expression to date of inner Islamic opposition to IS is the Open Letter to al-Baghdadi, dated September 19, 2014.[25] The Open Letter sets about its business in very organized fashion: it is a collaborative creation of more than a hundred Muslim religious dignitaries from all over the Islamic world, all leaders of religious scholarship and teaching in their various countries (to whom many more have been added in the time since its publication).[26] Its message, similar to that of the fatwas we have looked at, is laid out very formally, with the paragraphs of the letter numbered and ordered so as, first, to show how the writers see themselves as qualified and entitled to offer criticism of al-Baghdadi and IS; secondly, to demonstrate that al-Baghdadi and IS do not have the right qualifications to make legal judgments or define what is obligatory or forbidden in Islam; and thirdly, to show what is wrong with IS behavior and how it should be reformed. The impression of a business document or even a legal brief is strengthened by the presence of an "Executive Summary" listing the principal points of the Letter.[27]

The Open Letter presents several puzzles. It is cast as a letter but we have no way of knowing if it was ever sent to the caliph—we would wonder how it might have been delivered—or if he has ever seen and read it. Nor is it clear that al-Baghdadi is in fact the intended audience for the Letter. An open letter is generally intended for public consumption. A named addressee is rarely the real one; more often such an addressee is merely the hook on which the writer hangs an argument aimed at a wider audience. In this case, the formulation as an open letter shows that it is intended at least partly for a mass readership, composed of Muslims, in particular young ones potentially susceptible to IS propaganda. This is confirmed by the fact that the writers have also taken care to publish the Open Letter in a variety of languages.

Besides the original Arabic, and an accompanying English translation, the letter is available in German, Spanish, Bosnian, Hungarian, and Dutch, to which Turkish, Persian, and French have recently been added. The large number of versions indicates a desire for broad dissemination of the text, though the selection of languages suggests that new languages are added only as and when translators become available, rather than chosen strategically. The Marrakesh Declaration, too, was published in a curious, and in that case curiously limited, selection of versions: in addition to the original Arabic, it is available only in English, Italian, and Dutch.

Italian and Dutch are not the most obvious of languages for large audiences of young Muslims. More significantly, we do not have that document in Persian or Turkish, and neither the Marrakesh Declaration nor the Open Letter is available, to date at least, in such languages as Urdu, Malay, or Bahasa Indonesia, major languages of Muslims in the world today.

At the same time, the Open Letter addresses the caliph directly and in very formal and polite terms: "To Dr. Ibrahim Awwad al-Badri, alias 'Abu Bakr al-Baghdadi' and to the fighters and followers of the self-declared 'Islamic State.'" The word "alias," *laqab* in Arabic, carries none of the negative connotations that the word has in English. While the absence of any reference to al-Baghdadi as caliph, even as leader, and the description of the Islamic State as "self-declared" both indicate rejection of the claims of IS, the recognition of the addressee as having a doctorate and the overall formality of the address proffer politeness and even respect. The opening of what is technically a letter is similarly courteous: "Peace and the mercy of God be upon you." This tone is maintained throughout. Even though the caliph of the Islamic State is never called by that title, he is treated all through the document with kid gloves, rather as if he were what the New Testament calls an errant sheep.

The Open Letter sets out the conditions under which Islamic legal pronouncements may be issued and then proceeds to issue some. The writers construct their argument stone by stone, beginning systematically with fundamental generalities: only those with the necessary learning may issue fatwas, legal opinions; mastery of the Arabic language is a necessity; legal matters may not be simplified because, whatever casual reading of sources may suggest, a long tradition has introduced many complications that cannot be ignored; scholars may legitimately differ on legal matters; and, strikingly, it is necessary to consider the contemporary world—and not just look back to the foundational period of Islam—in deriving legal rulings. Not just anyone, in other words, however pious, may assume the right to give legal opinions. Qualifications are vital, and, especially in the modern world, opinions, even on legal matters, may differ.

Following this statement of general principles that define the qualifications that they themselves possess, the scholars proceed to list seventeen examples of IS behavior that they label forbidden. Most of these concern specific barbarities: killing the innocent; torture; killing aid workers and journalists; enslavement of captives; forcing people to convert to Islam; disfiguring the dead; mistreating Christians and other People of the Book, or Yazidis; denying women and children their rights; enacting such quranic punishments as cutting off hands; and destroying graves.[28] Others concern theological issues with a clear policy aspect to them: thus jihad is defined here as being only a defensive form of war, and IS is condemned for defining some of its enemies as non-Muslims, since the only way people can be so defined is if they themselves declare their unbelief. Similarly, "it is forbidden to attribute evil acts to God": this attacks the IS claim that their actions are supported by God and that it is He who is responsible for them. Finally, a small group of items deals with IS as a political movement with a religious basis: armed revolt against a ruler is forbidden unless he is an explicit unbeliever and prevents Muslims from praying; a caliphate cannot be declared without the consensus of all Muslims; it is permissible for Muslims to be loyal to the nations to which they belong; and, carrying this argument further, there is no obligation on Muslims to migrate, following the call of IS, to lands under Muslim control—which for IS means IS territory.

The implication—it is nowhere spelled out explicitly—is that these scholars have the requisite qualifications to make such definitions of what is legal and illegal, permitted and forbidden, in Islam. While the Open Letter thus issues what amounts to legal pronouncements—many of them are recast in the executive summary as explicit commands or prohibitions—it is noteworthy that the letter nowhere claims to be a fatwa. An open letter is not a fatwa.

Each of the topics is discussed in a paragraph or more, with elaborate arguments and citations of texts, often the Quran, supporting the writers' position. The impression of erudition is emphasized by an array of footnotes—sixty-five in all—that point to the work of other scholars, mainly from the first few centuries of Islam and all based solidly in Islamic tradition going back to the Prophet himself. As many as thirty or so early scholars and their works are cited here, alongside a few from the modern world.[29]

In arguing against IS practice, the writers of the Open Letter condemn outright the viciousness and brutality of IS. Nonetheless, they are engaged not just in moralizing but in legal discussion as well, and they see all that not simply as violence for violence's sake, but as a mistaken deduction from the teachings of the past. When an IS fighter asks people at a checkpoint how many prostrations are to be performed in a particular prayer and, on getting the wrong answer, kills the unfortunate respondents, the writers of the Open Letter urge that mercy is what the Prophet and Islamic tradition recommend.[30] Killing, extreme rejection of sinners, is rejected, and mercy preferred. But extreme interpretations of the sort that IS uses, though rejected by mainstream Islam these many centuries, have their place in the tradition, and it is for this reason both that IS reaches for them and practices them and that the writers of the Open Letter accept that they need to be discussed. That is not always a safe platform to stand on.

The language and style of the letter are simple and direct—recalling the common quranic refrain that the Quran itself is in "clear" Arabic—so that in theory the text is accessible to anyone literate in Arabic. But the Open Letter is constructed in the form of a legal argument, or learned article. It is not a popular sermon. It aims to persuade the mind, not appeal to the heart. At the very start of the letter, above the title, we find, in elaborately ornate and hard-to-read Arabic calligraphy, a quotation from the Quran: "Only those of his servants fear God who have knowledge" (*sura* 35:28). Those who read the letter face a choice—whose arguments are stronger, more persuasive? Who has the more powerful proofs?

In writing as they do, the authors of the Open Letter are taking a big risk. They are treating their opponent as a peer and addressing him with politeness and respect. They are claiming that erudition is what counts, and are then proceeding to swap interpretations of the Quran and of legal matters in Islam with him, and show off their erudition as against his, even as they imply that he and his advisers are not qualified to make such judgments. In doing all this they are granting potential legitimacy to some of the ideology and judgments that come from IS—for example, in the case of the correct number of prostrations for specific prayers—and admitting the possibility that IS laws and rules might, just might, be rooted in the same texts and arguments and manners of thinking as their own. They are recognizing that IS has some sort of standing within Islam, some sort of qualification, even if inadequate, to be making the kinds of demands that it is making. They are accepting that IS has a place within the shade of Islam, even perhaps taking up the challenge that IS is making on the intellectual level.

Granting that IS has a place within the shade of Islam is not, in fact, so extreme a position as it might appear. Regardless of President Obama's denial that ISIL is Islamic, the act of *takfir*, or declaring someone to be not a Muslim, is very rare in the Sunni world. Historically, Sunnis have been reluctant to practice what we know as excommunication and have made great efforts to avoid doing it. In the case of IS too, what we are witnessing is a preference to retain people within the fold of Islam, to draw them back to the true path. But doing so comes at a price: recognition of IS and its followers as Islamic.

IS and the World's Muslims

IS uses social media; it does not just issue leaflets and publish messages, using the Internet as a glorified newspaper or a press office. The group knows and understands how the Internet works and how to exploit modern media to its own ends. It directs its propaganda at a carefully selected set of audiences. Depending on the particular message of the day, its target audience is not just disaffected young Muslims, at home and abroad, but the entire Western world. It has created a brand that sells, with a name and packaging that attract especially its principal target audience. The movement has been very creative, not just in terms of its especially cruel modes of killing or the "slick" production values of the videos with which it publicizes its horrors and attracts its public. It also produces vast amounts of material in a variety of forms that it makes widely available via the Internet. And it has learned how to dominate the news cycle. Its latest production is an online app for the Arabic ABC that uses the alphabet to teach an IS message: B is for gun (*bundukiyya* in Arabic), D is for tank (*dabbaba* in Arabic), S for sword (*sayf* in Arabic), and so on.[31]

All of this IS propaganda is largely incomprehensible to its opponents. We cannot measure the effect of IS propaganda, beyond attempts to count recruits who travel to Syria to join the ranks. It is harder still to measure the effect of the erudite reactions by mainstream Muslim leaders. But the competition is unequal: on one side are the gray-haired old men with learning as deep as their beards are long; on the other are Internet and Android apps for the Arabic ABC. The old men have their erudition and the tomes of their medieval predecessors; IS has the practices of old and the promise of Dabiq.

Notes

Quran quotations generally follow A. J. Arberry, *The Koran Interpreted* (London: Allen and Unwin, 1955), which is frequently reprinted by Oxford University Press. Works frequently cited have been identified by the following abbreviations:

26 Unseen Documents	Aymenn Jawad al-Tamimi, online collection of 26 previously unseen IS documents, http://www.aymennjawad.org/17757/the-archivist–26-unseen-islamic-state
32 Fatwas	Cole Bunzel, online posting at *Jihadica: Documenting the Global Jihad*; see http://www.jihadica.com/32-islamic-state-fatwas/
Archive	Aymenn Jawad al-Tamimi, online collection of IS documents, http://www.aymennjawad.org/2015/01/archive-of-islamic-state-administrative-documents (A–12J); http://www.aymennjawad.org/2016/01/archive-of-islamic-state-administrative-documents–1 (12K–22Z); http://www.aymennjawad.org/2016/08/archive-of-islamic-state-administrative-documents–2 (23A–23Z)
EI²	*Encyclopaedia of Islam*, 2nd ed. (Leiden: Brill, 1954–2005).
Fatwas on Jihad and Slavery	Aymenn Jawad al-Tamimi, online collection "Fatwas on Jihad and Slavery," http://www.aymennjawad.org/17879/the-archivist-unseen-islamic-state-fatwas-on
Health Department	Aymenn Jawad al-Tamimi, online collection "Health Department," http://www.aymennjawad.org/17775/the-archivist-critical-analysis-of-the-islamic

Ninawa I   Aymenn Jawad al-Tamimi, online collection of IS state
                   administration documents "Ninawa I," http://www.
                   aymennjawad.org/15946/aspects-of-islamic-state-is-
                   administration-in
Ninawa II   Aymenn Jawad al-Tamimi, online collection of IS state
                   administration documents "Ninawa II," http://www.
                   aymennjawad.org/15952/aspects-of-islamic-state-is-
                   administration-in
Ninawa III   Aymenn Jawad al-Tamimi, online collection of IS state
                   administration documents "Ninawa III," http://www.
                   aymennjawad.org/15961/aspects-of-islamic-state-is-
                   administration-in

Introduction

1. See Michael Cook, *Ancient Religions, Modern Politics: The Islamic Case in Comparative Perspective* (Princeton, NJ: Princeton University Press, 2014), though Judaism is strikingly absent from his discussion.
2. William Shepard, "What Is 'Islamic Fundamentalism'?" *Studies in Religion* 17 (1988): 5–26.
3. For reactions to Darwin and Darwinism in (Arab) Islam see Najm A. Bezirgan, "The Islamic World," in Thomas F. Glick, ed., *The Comparative Reception of Darwinism* (Austin: University of Texas Press, 1974), pp. 375–387; Pew Research Center, Religion and Public Life, *The World's Muslims: Religion, Politics and Society*, April 30, 2013, at http://www.pewforum.org/2013/04/30/the-worlds-muslims-religion-politics-society-overview/ (accessed May 30, 2016), esp. pp. 132–133 and 181 (though it is instructive to compare this with Pew Research Center, "Public's Views on Human Evolution," December 2013 [at http://www.pewforum.org/files/2013/12/Evolution–12–30.pdf], for the United States); and especially Uriya Shavit, "The Evolution of Darwin to a 'Unique Christian Species' in Modernist Apologetic Arab-Islamic Thought," *Islam and Christian-Muslim Relations* 26, no. 1 (2015): 17–32. For some medieval background, see Mehmet Bayrakdar, "Al-Jahiz and the Rise of Biological Evolutionism," *Islamic Quarterly* 27, no. 2 (1983): 149–155, which is perhaps overstated; and for the Ottoman period, Alper Bilgili, "An Ottoman Response to Darwinism: Ismail Fenni on Islam and Evolution," *British Journal for the History of Science* 48, no. 4 (December 2015): 565–582. See now especially Marwa Elshakry, *Reading Darwin in Arabic, 1860–1950* (Chicago: University of Chicago Press, 2016).
4. See especially Pew Research Center, Religion and Public Life, *The World's Muslims: Unity and Diversity*, August 9, 2012, at http://www.pewforum.org/2012/08/09/the-worlds-muslims-unity-and-diversity-executive-summary/ (accessed May 30, 2016); Pew Research Center,

Religion and Public Life, *The World's Muslims: Religion, Politics and Society.*

5. For more on the importance of loudspeakers and broadcasting in Islam today, see particularly Brian Larkin, "Techniques of Inattention: The Mediality of Loudspeakers in Nigeria," *Anthropological Quarterly* 87, no. 4 (Fall 2014): 989–1015. Other papers on this topic in the same volume, subtitled "Islamic Sounds and the Politics of Listening," are also well worth reading, esp. the "Introduction," by Jeanette S. Jouili and Annette Moors, pp. 977–988; Isaac A. Weiner, "Calling Everyone to Pray: Pluralism, Secularism and the Adhān in Hamtramck, Michigan," pp. 1049–1077; and Jeanette S. Jouili, "Refining the Umma in the Shadow of the Republic: Performing Arts and New Islamic Audio-Visual Landscapes in France," pp. 1079–1104. See also Lauren E. Osborne, "The Experience of the Recited Qur'an," *International Journal of Middle East Studies* 48 (2016): 124–128.

6. "Discourage" is a relative term. The *New York Times* carried a report on Ramadan in Indonesia, offering insight into differing levels of "discouragement," ranging from mere neighborly disapproval to crowd violence to legal challenges; see Joe Cochrane, "Raid on Indonesian Food Stall Stokes Fears of Fundamentalism," *New York Times*, July 10, 2016, at http://www.nytimes.com/2016/07/10/world/asia/indonesia-ramadan-raid-islam-fundamentalism.html (accessed July 10, 2016).

7. For a striking example, see the discussion of prayer as a religious-cum-political activity in Aaron Rock-Singer, "Prayer and the Islamic Revival: A Timely Challenge," *International Journal of Middle East Studies* 48 (2016): 293–312.

8. For the figures see Pew Research Center, Religion and Public Life, *The World's Muslims: Unity and Diversity*, p. 46. Uzbekistan lay at 9 percent, Albania at 5. Azerbaijan strikes several odd notes in the Pew surveys. Its population is almost entirely Muslim, Shi'i rather than Sunni, and its figures for practice are generally very low, but it also reports a very high figure for the importance of religion to people in general: 36 percent said it was very important and a further 37 percent somewhat important, comparable to other countries in the region, where reported practice is much higher (p. 131).

9. See ibid., pp. 43–44.

10. For the figures, see ibid., p. 50.

11. Ibid., p. 79.

12. For a sensitive expression of this point, see Richard Ettinghausen, "Arabic Epigraphy: Communication or Symbolic Affirmation?" in *Near Eastern Numismatics, Iconography, Epigraphy and History: Studies in Honor of George C. Miles*, ed. Dickran K. Kouymjian (Beirut: American University in Beirut, 1974), pp. 297–317.

13. Pew Research Center, Religion and Public Life, *The World's Muslims: Unity and Diversity*, p. 54.

14. See Archive, specimens N, Q, 3L, 5B, 5J, 6A, 9S, 11B.
15. See Royal Embassy of Saudi Arabia, Washington, DC, *The Basic Law of Governance*, at http://www.constitutionnet.org/files/the_basic_law_of_ governance.pdf (accessed June 12, 2016). As the country's legal system shows, this is more a statement of aspiration than a fully worked out legal position.
16. See Mark Tran, "Dutch Woman Arrested in Qatar after Reporting Rape to Appear in Court," *Guardian*, June 12, 2016, at https://www.theguardian. com/world/2016/jun/12/dutch-woman-arrested-qatar-after-reporting- rape-court-doha-hotel (accessed June 12, 2016). The woman in question was both a foreigner and, apparently, a non-Muslim. Al-Jazeera reported on June 13, 2016, that the woman had been convicted and given a one- year suspended sentence. She was to be deported to Holland. The *New York Times*, June 14, 2016, added that she had been detained for three months and also fined nearly 850 dollars. The man she accused of raping her was convicted, but not of rape, only of having sex outside marriage. He was to be given one hundred lashes for that crime, with an additional forty lashes for public drunkenness. He was also to be deported. Because he was apparently a Syrian, that may turn out to be the worst punishment; see http://www.aljazeera.com/news/2016/06/qatar-dutch-woman-alleged- rape-guilty-adultery–160613073219724.html (accessed June 13, 2016). According to the *New York Times*, such cases are an added source of con- cern to human rights groups, because Qatar is to host the World Cup in 2022.
17. Pew Research Center, "The Divide over Islam and National Laws in the Muslim World," April 2016, at http://www.pewglobal.org/files/2016/04/ Pew-Research-Center-Political-Islam-Report-FINAL-April–27–2016. pdf (accessed June 8, 2016). For similar results, see Pew Research Center, Religion and Public Life, *The World's Muslims: Religion, Politics and Society*, pp. 46–48, 201.
18. Harriet Sherwood, "People of No Religion Outnumber Christians in England and Wales—Study," *Guardian*, May 23, 2016; and Stephen Bullivant, *Contemporary Catholicism in England and Wales: A Statistical Report Based on Recent British Social Attitudes Survey Data*, Twickenham, St Mary's University, Benedict XVI Centre for Religion and Society, Catholic Research Forum Reports, no. 1, 2016, at http://www.stmarys. ac.uk/benedict-xvi/docs/2016-may-contemporary-catholicism-report.pdf (accessed May 30, 2016).
19. See Pew Research Center, "U.S. Public Becoming Less Religious," November 3, 2015, at http://www.pewforum.org/files/2015/11/201.11.03_ RLS_II_full_report.pdf (accessed June 8, 2016).
20. Current pressure to de-secularize Aya Sofya (formerly the Greek church of Hagia Sophia), on the pattern of the de-secularization of the Aya Sofya in Trabzon, exemplifies this. See for Trabzon Amberin Zaman, "Another

Byzantine Church Becomes Mosque in Turkey," *Al-Monitor*, August 7, 2013, at http://www.al-monitor.com/pulse/originals/2013/08/another-byzantine-church-becomes-a-mosque.html (accessed July 10, 2016). For Istanbul see "Muezzin Recites Azan from Inside Istanbul's Hagia Sophia for First Time in 85 Years," *Daily Sabah* (Istanbul) July 2, 2016, at http://www.dailysabah.com/istanbul/2016/07/02/muezzin-recites-azan-from-inside-istanbuls-hagia-sophia-for-first-time-in-85-years (accessed July 10, 2016). A video of the event is available at http://portalsatu.com/read/news/video-azan-berkumandang-di-ayasofya-istanbul-2-juli-2016-setelah-85-tahun-dilarang-14043 (accessed July 10, 2016).

21. On Islamic gardens, see D. Fairchild Ruggles, *Islamic Gardens and Landscapes* (Philadelphia: University of Pennsylvania Press, 2008). The supply of virginal women seems to presuppose exclusively male applicants for entry.

22. For a look at their families, see Shiraz Maher and Peter R. Neumann, *Pain, Confusion, Anger, and Shame: The Stories of Islamic State Families*, International Centre for the Study of Radicalisation and Political Violence, 2016, at http://icsr.info/wp-content/uploads/2016/04/ICSR-Report-Pain-Confusion-Anger-and-Shame-The-Stories-of-Islamic-State-Families1.pdf (accessed June 29, 2016). See also Peter R. Neumann, *Victims, Perpetrators, Assets: The Narratives of Islamic State Defectors*, International Centre for the Study of Radicalisation and Political Violence, 2015, at http://icsr.info/wp-content/uploads/2015/09/ICSR-Report-Victims-Perpertrators-Assets-The-Narratives-of-Islamic-State-Defectors.pdf (accessed July 4, 2016).

23. Samuel P. Huntington, *The Clash of Civilizations and the Remaking of World Order* (New York: Simon and Schuster, 1996).

24. For the seizure and two-week siege of the Grand Mosque, see Joseph A. Kechichian, "The Role of the Ulama in the Politics of an Islamic State: The Case of Saudi Arabia," *International Journal of Middle East Studies* 18 (1986): 53–71; Joseph A. Kechichian, "Islamic Revivalism and Change in Saudi Arabia: Juhaymān al-'Utaybī's 'Letters' to the Saudi People," *Muslim World* 80 (1990): 1–16; Thomas Hegghammer and Stéphane Lacroix, "Rejectionist Islamism in Saudi Arabia: The Story of Juhayman al-'Utaybi Revisited," *International Journal of Middle East Studies* 39 (2007): 103–122; Yaroslav Trofimov, *The Siege of Mecca: The Forgotten Uprising in Islam's Holiest Shrine and the Birth of al Qaeda* (New York: Doubleday, 2007).

25. Thus Michael Cook, *Commanding Right and Forbidding Wrong in Islamic Thought* (Cambridge, Eng.: Cambridge University Press, 2000), p. 192, n. 263, points out that Juhayman's tract on *al-amr bil-maʿruf*, "On Commanding Right," is in fact largely an abridgment of that on the same subject by the great thirteenth- to fourteenth-century scholar Ibn Taymiyya.

26. Similarly, following the IS-claimed attack on a café in Dhaka in July 2016, the son of the Bangladeshi prime minister, Sajeeb Wazed Joy, wrote on his Facebook page, "I have been trying to think of what to write but I have been at a loss for words. It was a terrible, heinous attack. These killers were not Muslims. Terrorists have no religion." The internal Islamic context, unlike that in which U.S. presidents operate, means that such statements carry a potential religious significance going beyond the demands of immediate political advantage and rhetorical hyperbole; see http://www.risingbd.com/english/gulshan-caf%C3%A9-attackers-not-muslims-joy/36639 (accessed July 4, 2016).

27. See a White House announcement on the human costs, in terms of collateral deaths, involved in some drone activity: https://www.whitehouse.gov/the-press-office/2016/07/01/fact-sheet-executive-order-us-policy-pre-post-strike-measures-address, issued July 1, 2016, with Charlie Savage and Scott Shane, "U.S. Reveals Death Toll from Airstrikes outside War Zone," *New York Times*, July 1, 2016, at http://www.nytimes.com/2016/07/02/world/us-reveals-death-toll-from-airstrikes-outside-of-war-zones.html?_r=0; also *The Drone Papers*, "a cache of secret documents detailing the inner workings of the U.S. military's assassination program," revealed by a whistleblower, that give a less rosy picture, available at https://theintercept.com/drone-papers/ (all accessed July 4, 2016).

28. A large number of others both from IS itself and from earlier incarnations of the organization are available, in Arabic and in English, on the website of the Combating Terrorism Center at West Point, at https://www.ctc.usma.edu/isil-resources. Navigation is tricky, but worthwhile. *Al-Monitor* recently reported on the capture and its own examination of many more, of administrative and operational character; see Mahmut Bozarslan, "Turkish Court Documents Reveal New Details about IS Operations," *Al-Monitor*, July 21, 2016, at http://www.al-monitor.com/pulse/originals/2016/07/turkey-syria-isis-in-court-documents.html?utm_source=Boomtrain&utm_medium=manual&utm_campaign=20160722&bt (accessed July 23, 2016), but these documents do not seem to have become publicly available.

29. See Armin Rosen, "The Remarkable Story of a Rising Terrorism Analyst Who Got Too Close to His Subjects," *Business Insider*, July 22, 2014, http://www.businessinsider.com/tamimi-2014-7 (accessed December 2, 2015), cited at Charles C. Caris and Samuel Reynolds, *ISIS Governance in Syria*, Washington, Institute for the Study of War, Middle East Security Report, 22, http://www.understandingwar.org/sites/default/files/ISIS_Governance.pdf (accessed December 10, 2016), 2014:31, n.14.

30. Al-Tamimi adds new documents to the file from time to time. They are in several series, numbered consecutively A-Z, 1A-1Z, 2A-2Z, … 10A-10Z, 11A-11P … 17E by July 2016. There is no 7K.

31. See, e.g., S. D. Goitein, *A Mediterranean Society: The Jewish Communities of the Arab World as Portrayed in the Documents of the Cairo Geniza*, 6 vols. (Berkeley: University of California Press, 1967–1993), with a useful introduction at vol. 1, pp. 1–28; and for the history of the Geniza and its study, Adina Hoffman and Peter Cole, *Sacred Trash: The Lost and Found World of the Cairo Geniza* (New York: Nextbook, Schocken, 2011).

32. They are referred to here as "Archive," "Fatwas on Jihad and Slavery," "Health Department," "Ninawa I," "Ninawa II," "Ninawa III," "26 Unseen Documents", and "32 Fatwas" (for the websites, see the Abbreviations list). Several other smaller items are also used here.

33. Omar, or Abu Omar, al-Shishani ("the Chechen"), has been reported dead several times, most recently in July 2016. As it was IS that announced his death on this occasion, it may well be the truth.

34. For one egregious example of the daily dose problem, see Chapter 3.

35. So too the al-Amq news agency, very closely associated with IS, whose name, as we shall see, echoes that of a place in the hadith mentioning Dabiq (see Chapter 7).

36. See, e.g., "Islamic State Video Suspect Thought to Be Briton Siddhartha Dhar," http://www.bbc.com/news/uk–35228558 (accessed January 6, 2016).

37. References to the *New York Times* generally carry web references. It should be noted that the dates of the appearance of articles in the web publication, as well as their titles, do not always match those in the print version of the paper. Thus, http://www.nytimes.com/2015/11/27/world/asia/indonesia-islam-nahdlatul-ulama.html?_r=0 is an article entitled "From Indonesia, a Muslim Challenge to the Ideology of the Islamic State" in the web edition of the newspaper dated November 26, 2015. It is the same article as that appearing in the print issue dated November 26, 2015, under the title "Muslims in Indonesia Challenge ISIS Ideology."

Chapter One. Caliphate

1. The text of the announcement is available online, at https://ia902505.us.archive.org/28/items/poa_25984/EN.pdf in various languages (accessed December 6, 2016). The English version lacks the introductory *Basmala* or invocation, *bism Allah al-Rahman al-Rahim*, "In the Name of God the Compassionate the Merciful." This seems to be a slip. The Arabic has it and it occurs in some (but not all) of the translations.

2. Einhard, *Vita Karoli Magni*, section 16 (Einhard and Notker the Stammerer, *Two Lives of Charlemagne*, trans. Lewis Thorpe [Harmondsworth, Eng.: Penguin, 1969], p. 70); Einhard, *Vita Karoli Magni: Das Leben Karls des Grossen*, Lateinisch/Deutsch, trans. Evelyn Scherabon

Firchow (Stuttgart: Philipp Reclam Jun., 1981), p. 34. As the wording shows, the true story of the gift of an elephant is shaped by the Latin writer in such a way as to magnify Charlemagne by demonstrating the honor in which he is held by the great caliph of Baghdad.

3. It is under this title, in various languages, that the document can be found on the Web.

4. The commentator is al-Qurtubi, who died in 1272.

5. For Taha Husayn's autobiography, *al-Ayyam* ("The Days"), see *The Days: Taha Hussein; His Autobiography in Three Parts*, trans. E. H. Paxton (Cairo: American University in Cairo Press, 2001). See also Fedwa Malti-Douglas, *Blindness and Autobiography: Al-Ayyām of Ṭāhā Ḥusayn* (Princeton, NJ: Princeton University Press, 1988).

6. See, e.g., Kristina Nelson, *The Art of Reciting the Qur'an* (Austin: University of Texas Press, 1985).

7. We might think of some radio and TV channels in the United States with Bible readings and evangelical preaching as a sort of parallel, but these are essentially minority media. The Quran is a major everyday presence in the Islamic world.

8. See, e.g., Hillel Frisch, "Nationalizing a Universal Text: The Qur'an in Arafat's Rhetoric," *Middle Eastern Studies* 41 (2005): 321–336.

9. See, e.g., *EI²*, IX, pp. 504–505, art. 'Shura,' section 1 (C. E. Bosworth), and p. 506, art. 'Shura,' section 3 (A. Ayalon).

10. See David J. Wasserstein, *The Caliphate in the West: An Islamic Political Institution in the Iberian Peninsula* (Oxford, Eng.: Clarendon Press, 1993), p. 11, with references.

11. David Wasserstein, *The Rise and Fall of the Party-Kings: Politics and Society in Islamic Spain, 1002–1086* (Princeton, NJ: Princeton University Press, 1985); and *Caliphate in the West*. It is noteworthy that *servus servorum Dei*—"servant of the servants of God"—is one of the titles used by popes.

12. Al-Mawardi, *The Ordinances of Government: Al-Ahkam al-Sultaniyya w'al-Wilayat al-Diniyya*, trans. Professor Wafaa H. Wahba (Reading, U.K.: Garnet Publishing, The Center for Muslim Contribution to Civilization, 1996), p. 4.

13. For the battle see *The Life of Muhammad: A Translation of Ibn Isḥāq's Sīrat Rasūl Allāh*, with introduction and notes by A. Guillaume (Lahore, Karachi: Oxford University Press Pakistan Branch, 1955), pp. 289–360; *EI²*, I, pp. 867–868 (W. Montgomery Watt).

14. Such happy coincidences do occur: the father of the Prophet Muhammad was named Abd Allah. Given the rich polytheistic theophoric onomastic possibilities of the time, this was very fortunate.

15. For the habit of using simply the given name, and deliberately avoiding the *kunya*, as a form of humiliation, in addressing non-Arabs in the classical period of Islam, see Ignaz Goldziher, *Muslim Studies (Muhammedanische Studien)*, ed. S. M. Stern, trans. C. R. Barber and S. M. Stern (London:

George Allen & Unwin, 1967–1971), vol. 1, p. 242. See also Ignaz Goldziher, "La *kunya* selon la loi musulmane" ("Etudes islamologiques d'Ignaz Goldziher," traduction analytique [II] VIII par G.-H. Bousquet), *Arabica* 7 (1960): 113–115, which originally appeared in *Zeitschrift der deutschen morgenländischen Gesellschaft* 51 (1897): 256–258; and Milka Levy-Rubin, *Non-Muslims in the Early Islamic Empire: From Surrender to Coexistence* (Cambridge, Eng.: Cambridge University Press, 2011), pp. 149–150.

16. Or simply some other name: the Prophet Muhammad, who had a son called Ibrahim, had the *kunya* Abu al-Qasim.

17. For the use of Abu Bakr as a given name, not as a *kunya*, see Jacqueline Sublet, *Le voile du nom: Essai sur le nom propre arabe* (Paris: Presses universitaires de France, 1991), pp. 53–56. In the huge medieval biographical dictionary *Siyar Alam al-Nubala*, of the Damascene scholar al-Dhahabi (1274–1348), for example, there are fifteen biographees with the given name Bakr as opposed to thirty-two with the given name (not the *kunya*) Abu Bakr.

18. That Abu Bakr should be seen here as an extra name and not as a *kunya* is suggested also by a statistical observation: Ibrahim as a name is very commonly accompanied by the *kunya* Abu Ishaq, "father of Isaac," reflecting the biblical relationship. In al-Dhahabi's *Siyar Alam al-Nubala*, for example, we find a total of 135 men named Ibrahim who have a *kunya* (not all have one; not all are known). Of these fully 111, or 82 percent, have the *kunya* Abu Ishaq, while the remaining twenty-four share some eighteen different *kunyas*. None has the *kunya* Abu Bakr. In other words, what this little exercise tells us is that some names carry with them almost automatic *kunyas*. And from that it follows that, if an Ibrahim carries a *kunya* other than Abu Ishaq, or is known by what looks like a *kunya* other than Abu Ishaq, we are justified in asking whether that choice of *kunya* can tell us something, about for example political or religious attitudes or intentions. In the present case, the adoption of the name-form Abu Bakr, which happens to be a given name but in the shape of a *kunya*, suggests very strongly that Ibrahim, as caliph, wishes to stress a connection not only with early caliphs as a class but also with the very first caliph of all, that first successor to the Prophet. Another example of this, showing that *kunyas* can change reflecting their bearers' choices and specific intentions, occurs in the case of an early Abbasid caliph, al-Mamun (who ruled 813–833): his *kunya* was Abu al-Abbas. "But when he became caliph, his *kunya* became Abu Jafar." Abu Jafar was the *kunya* of the powerful second caliph of the Abbasid house, al-Mansur (who reigned 754–775), al-Mamun's great grandfather. We should see this as a deliberate choice intended to echo al-Mansur's *kunya* and remind people of the new caliph's relationship to his great predecessor (see al-Dhahabi, *Siyar Alam al-Nubala*, 25 vols. [Beirut: Muassasat al-Risala, 1981–1988], vol. 10, pp. 272–290, and p. 274, n. 72).

19. See Bernard Lewis, "The Regnal Titles of the First Abbasid Caliphs," *Dr Zakir Husain Presentation Volume*, New Delhi, pp. 13–22, reprinted in Bernard Lewis, *Studies in Classical and Ottoman Islam (7th–16th Centuries)* (London, 1976).

20. Sublet, *Le voile du nom*, pp. 84–86.

21. Pierre Guichard, "*Al-Mansūr* and *al-Mansūr bi-Llāh?* Les *laqab/s* des Amirides d'après la numismatique et les documents officiels," *Archéologie Islamique* 5 (1995): 47–53.

22. Wasserstein, *Rise and Fall*.

23. See D. Gershon Lewental, "'Saddam's Qadisiyyah': Religion and History in the Service of State Ideology in Ba'thi Iraq," *Middle Eastern Studies* 50, no. 6 (2014): 891–910, at 900, n. 84. For more on Saddam's use of religiously charged titles, see p. 907, n. 46.

24. David J. Wasserstein, "Ibn Hazm on Names Meet for Caliphs: The Textual History of a Medieval Arabic Onomastic Catalogue and the Transmission of Knowledge in Classical Islam," *Cahiers d'Onomastique Arabe, 1988–1992* (1993): 61–88.

25. Al-Mas'udi, *Kitab al-Tanbih wal-Ishraf*, ed. M. J. de Goeje (Leiden: E. J. Brill, 1893), pp. 335–337; Maçoudi, *Le livre de l'avertissement et de la révision*, trans. Baron Carra de Vaux (Paris: Imprimerie Nationale, 1896), pp. 431–434.

26. For these coins see David J. Wasserstein, "The Coinage of the Islamic State," *Israel Numismatic Research* 11 (2016): 181–204.

27. For some important partial exceptions to this statement, see Patricia Crone and Martin Hinds, *God's Caliph: Religious Authority in the First Centuries of Islam*, University of Cambridge Oriental Publications no. 37 (Cambridge, Eng.: Cambridge University Press, 1986), p. 7.

28. See David J. Wasserstein, "Khalifa—A Word Study," in *Words in Time: Diachronic Semantics from Different Points of View*, ed. Regine Eckardt, Klaus von Heusinger, and Christoph Schwarze, Mouton de Gruyter Trends in Linguistics Studies and Monographs, 143 (Berlin: Mouton de Gruyter, 2003), pp. 115–133. For the argument that the title was originally "khalifat Allah," rather than "khalifat rasul Allah," see Crone and Hinds, *God's Caliph*.

29. A. J. Wensinck, *Concordance et Indices de la Tradition Musulmane: Les Six livres, le Musnad d'al-Dārimī, le Muwaṭṭa' de Mālik, le Musnad de Aḥmad Ibn Ḥanbal*, 8 vols. (Leiden: Brill, 1943), vol. 7, p. 5, referring to the old edition, vols. 4:273; 5:404 (new ed.: Beirut, Dar Ihya al-Turath al-Arabi, 9 vols., 1991, vols. 6:560, no. 22922; and 5:341–342, no. 17939).

30. For Hudhayfa ibn al-Yaman, see al-Dhahabi, *Siyar Alam al-Nubala*, 2:361–369, no. 76.

31. For al-Numan ibn Bashir, see al-Dhahabi, *Siyar Alam al-Nubala*, 3:411–412, no. 66. He lived from 624 to 684, governed Kufa for the caliph Muawiya, then served as *qadi* (judge) of Damascus, and finally as governor of Hims.

32. The translation "cruel" here is from a rare root in Arabic, with meanings like "biting." The precise meaning here is uncertain, but it must mean

something like cruel, biting, cunning. For "insolence/haughtiness" see Edward William Lane, *An Arabic-English Lexicon* (London: Williams and Norgate, 1863–1893). Page 374 of Lane's work has a generalized version of this, taken from the medieval al-Zamakhshari and the *Taj al-Arus*, which he translates as follows: "There has been no prophetic office but a kingly office has succeeded in its place through some one's self-magnification, pride, haughtiness or insolence," and explains thus: but kings have magnified themselves, or behaved proudly or haughtily or insolently, after it. As can be seen, as well as suggesting that it was by means of their haughtiness that those kings reached their office, which the Arabic does not support, the generalization greatly changes, and weakens, the point of the hadith.

33. Hudhayfa ibn al-Yaman, who is said to have transmitted the first version of this hadith, died, as we have seen, in 656, "forty nights after" the third caliph, Uthman. He thus did not see any of the later historical developments alluded to in the second version of the hadith, but he did see the period of the first three of the Rightly Guided caliphs and his version of the hadith makes excellent sense as a description of the (very recent) past.

Chapter Two. Administration

1. Salman Rushdie, *Two Years Eight Months and Twenty-Eight Nights: A Novel* (New York: Random House, 2015), p. 209.

2. Archive, specimen 7V.

3. Ninawa I, specimen A.

4. Darwin, along with much of modern science, is to be done away with. See the Introduction. The similarity to some Texan ideas in education should come as little surprise.

5. 26 Unseen Documents, specimen H. These maps should be of particular interest, when they become available, for how they indicate international boundaries and sovereignties. Maps are a source of special upset in many contexts. For examples see http://palwatch.org/main.aspx?fi=413&fld_id=556&doc_id=4928, which illustrates Palestinian erasure of Israel; and http://www.mfa.gov.il/MFA/AboutIsrael/Maps/Pages/Israel-Size-and-Dimension.aspx (the website of the Ministry of Foreign Affairs of Israel), showing "Israel—Size and Dimension," where the West Bank (Judea and Samaria), officially not part of Israel, is in a very slightly different color from Israel proper—but the Golan Heights, in effect annexed by Israel in 1981, appears in what seems to be the same color. (It is but fair to add that the website carries a note to the effect that the "map is for illustrative purposes only and should not be considered authoritative," though one might have expected the Ministry of Foreign Affairs to be fairly authoritative.) (Both websites accessed December 6, 2016.)

6. 26 Unseen Documents, specimen K; undated but after the IS capture of Palmyra in May 2015.

7. See, for exam timetables, Ninawa I, Archive, specimens T, U, 2E, 2F, 2G, 4C, and 7L, as well as 4A (an examination card), 8R (how to deal with problems), 9M, 9W, and 10X; for registration, Archive, specimens F, 2Y, 3G (for girls), 8V, 9F, and 9H; for term dates, Archive, specimens H and 7M; for (re-)opening of kindergartens, etc., Archive, specimens 2W and 8B; for application forms, Archive, specimens 3I, 8G, as well as 8J (a form for indicating subject preferences), 9O (similar), 8H (helpful advice for filling in forms), and 9N; and, for entry by strangers into schools, Archive, specimen V.

8. Archive, specimen Y.

9. For the textbooks, see Archive, specimens 1X (mathematics and Arabic language), 2O (Grade 1, creed and Islamic jurisprudence), and 3M, 3N, 3O, 3P; for the elementary school reader, see Archive, specimen 6X.

10. See Archive, specimens 10C, 10D, and 10E, "Prices for Printing Islamic State" textbooks.

11. Archive, specimen 1W.

12. Archive, specimens L, 3A, 5D, 5K, 5A deal with sharia sessions for teachers, training, preparation, doctrinal instruction of teachers, and a "meeting on reforms." The parallel with the Cultural Revolution in China cannot be ignored.

13. Archive, specimens Z, 1V, 3B, 3C, 3D, 4U, and 5N (the last two both for women).

14. For the firing of teachers, see Archive, specimen 4T; for job announcements for teachers, see Archive, specimens 3J, 4O.

15. This may be the same as the Ramadi General Hospital. In early January 2016, it was reported that IS had "detonated explosives on the ground floor of the Ramadi General Hospital, the largest in the province, damaging the building as security forces approached" (*New York Times*, January 8, 2016; see also http://www.iraqinews.com/iraq-war/isis-detonates-large-parts-ramadi-general-hospital/ (accessed December 6, 2016).

16. Archive, specimens 4B, 5I, 8O, 10Q, 10A.

17. Archive, specimens 4X, 5Y.

18. Archive, specimen W.

19. See Warren Strobel, Jonathan Landay, and Phil Stewart, "Exclusive: Islamic State Sanctioned Organ Harvesting in Document Taken in U.S. Raid," Reuters, December 25, 2015, at http://www.reuters.com/article/us-usa-islamic-state-documents-idUSKBN0U805R20151225, with a translation of the document at http://graphics.thomsonreuters.com/doc/document.pdf (accessed January 4, 2016).

20. Joseph Schacht, *An Introduction to Islamic Law* (London: Clarendon Press, 1964), p. 162, cited by Miri Shefer-Mossensohn, *Ottoman Medicine, Healing and Medical Institutions, 1500–1700* (Albany: State University of New York Press, 2009), at p. 227, n. 86 to p. 129; see generally also pp. 128–132.

21. Shefer-Mossensohn, *Ottoman Medicine*, p. 130, mentions that doctors in the Mansuri hospital that operated in Cairo from the thirteenth until the nineteenth century dealt with the problem in a very elegant manner: doctors were described legally as *mahrims*. "By this legal stratagem the problem of privacy between doctors who were male and patients who were female was avoided. The male physician was not considered to be transgressing, but was given the status of a close relative in order to sanction their proximity." See also Peter E. Pormann and Emilie Savage-Smith, *Medieval Islamic Medicine* (Washington, DC: Georgetown University Press, 2007), pp. 103–108.

22. Shefer-Mossensohn, *Ottoman Medicine*. See also Avner Giladi, *Infants, Parents and Wet Nurses: Medieval Islamic Views on Breastfeeding and Their Social Implications* (Leiden: Brill, 1999); Avner Giladi, *Muslim Midwives: The Craft of Birthing in the Premodern Middle East* (Cambridge, Eng.: Cambridge University Press, 2015); and Ahmed Ragab, *The Medieval Islamic Hospital: Medicine, Religion and Charity* (New York: Cambridge University Press, 2015).

23. Archive, specimen 2L, Fatwa no. 42.

Chapter Three. Revenue

1. Kidnapping of foreigners for ransom is also regularly mentioned in news reports, but this does not appear to involve large numbers of victims or of ransom payments. See FATF (2015), *Financing of the Terrorist Organisation Islamic State in Iraq and the Levant (ISIL), FATF,* at http://www.fatf-gafi.org/topics/methodsandtrends/documents/financing-of-terrorist-organisation-isil.html (accessed December 6, 2016), pp. 18 (where a guestimate of $20–45 million in ransom payments is suggested. But evidence in its support is lacking), 35.

2. Archive, specimen 9Z.

3. The caliphal fifth is based not only on older traditions but specifically, in Islam, on Quran 8:41, "Know that, whatever booty you take, the fifth of it is God's, and the Messenger's, and the near kinsman's, and the orphans', and for the needy, and the traveler."

4. On taxation in early Islam, see Frede Løkkegaard, *Islamic Taxation in the Classic Period, with Special Reference to Circumstances in Iraq* (1950; Philadelphia: Porcupine Press, 1978); and Daniel C. Dennett, *Conversion and the Poll Tax in Early Islam* (1950; New York, Arno Press, 1973); A. Ben Shemesh, *Taxation in Islam,* vol. 2: *Qudama b. Ja'far's Kitab al-Kharaj Part Seven, with Excerpts from Abu Yusuf's Kitab al-Kharaj Translated and Provided with an Introduction and Notes* (Leiden: E. J. Brill, 1965); Abd al-Aziz Duri, *Early Islamic Institutions: Administration and Taxation from the Caliphate to the Umayyads and Abbasids* (London: I. B. Tauris, 2011).

5. For a heartfelt lament over the destruction wrought by IS at Palmyra, by a scholar who has done much to increase our knowledge of the city and its past, see Paul Veyne, *Palmyre: L'irremplaçable trésor* (Paris: Albin Michel, 2015). For the damage itself see, e.g., Cheikhmous Ali, *Palmyra Heritage Adrift: Detailed Report on All Damage Done to the Archaeological Site between February 2012 and June 2015*, http://www.asor-syrianheritage. org/palmyra-heritage-adrift/ (accessed July 7, 2015). Also available in French, at http://apsa2011.com/apsanew/palmyre-patrimoine-a-la-derive/ ?lang=fr); an Arabic version, at http://apsa2011.com/apsanew/%D8%AA %D8%AF%D9%85%D8%B1%D9%86%DA%BE%D8%A8%D9%88 %D8%AA%D8%AF%D9%85%D9%8A%D8%B1%D8%A7%D9%84 %D8%AA%D8%B1%D8%A7%D8%AB/?lang=ar, is no longer available. And for evidence that much is fuzzy even in this sort of area, see "Syrian Troops Looting Ancient City Palmyra, Says Archaeologist," *Guardian*, June 1, 2016 (from AFP), at https://www.theguardian.com/ world/2016/jun/01/syrian-troops-looting-ancient-city-palmyra-says- archaeologist (accessed December 6, 2016); the archeologist in question is Professor Hermann Parzinger, head of the Stiftung Preußischer Kulturbesitz. See also "Nichts ist gut in Palmyra," *Frankfurter Allgemeine Zeitung*, June 1, 2016; together with the odd views of Franklin Lamb, "How 100 Syrians, 200 Russians and 11 Dogs Out-Witted ISIS and Saved Palmyra," *Counterpunch*, June 27, 2016, at http://www.counterpunch. org/2016/06/27/how–100-syrians–200-russians-and–11-dogs-out- witted-isis-and-saved-palmyra/; and "About the Accusation That Syrian and Russian Troops Are Looting Palmyra," *Counterpunch*, June 29, 2016, at http://www.counterpunch.org/2016/06/29/about-the-accusation-that- syrian-and-russian-troops-are-looting-palmyra/ (all accessed July 8, 2016). An exhibition entitled "La Syrie et le désastre archéologique du Proche-Orient: Palmyre, cité martyre," devoted to the destruction at Palmyra and elsewhere, was open during the Beiteddine Arts Festival in Lebanon between July 8 and August 10, 2016.

6. For the British Institute statement of March 9, 2015, see http://www.bisi. ac.uk/content/statement-bisi-council–9-march–2015 (accessed January 20, 2016). A useful description of the sculptures at Hatra can be found in Harald Ingholt, *Parthian Sculptures from Hatra, Orient and Hellas in Art and Religion*, vol. 12 of *Memoirs of the Connecticut Academy of Arts and Sciences* (New Haven, CT: Connecticut Academy of Arts and Sciences, 1954).

7. See Graham Bowley and Robert Mackey, "Destruction of Antiquities by Militants Is Denounced," *New York Times*, February 28, 2015.

8. UN General Assembly, at http://www.un.org/en/ga/search/view_doc. asp?symbol=A/RES/69/281 (accessed January 20, 2016); Security Council: http://www.un.org/en/ga/search/view_doc.asp?symbol=S/RES/ 2199 (2015) (accessed January 20, 2016).

9. Quoted in Rick Gladstone, "Antiquities Still at Risk, Experts Warn," *New York Times*, September, 25, 2015.

10. Maybe not so new as all that—consider the Taliban destruction of the huge statues of Buddha at Bamiyan in 2001.

11. Julian Pecquet, "Congress Deals Blow to IS Looting in Syria," *Al-Monitor*, June 1, 2015, at http://www.al-monitor.com/pulse/originals/2015/06/congress-illegal-isis-looting-syria-artifacts.html (accessed January 20, 2016).

12. For more on Keller's presentation and for context, see the following U.S. Department of State documents: http://eca.state.gov/cultural-heritage-center/conflict-antiquities; http://www.state.gov/e/eb/rls/rm/2015/247610.htm; and http://www.state.gov/e/eb/rls/rm/2015/247739.htm. See also, for details of the items seized at Abu Sayyaf's compound, http://eca.state.gov/cultural-heritage-center/iraq-cultural-heritage-initiative/isil-leaders-loot (all accessed January 20, 2016).

13. For the Red Lists database, see http://icom.museum/resources/red-lists-database/red-list/syria/ with versions in English, French, Arabic, and German (accessed January 20, 2015); http://icom.museum/fileadmin/user_upload/pdf/Press_Releases/Red_List_Iraq_EN_2015.pdf (accessed January 20, 2016).

14. Ute Wartenberg Kagan, "Collecting Coins and the Conflict in Syria," https://eca.state.gov/files/bureau/wartenbergsyria-coincollecting.pdf (accessed January 20, 2016).

15. See "'Antiques' from Iraq: Trade Stats Raise Questions," http://cultural-heritagelawyer.blogspot.com/2016_01_01_archive.html, January 5, 2016 (accessed January 23, 2016). For Red Arch Cultural Heritage Law & Policy Research itself see http://www.redarchresearch.org/About-Us.html (accessed on January 23, 2016).

16. For the Census data see https://www.census.gov/foreign-trade/statistics/product/enduse/imports/c5050.html (for Iraq) and https://www.census.gov/foreign-trade/statistics/product/enduse/imports/c5020.html#questions (for Syria), at line 41300 in each (both accessed December 6, 2016).

17. See ibid., at line 41320.

18. For a list of possible sources of error in the Census Bureau statistics, see https://www.census.gov/foreign-trade/reference/guides/tradestatsinfo.html#errors and https://www.census.gov/foreign-trade/aip/quality_profile10032014.pdf (both accessed on January 23, 2016). Errors of the types studied do not appear to have meaningful significance here.

19. For U.S. imports from Monaco, see https://www.census.gov/foreign-trade/statistics/product/enduse/imports/c4272.html, line number (00120) (accessed January 23, 2016).

20. For this general point, see also Ben Taub, "The Real Value of the ISIS Antiquities Trade," http://www.newyorker.com/news/news-desk/the-real-

value-of-the-isis-antiquities-trade, December 4, 2015 (accessed January 24, 2016).

21. Adel H. Yahya, "Managing Heritage in a War Zone," *Archaeologies: Journal of the World Archaeological Congress* 4, no. 3 (December 2008): 495–505; and Yahya, "Looting and 'Salvaging': How the Wall, Illegal Digging and the Antiquities Trade Are Ravaging Palestinian Cultural Heritage," *Jerusalem Quarterly* 33 (Winter 2008): 39–55. (These are essentially two versions of the same piece.)

22. See, for example, Colin P. Clarke, *Terrorism, Inc.: The Financing of Terrorism, Insurgency and Irregular Warfare* (Santa Barbara, CA: Praeger Security International, 2015), p. 158 (though his reference is mainly to the seizure of cash from the central bank in Mosul).

23. See, for example, among many such reports, Hamza Hendawi and Qassim Abdul-Zahra, "ISIS Is Making up to $50 Million a Month from Oil Sales," *Business Insider*, October 23, 2015, at http://www.businessinsider. com/isis-making-50-million-a-month-from-oil-sales-2015-10 (accessed December 28, 2015). See also, for further details of similar type, Richard Engel and Robert Windrem, "ISIS Makes Three Times as Much from Oil Smuggling as Previously Thought: Officials," at http://www.nbcnews. com/storyline/isis-uncovered/isis-makes-three-times-much-oil-smuggling-previously-thought-officials-n397836 (accessed December 28, 2015); Jose Pagliery, "Inside the $2 billion ISIS War Machine," CNN Money, December 11, 2015, at http://money.cnn.com/2015/12/06/news/ isis-funding (accessed December 28, 2015).

24. For the figure of $1,000 per month, which is higher than some other estimates, see Engel and Windrem, "ISIS Makes Three Times as Much from Oil Smuggling." The figures available for numbers of IS fighters appear no more reliable than most others concerning IS.

25. Hans Delbrück, *Numbers in History: How the Greeks Defeated the Persians, the Romans Conquered the World, the Teutons Overthrew the Roman Empire, and William the Norman Took Possession of England* (London: University of London Press, 1913).

26. Ibid., p. 15.

27. Ibid., p. 11.

28. Ibid., pp. 22–23.

29. Hendawi and Abdul-Zahra, "ISIS Is Making up to $50 Million a Month."

30. How IS actually receives the money it is paid for its oil presents further problems. One report claims that the money is being wired to women in Istanbul and Ankara who then hand-deliver it into IS territory. Whether or not such a story is credible, and regardless of the security problems involved, it is hard to believe that substantial sums can be transported in this way. See ibid.

31. See "Russian Intel Spots 12,000 Oil Tankers and Trucks on Turkey-Iraq Border—General Staff," https://www.rt.com/news/327063-russian-intelligence-oil-tankers-turkey/ (accessed December 28, 2015).

32. See ibid. The quotation itself and the entire report, it should be noted, come in a Russian publication.

33. See also Ben Taub, "The ISIS Oil Trade, from the Ground Up," http://www.newyorker.com/news/news-desk/the-isis-oil-trade-from-the-ground-up, December 4, 2015 (accessed January 24, 2016).

34. See Archive, specimens 13Z, 14A, 14B, 14L, 16I, 16J, 16K, 16L, 16M, 16N, 16O, 16P, 16Q, 16R.

35. See FATF (2015), *Financing of the Terrorist Organisation Islamic State in Iraq and the Levant (ISIL), FATF,* at http://www.fatf-gafi.org/topics/methodsandtrends/documents/financing-of-terrorist-organisation-isil.html.

36. See, e.g., Jose Pagliery, "ISIS Cuts Its Fighters' Salaries by 50%," CNN Money, January 19, 2016, at http://money.cnn.com/2016/01/19/news/world/isis-salary-cuts/ (accessed July 5, 2016).

37. Matthew Rosenberg, "U.S. Drops Bombs Not Just on ISIS, But on Its Cash Too," *New York Times*, January 20, 2016, at http://www.nytimes.com/2016/01/21/us/politics/us-drops-bombs-not-just-on-isis-but-on-its-cash-too.html (accessed July 3, 2016).

38. See "Video of U.S. Dropping Two 2,000-pound Bombs in Airstrike over ISIS Bank Show (*sic*) 'Clouds of Paper Money Torched That Terror Group Used to Pay Fighters,'" *Daily Mail*, January 15, 2016, at http://www.dailymail.co.uk/news/article-3402095/Pentagon-releases-video-U-S-airstrike-ISIS-bank-torched-millions-dollars-used-pay-terror-group-s-fighters.html (accessed July 5, 2016).

39. Jim Miklaszewski and Corky Siemaszko, "Millions in ISIS Cash Destroyed in U.S. Airstrike," NBC News, January 11, 2016, at http://www.nbcnews.com/storyline/isis-terror/millions-isis-cash-destroyed-u-s-airstrike-n494261 (accessed July 5, 2016).

40. See Rosenberg, "U.S. Drops Bombs."

41. Luis Martinez, "US Airstrikes Destroy More than $500 Million in ISIS Cash Reserves," ABC News, February 17, 2016, at http://abcnews.go.com/International/us-airstrikes-destroy–500-million-isis-cash-reserves/story?id=37010061 (accessed July 3, 2016).

42. Simon Lewis, "Money to Burn: Up to $800 Million of ISIS Cash Destroyed in Air Strikes," *Time*, April 26, 2016, at http://time.com/4308912/airstrikes-isis-cash-money-funds-daesh/ (accessed July 3, 2016); Simon Tomlinson, "Air Strikes Have Blown up $800 Million of ISIS Cash as the Terror Group's Dwindling Finances Spark a Rise in Defections, U.S. General Reveals," *Daily Mail*, April 27, 2016, at http://www.dailymail.co.uk/news/article–3560950/Air-strikes-blown–800million-ISIS-cash-terror-group-s-dwindling-finances-spark-rise-defections-U-S-

General-reveals.html (accessed July 3, 2016), with video and a picture apparently showing "clouds of paper, presumably some form of foreign currency . . . floating above the site."

43. Jim Michaels, "U.S.-led Coalition Blows up $500 Million in Islamic State Cash," *USA Today*, April 21, 2016, at http://www.usatoday.com/story/ news/world/2016/04/21/united-states-coalition-blows-up-cash-islamic- state/83346102/ (accessed July 3, 2016).

44. In 1198, for example, Pope Innocent III explicitly excommunicated those Venetians who sold the "Saracens" "arms, iron, or wood." See J. P. Migne, ed., *Patrologiae Cursus Completus* (Paris, 1855), vol. 214, p. 493, reprinted in Roy C. Cave and Herbert H. Coulson, *A Source Book for Medieval Economic History* (1936; New York: Biblo & Tannen, 1965), pp. 104–105, at https://legacy.fordham.edu/halsall/source/1198popevenz.asp (accessed January 24, 2016). More generally see, e.g., Leor Halevi, "Religion and Cross-Cultural Trade: A Framework for Interdisciplinary Inquiry," in *Religion and Trade, Cross-Cultural Exchanges in World History, 1000–1900*, ed. Francesca Trivellato, Leor Halevi, and Cátia Antunes (New York: Oxford University Press, 2014), pp. 24–61.

Chapter Four. Religion

Epigraph: A Tunisian preacher in Raqqa, quoted in Hadil Aarja, "Al-Raqqa, Province of 'Dragging to Paradise . . . in Chains': 'The Muhajirun' and Their Women Rule by the Edge of the Sword," *Al-Hayat*, March 21, 2014, at http:// www.alhayat.com/Articles/1246862; translated at *Al-Monitor—Pulse of the Middle East*, March 21, 2014, as "ISIS Enforces Strict Religious Law in Raqqa," at http://www.al-monitor.com/pulse/security/2014/03/isis-enforces- islamic-law-raqqa-syria.html# (both accessed January 3, 2015).

1. See Maribel Fierro, "The Treatises against Innovations (*kutub al-bidaʿ*)," *Der Islam* 69 (1992): 204–246. For a Christian example cf. Epiphanius of Salamis (in Cyprus), a fourth-century writer whose *Panarion* is a rich treasury of information on Christian sects of his time and earlier that he opposed.

2. For the history of Islamic law, see Wael Hallaq, *An Introduction to Islamic Law* (Cambridge, Eng.: Cambridge University Press, 2009); *The Origins and Evolution of Islamic Law* (Cambridge, Eng.: Cambridge University Press, 2005); also *Shar'ia: Theory, Practice, Transformation* (Cambridge, Eng.: Cambridge University Press, 2009); also N. J. Coulson, *A History of Islamic Law* (Edinburgh: Edinburgh University Press, 1964); Joseph Schacht, *An Introduction to Islamic Law* (Oxford, Eng.: Clarendon Press, 1964).

3. Reading a blasphemy can itself constitute blasphemy. So too hearing one: a blackmail-blasphemy case in Pakistan in 2016, in which a Christian was charged with blasphemy against Islam with the alleged

blasphemous remarks recorded on a cellphone, exposed one major difficulty in proving the charge: "Islam prohibits listening to blasphemy," and
according to the defense lawyer in the case for this reason the recording
was never played for the court. See "Blasphemy Law in Pakistan Claims
Another Victim—and His Accusers," *International Christian Response*, July
1, 2016, at http://christianresponse.org/news/blasphemy-law-in-pakistan-
claims-another-victim-and-his-accusers/ (accessed July 6, 2016) (not all
reports on the case include this detail).

4. The fatwa can be read, in English translation, at the Wikipedia entry for
   "*The Satanic Verses* controversy." As can be seen, it is very short—and was
   published as a radio announcement by the Ayatollah himself. It was criti-
   cized widely for not giving the legal grounds for the judgment—which is
   what it was, as distinct from a legal opinion. The whole episode generated a vast amount of newsprint, articles, and books, some of it worth
   reading. See, for example, Daniel Pipes, *The Rushdie Affair: The Novel, the
   Ayatollah, and the West* (1990; New Brunswick, NJ: Transaction
   Publishers, 2003); Kenan Malik, *From Fatwa to Jihad: The Rushdie Affair
   and Its Aftermath* (Brooklyn, NY: Melville House, 2010).

5. For the fatwas of Ibn Rushd, see Camilo Gomez-Rivas, *Law and the
   Islamization of Morocco under the Almoravids: The Fatwas of Ibn Rushd al-
   Jadd to the Far Maghreb* (Leiden: Brill, 2014); for al-Wazzani, see Etty
   Terem, *Old Texts, New Practices: Islamic Reform in Modern Morocco*
   (Stanford, CA: Stanford University Press, 2014); and for al-Wansharisi
   see Vincent Lagardère, *Histoire et Société en occident musulman au moyen
   âge: Analyse du "Mi'yar" d'al-Wansarisi* (Madrid: Casa de Velázquez, 1995);
   and David S. Powers, *Law, Society and Culture in the Maghreb, 1300–1500*
   (Cambridge, Eng.: Cambridge University Press, 2002).

6. See the Introduction.

7. For examples of these see (for repentance for sin) 26 Unseen Documents,
   G; Archive, specimens 1B, 1V, 3U, 3V, 5W, 6Q, 6R, 7W; (for prayer times
   and rules for mosques) Archive, specimens E, Z, 3L, 4S, 4W, 5B, 5J, 5L;
   (for *zakat*) Archive, specimens 2U; (for beards) 6J, 8Q; (for Wi-Fi and
   closing of shops) 26 Unseen Documents, Z; Archive, specimen 7U; (for
   plunder, etc.) Archive, specimens 6E, 13I; (for *hudud* punishments, etc.)
   Archive, specimens 1C, 1D, 6F, 7X. For the "orphans' share" see Quran
   8:41, "Know that, whatever booty you take, the fifth of it is God's, and
   the Messenger's, and the near kinsman's, and the orphans', and for the
   needy, and the traveler."

8. Michael R. Gordon, "ISIS Captives Say They Faced Blade as Rescue
   Came," *New York Times*, October 28, 2015.

9. 32 Fatwas, no. 55 (January 18, 2015).

10. The tradition is recorded by Ibn Maja and Ibn Hanbal. For these and for
    other hadiths with a similar message, see A. J. Wensinck, *Concordance et
    indices de la tradition Musulmane: Les Six livres, le Musnad d'al-Dārimī, le*

Muwaṭṭa' de Mālik, le Musnad de Aḥmad Ibn Ḥanbal, 8 vols. (Leiden: Brill, 1943), vol. 2, p. 404. The Arabic term here is *isbal.*

11. Cf. the biblical account in Joshua, chapter 10, where God halts the sun and the moon at the request of Joshua so that he can win the battle against the Amorites.

12. Al Arabia News, "Thursday First Day of Ramadan: Saudi Arabia," June 16, 2015, at http://english.alarabiya.net/en/News/middle-east/2015/06/16/Thursday-first-day-of-Ramadan-Saudi-Arabia.html (accessed November 19, 2016).

13. For Muslims (as for Jews) a day begins not in the morning, or at midnight, but at nightfall. Thus a month that begins on Wednesday calls for the sighting of the new moon as its starting signal as early as Tuesday. If the new moon is not seen on the Tuesday, but on Wednesday, the month is reckoned to begin at nightfall on Wednesday evening; hence the first day is Thursday.

14. R. J. C. Broadhurst, trans., *The Travels of Ibn Jubayr* (London: Jonathan Cape, 1952), p. 145. It is noteworthy that the Muslim writer uses, even when he is in Arabia, the Christian dating system to say when the new moon occurred. He does this extremely often.

15. See, e.g., Dimitri Gutas, *Greek Thought, Arabic Culture: The Graeco-Arabic Translation Movement in Baghdad and Early 'Abbāsid Society (2nd–4th/8th–10th Centuries)* (London: Routledge, 1998); Juan Vernet, *Lo que Europa debe al Islam de España* (Barcelona: El Acantilado, 1999); George Saliba, *A History of Arabic Astronomy: Planetary Theories during the Golden Age of Islam* (New York: New York University Press, 1994).

16. H. St. John Philby, *Arabia of the Wahhabis* (London: Frank Cass, 1977), pp. 11–12; see also G. E. von Grunebaum, *Muhammadan Festivals* (London: Curzon Press, 1951), pp. 62–63.

17. "ISIS: The Tarawih Prayer Is an Innovation and a Deviation" (in Arabic), http://alwatan.kuwait.tt/articledetails.aspx?id=439790 (accessed December 10, 2016).

18. Archive, specimen 2P.

19. The *New York Times* reported on October 27, 2015, on a paper in *Nature Climate Change,* published online October 26, 2015, "Future Temperature in Southwest Asia Projected to Exceed a Threshold for Human Adaptability," by Jeremy S. Pal and Elfatih A. B. Eltahir, who point out that, as the century goes on, "These extreme conditions are of severe consequence to the Muslim rituals of Hajj, when Muslim pilgrims (~2 million) pray outdoors from dawn to dusk near Mecca. The exact date for this ritual is fixed according to the lunar calendar and can therefore occur during the boreal summer for several consecutive years. This necessary outdoor Muslim ritual is likely to become hazardous to human health, especially for the many elderly pilgrims, when the Hajj occurs during the boreal summer." See also Justin Gillis, "2015 Far Eclipsed

2014 as World's Hottest Year, Climate Scientists Say," *New York Times*, January 21, 2016; Rebecca Hersher, "'Heat Dome' Causing Excessive Temperatures in Much of U.S.," NPR, July 22, 2016, at http://www.npr. org/sections/thetwo-way/2016/07/22/487031278/heat-dome-causing-excessive-temperatures-in-much-of-u-s (accessed July 23, 2016), pointing out that the first six months of 2016 were the hottest since reliable records began in 1880; see also Jason Samenow, "Two Middle East Locations Hit 129 Degrees, Hottest Ever in Eastern Hemisphere, Maybe the World," *Washington Post*, July 22, 2016, at https://www.washingtonpost .com/news/capital-weather-gang/wp/2016/07/22/two-middle-east-locations-hit–129-degrees-hottest-ever-in-eastern-hemisphere-maybe-the-world/ (accessed July 23, 2016).

20. This document has been made available, with an introduction and notes as well as a translation, by Aymenn Jawad al-Tamimi: see http://www .aymennjawad.org/2015/10/unseen-islamic-state-treatise-on-calendars-full (accessed July 6, 2016). For a specimen calendar, see Archive, specimen 2Q.

21. See Archive, specimen 6J for the prohibition on shaving beards. Archive, specimen 8Q is a notice of the closure of a barber shop for shaving beards.

22. IS is not entirely alone in seeking to impose Islamic time: some years ago, according to a BBC report, a conference of Muslim scientists and clerics in Qatar, on the subject Mecca the Centre of the Earth, Theory and Practice, called for the replacement of GMT (Greenwich Mean Time) with Mecca time, on the ground that, as one of the scholars, Yusuf al-Qaradawi, said, "modern science had at last provided evidence that Mecca was the true centre of the earth." Magdi Abdelhadi, "Muslim Call to Adopt Mecca Time," BBC News, April 21, 2008, at http://news.bbc. co.uk/2/hi/middle_east/7359258.stm (accessed July 6, 2016).

23. A picture of the queen holding the placard is at http://www.thedailystar. net/jordan-vows-to-eradicate-isis–63610 (accessed June 22, 2016). For the bombing see "Jordanian Airstrikes Kill 55 ISIS Militants," Al Arabiya, February 2015, at http://english.alarabiya.net/en/News/middle-east/ 2015/02/05/Jordanian-airstrikes-kill–55-ISIS-militants-one-commander. html (accessed June 22, 2016).

24. See "ISIS Issues Fatwa to Justify Burning of Jordanian Pilot," *MEMRI: Jihad and Terrorism Threat Monitor*, February 4, 2015, http://www. memrijttm.org/isis-issues-fatwa-to-justify-burning-of-jordanian-pilot. html (accessed June 22, 2016).

25. According to Cassandra Vinograd, "When Did Jordan Find Out Hostage Pilot Muath al-Kasasbeh Was Dead?" NBC News, February 4, 2015, http://www.nbcnews.com/storyline/isis-uncovered/when-did-jordan-find-out-hostage-pilot-muath-al-kasasbeh-n299896 (accessed June 22, 2016), which states also that "As early as Jan. 8, tweets suggested the pilot

had met a fiery end." The fact that all these revelations came as soon as the video was released suggests that in fact some considerable knowledge of the true circumstances was circulating long before public release of the video in early February.

26. Vinograd, NBC News, February 4, 2015, says that "State media reported on Tuesday [February 3, 2015] that al-Kasasbeh was killed on Jan. 3." "ISIS Snuff Films' Sleight of Hand," *Daily Beast*, February 3, 2015, says that "Kasasbeh was killed weeks before the video aired—as early as January 3," according to Jordanian officials, while "British security sources told *The Daily Beast* that they had come to the conclusion Kasasbeh was murdered between Jan. 5 and 8; shortly thereafter, they informed their Jordanian counterparts of their suspicion." It is not clear from this whether the words "between Jan. 5 and 8" refer to the time of the murder or to that of the conclusion. The date of January 8 for the killing is supported by the detail of the tweet and an interview with its author in the *Daily Beast*, but neither appears conclusive. See http://www.thedailybeast.com/articles/2015/02/03/isis-snuff-films-sleight-of-hand.html (accessed July 10, 2016). For the January 3 date see also Rod Nordland and Ranya Kadri, "Jordanian Pilot's Death, Shown in ISIS Video, Spurs Jordan to Execute Prisoners," *New York Times*, February 3, 2015, at http://www.nytimes.com/2015/02/04/world/middleeast/isis-said-to-burn-captive-jordanian-pilot-to-death-in-new-video.html?_r=0 (accessed June 22, 2016), who add that the Jordanian officials "did not, however, explain where they got the information." It remains unclear when they got the information too. And "Jordan Pilot Hostage Moaz al-Kasasbeh 'Burned Alive,'" BBC, February 3, 2015, at http://www.bbc.com/news/world-middle-east-31121160 (accessed June 22, 2016).

27. See David J. Wasserstein, "The Coinage of the Islamic State," *Israel Numismatic Research* 11 (2016): 181–204.

28. Orthodox Christians display an attachment to a different calendar, their own, in celebrating Christmas and Easter at different dates from Western Christians. Jews use their own calendar for religious festivals, which is why their New Year seems to wander from year to year. And in June 2016, Bolivia, under its president Evo Morales, proposed a return to a pre-Colombian calendar, for similar reasons: finding the Gregorian calendar that we all use "untidy," he wants Bolivia to "reclaim its ancestral calendar as part of the rebuilding of our identity." See http://www.bbc.com/news/world-latin-america-36595192 (accessed June 22, 2016).

29. 17 Rabi I represents simply an alternative tradition for the date of the event in question.

30. For the date see A. Guillaume, *The Life of Muhammad: A Translation of Ibn Ishaq's Sirat Rasul Allah* (London: Oxford University Press, 1955), p. 69. G. E. von Grunebaum, *Muhammadan Festivals* (New York: Schuman, 1951), p. 73, says, "Muhammad died on Monday, the twelfth of the First

Rabi' and his birthday, the date of which is not known, has been arbitrarily placed on the same date." This is an attractive explanation: deaths of important men—and who, in Islam, could be more important than the Prophet?—make more noise and are more noticeable than the births of infants, but it is noteworthy, against this background, that Ibn Ishaq, at least, gives the precise day and date for the birth, assigning merely a Monday in late Safar or early Rabi I, with no exact date, to the death.

31. See von Grunebaum, *Muhammadan Festivals*, pp. 73–76, which is a translation of an extensive passage from the Arab writer Ibn Khallikan, of the thirteenth century, describing the festivities in his own time; see also Edward William Lane, *An Account of the Manners and Customs of the Modern Egyptians, Written in Egypt during the Years 1833–1835* (London: Ward Lock, n.d.), chapter 24, which is an even more extensive modern account by an English visitor to Cairo, and includes descriptions of the dervish participants.

32. See N. J. G. Kaptein, *Muhammad's Birthday Festival, Early History in the Central Muslim Lands and Development in the Muslim West until the 10th/16th century* (Leiden: Brill, 1993); Marion Holmes Katz, *The Birth of the Prophet Muhammad: Devotional Piety in Sunni Islam* (London: Routledge, Culture and Civilization in the Middle East, 2007). It is usually possible to find videos of *mawlid* celebrations on YouTube.

33. The phrase comes from von Grunebaum, *Muhammadan Festivals*, p. 77.

34. See for the larger discussion especially the works of Kaptein and Katz.

35. See for example, Arthur Hertzberg, *A Jew in America: My Life and a People's Struggle for Identity* (New York: HarperSanFrancisco, 2002), p. 163, who stresses "how far the established, mainline, synagogues and churches in America, in all their varieties, have moved away from expressing religious emotion and religious passion."

36. Archive, specimens 1Z (billiards), 2A (foosball).

37. What follows depends on James M. Dorsey, "Jihad v. Soccer: The Islamic State's Convoluted Love-Hate Relationship," at https://mideastsoccer. blogspot.sg/2016/07/jihad-v-soccer-islamic-states.html (accessed July 11, 2016). See also, at greater length, Dorsey's study *The Turbulent World of Middle East Soccer* (2013; New York: Oxford University Press, 2016).

38. Amnon Shiloach, "Music," *New Cambridge History of Islam*, vol. 4, ed. Robert Irwin (Cambridge, Eng.: Cambridge University Press, 2010), pp. 743–750, with further references; see also the classic work of Henry George Farmer, *A History of Arabian Music, to the XIIIth Century* (London: Luzac, 1929).

39. Examples of singing slave-girls can be found all over classical and medieval Arabic literature; for some, see Ibn al-Sa'i, *Consorts of the Caliphs: Women and the Court of Baghdad*, ed. Sh. M. Toorawa, trans. by the editors of the Library of Arabic Literature (New York: New York University Press, 2015). The epistle on this subject by al-Jahiz (ninth century) was

translated with notes by A. F. L. Beeston, as *The Epistle on Singing-Girls of Jahiz* (Warminster, UK: Aris and Phillips, 1980).

40. Archive, specimen 10H.

41. See Archive, specimen 5J; "ISIS: Tarawih Prayers Is Heresy and Straying from the True Path of Islam," Abna24, June 21, 2015, at http://en.abna24.com/service/middle-east-west-asia/archive/2015/06/21/696487/story.html (accessed July 11, 2016; Abna24 is an Iranian news agency located in Qom); Johnlee Varghese, "Mosul: Isis Bans Taraweeh Prayers for Ramadan; Worshippers Flogged Publicly for Disobeying Decree," *International Business Times*, July 1, 2015, at http://www.ibtimes.co.in/mosul-isis-bans-taraweeh-prayers-ramadan-worshippers-flogged-publicly-disobeying-decree–637724; Joanna Paraszczuk, "Ramadan in Mosul: IS Bans Backgammon, Dominoes—and Prayers," Radio Free Europe Radio Liberty, June 22, 2015, at http://www.rferl.org/content/islamic-state-ramadan-mosul/27086743.html (accessed July 11, 2016); "'Daesh' Forbids the Tarawih Prayer and Threatens Those Who Perform It with Flogging," *Deutsche Welle*, June 7, 2016, in Arabic at http://dw.com/p/1FjHj (accessed July 12, 2016).

42. Broadhurst, *Ibn Jubayr*, p. 146.

43. Ibid., p. 346.

44. Lane, *An Account of the Manners and Customs of the Modern Egyptians*, chapter 25, "Periodical public festivals, etc. *continued* (Those of the fourth and following months of the Muslim year)."

45. See the ninth-century collector of hadiths, al-Bukhari, *Sahih*, book 32, Praying at Night in Ramadan, 3.226–230.

46. See Fierro, "Treatises against Innovations," p. 222 and n. 106, with further references.

47. See Letter to al-Baghdadi, at http://www.lettertobaghdadi.com/, English version, pp. 9–10.

48. Archive, specimen 1G.

Chapter Five. Women, and Children Too

1. Christopher Miller, "What We Know about Hasna Aitboulahcen, Woman Killed in Paris Raid," *Mashable*, November 19, 2015, updated November 21, 2015, retrieved November 28, 2015. See also the report by Karin Bennhold, "Woman Killed in French Police Raid Had Unlikely Path to Extremism," *New York Times*, November 21, 2015 (accessed November 28, 2015). For alternative explanations of her death see http://www.bbc.com/news/world-europe–35375297 (accessed June 27, 2016). A longer account is at http://mtv.com.lb/news/english_highlights/543464/hasna_ait_boulahcen_is_suicide_bomber_who_liked_to_party_hard (accessed June 27, 2016).

2. A general study of media presentation of women terrorists is offered by Maura Conway and Lisa McInerney, "What's Love Got to Do with It?

Framing 'JihadJane' in the US Press," *Media, War & Conflict* 5, no. 1 (2012): 6–21. See also Laura Sjoberg and Caron E. Gentry, "Reduced to Bad Sex: Narratives of Violent Women from the Bible to the War on Terror," *International Relations* 22, no. 1 (2008): 5–23.

3. For a more mainstream example of the attitudes involved here, see the autobiography of a recent American woman convert to Islam, G. Willow Wilson, *The Butterfly Mosque* (New York: Grove Press, 2010).

4. See Erin Marie Saltman and Melanie Smith, *"Till Martyrdom Do Us Part": Gender and the ISIS Phenomenon* (London: Institute for Strategic Dialogue, 2015), pp. 43–47.

5. For an analysis of a recent ISIS propaganda campaign on social media, see Gilad Shiloach, "A Demonstration of Virtual Power by Supporters of the Islamic State," *Beehive: Middle East Social Media* 4, no. 6 (June 2016), at http://dayan.org/content/demonstration-virtual-power-supporters-islamic-state (accessed July 8, 2016).

6. See Darren Boyle, "Teenage Islamist 'Poster Girl' Who Fled Austria to Join ISIS 'Is Beaten to Death by the Terror Group after Trying to Escape from Syria,'" *Daily Mail*, November 24, 2015, at http://www.dailymail. co.uk/news/article-3331846/Teenage-Islamist-poster-girl-fled-Austria-join-ISIS-beaten-death-terror-group-trying-escape-Syria.html (accessed January 31, 2016). The exact ages of the two girls remain unclear.

7. For female Western volunteers, see generally Saltman and Smith, *"Till Martyrdom"*; Anita Peresin and Alberto Cervone, "The Western *Muhajirat* of ISIS," *Studies in Conflict and Terrorism* 38 (2015): 495–509 (for the 10 percent estimate, see p. 499, and n. 18, citing a report in the *Guardian* of September 29, 2014).

8. Kareem Fahim, "Militants Tied to IS Kill 7 at Sinai Hotel," *New York Times*, November 25, 2015.

9. See in particular Samuel Osborne, "Isis Burns 19 Yazidi Women to Death in Mosul for 'Refusing to Have Sex with Fighters,'" *Independent*, June 6, 2016, at http://www.independent.co.uk/news/world/middle-east/isis-burn-19-yazidi-women-to-death-in-mosul-for-refusing-to-have-sex-with-isis-militants-a7066956.html (accessed June 29, 2016). A series of poems by Yezidis reacting to the events of the summer of 2014, when IS made an attempt to destroy the Yezidi community, is translated in *Journal of Levantine Studies* 15, no. 1 (Summer 2015), at http://www.levantine-journal.org/ISSN+2222-9973_cid_21.aspx (accessed June 30, 2016). Rukmini Callimachi, "ISIS Uses Birth Control to Maintain Rapes," *New York Times*, March 13, 2016, looked at one of the ways in which IS takes care both to observe Islamic law as it understands it and to maintain a supply of young women for sexual purposes outside marriage.

10. For comparative figures for 1990 and 2014 see the World Bank data at http://data.worldbank.org/indicator/SL.TLF.CACT.FE.ZS (accessed June 30, 2016). Strikingly, though, Syria and Iraq do not rank very high

among Islamic countries—Malaysia and Indonesia are both not far behind the United Kingdom and the United States and other Western
countries; Syria and Iraq both rank behind Saudi Arabia, below the aver-
age for the Arab world as a whole, well behind Egypt and Turkey, and
stand more or less on a par with Iran and Jordan. Such figures must conceal a good deal of real-time variation in detail, as well as other variables
like economic structures, education, and social attitudes, but they are a
pointer nevertheless.

11. For Indian film in Nigeria, see Brian Larkin, *Signal and Noise: Media,
Infrastructure, and Urban Culture in Nigeria* (Durham, NC: Duke
University Press, 2008).

12. *Women's Economic Empowerment: Integrating Women into the Iraqi Economy*,
United Nations Development Program, March 2012, at http://www.undp.
org/content/dam/rbas/doc/Women's%20Empowerment/Report%
20on%20Women%E2%80%99s%20Economic%20Empowerment%20
in%20Iraq,%20Integrating%20Women%20in%20the%20Iraqi%20
Economy-.pdf. More formalistically, *Syrian Arab Republic*, OECD
Development Centre, Social Institutions and Gender Index http://www.
genderindex.org/sites/default/files/datasheets/SY.pdf, and *Iraq*, OECD
Development Centre, Social Institutions and Gender Index http://www.
genderindex.org/sites/default/files/datasheets/IQ.pdf. Also *Background on
Women's Status in Iraq Prior to the Fall of the Saddam Hussein Government*,
Human Rights Watch Briefing Paper, November 2003, at https://www.hrw.
org/legacy/backgrounder/wrd/iraq-women.htm (all accessed June 27, 2016).

13. See, e.g., from a large literature, *Are We Listening? Acting on our
Commitments to Women and Girls Affected by the Syrian Conflict*,
International Rescue Committee, September 2014, at http://www
.peacewomen.org/sites/default/files/irc_womeninsyria_report_web_1_0.
pdf; this is the website of the Women's International League for Peace
and Freedom, United Nations Office. The document seems no longer to
be available on the website of the International Rescue Committee itself;
#R2P10: The Impact of the Syrian Conflict on Women, International
Coalition for the Responsibility to Protect, June 17, 2015, at https://
icrtopblog.org/2015/06/17/r2p10-the-impact-of-the-syrian-conflict-on-
women/; Sarah Williamson, "Syrian Women in Crisis: Obstacles and
Opportunities," *Women's Economic Participation in Conflict-Affected and
Fragile Settings*, Georgetown Institute for Women, Peace and Security,
Occasional Paper Series, January 2016, pp. 26–40, at https://giwps.
georgetown.edu/sites/giwps/files/occasional_paper_series_volume_i_-_
womens_economic_participation.pdf; Beatrix Buecher and James
Rwampigi Aniyamuzaala, *Women, Work and War: Syrian Women and the
Struggle to Survive Five Years of Conflict*, CARE Research Study, March
2016, at http://www.care-international.org/files/files/CARE_Women_
Work_War_report.pdf; Laila Alodaat, "The Armed Conflict in Syria and

Its Disproportionate Impact on Women," at https://www.fes.de/gender/infobrief/pdf_content/FES_IL5_FOCUS02.pdf (also in German at https://www.fes.de/gender/infobrief/pdf_content/FES_IL5_FOKUS02.pdf), (all accessed June 28, 2016).

14. See 32 Fatwas, no. 44. For others on women from that date see ibid., nos. 40, 41, 42, 43, 45, 46, and, from the following month, no. 61. An earlier and much more detailed decree (not a fatwa) is at 12V (of 19 Rabi I 1435 = January 20, 2014).

15. 32 Fatwas, no. 44.

16. See 32 Fatwas, no. 40.

17. For this recommendation see 32 Fatwas, no. 61.

18. See 32 Fatwas, no. 41.

19. Archive, specimen 3T.

20. See 32 Fatwas, no. 45 (no. 46 is similar in inspiration); Archive, specimens M, 1Y; 26 Unseen Documents, specimen M.

21. See Health Department, p. 3; 32 Fatwas nos. 42, 43; Archive, specimens 2L, 7Y.

22. See *Saudi Arabia: Gross Human Rights Abuses Against Women*, Amnesty International, September 27, 2000, at https://www.amnesty.org/en/documents/mde23/057/2000/en/ (accessed June 30, 2016). Released in 2000, this report is now sixteen years old; many subsequent reports, however, both from Amnesty International itself and in the press, demonstrate that it is not out of date.

23. 26 Unseen Documents, specimen O; see also 26 Unseen Documents, specimen P; Archive, specimen 2Z; also Mona Mahmood, "Double-Layered Veils and Despair: Women Describe Life under ISIS," *Guardian*, February 17, 2015, https://www.theguardian.com/world/2015/feb/17/isis-orders-women-iraq-syria-veils-gloves (accessed June 27, 2016); and an extensive report, Azadeh Moaveni, "For ISIS Women, Fraught Choices," *New York Times*, November 22, 2015.

24. Not from an IS background, *A Woman in the Crossfire: Diaries of the Syrian Revolution*, by Samar Yazbek, translated by Max Weiss (London: Haus Publishing, 2011), offers something more than a plain diary though less than a full-scale autobiography.

25. The quotation comes from Thomas Pierret and Mériam Cheikh, "'I Am Very Happy Here': Female Jihad in Syria as Self-Accomplishment," *Hawwa: Journal of Women in the Middle East and the Islamic World* 13 (2015): 242–243.

26. See "Islamic State Jihadists Open 'Marriage Bureau,'" *Naharnet*, July 28, 2014, at http://www.naharnet.com/stories/en/140865, citing Agence France Presse (accessed July 2, 2016).

27. Saltman and Smith, *Till Martyrdom Do Us Part*, pp. 27–31.

28. For Shams see Saltman and Smith, *Till Martyrdom Do Us Part*, pp. 36–43; Ellie Hall, "An ISIS Love Story: 'Till Martyrdom Do Us Part,'" *BuzzFeed*,

September 17, 2014, at https://www.buzzfeed.com/ellievhall/an-isis-love-story-till-martyrdom-do-us-part?utm_term=.tgXbBDgmd3#.poNY8J2MKW (accessed July 2, 2016).

29. See, e.g., Peresin and Cervone, "The Western *Muhajirat*," p. 500, which stresses that "by leaving the West to perform *Hijra*, women demonstrate that they see a superiority of ISIS's ideology over the Western worldview, providing an important gratification and a significant morale booster for the *jihadist* fighters."

30. For Ahlam al-Nasr see especially Pierret and Cheikh, "'I Am Very Happy Here,'" pp. 241–269, with details of her writings (the quotations that follow are from this article unless otherwise stated). Also Halla Diyab, "Ahlam al-Nasr: Islamic State's Jihadist Poetess," *Militant Leadership Monitor* 6, no. 6, June 10, 2015, at http://www.jamestown.org/single/?tx_ttnews%5Btt_news%5D=44108&no_cache=1#.V3Gmcv4UXIU (accessed June 27, 2016). For her marriage, see "The Poetess of Daesh Marries Abu Usama al-Gharib in Syrian Raqqa," al-Quds News, October 14, 2014, where there is a photograph showing the happy groom, but not the bride, at http://www.alquds.co.uk/?p=234717 (accessed June 27, 2016; in Arabic).

31. The quotation here comes from Pierret and Cheikh, "'I Am Very Happy Here'"; the original article by Iman al-Bugha is available online (in Arabic) at http://justpaste.it/hn3O (accessed July 3, 2016). It is worth reading.

32. See Archive, specimen 6J for the prohibition on shaving beards. Archive, specimen 8Q is a notice of the closure of a barber shop for shaving beards.

33. It can be seen online at the top of Halla Diyab, "Ahlam al-Nasr." The meter is *wafir*, a fairly common poetic form.

34. The manifesto has been translated, with an introduction and notes, by Charlie Winter: see *Women of the Islamic State: A Manifesto on Women by the Al-Khanssaa Brigade*, Quilliam Foundation, February 2015, at https://www.quilliamfoundation.org/wp/wp-content/uploads/publications/free/women-of-the-islamic-state3.pdf (accessed June 28, 2016). All quotations here are taken from the unnumbered pages of this translation.

35. Much about the life of al-Khansa remains obscure or unknown. See the article on her in *EI²*, IV, p. 1027 (by F. Gabrieli). There is a French translation of her poems, by Père de Coppier, S.J., *Le Diwan d'al-Hansa': Précédé d'une étude sur les femmes poètes de l'ancienne Arabie* (Beyrouth: Imprimerie Catholique, 1889); and a not as good (and less complete) English version: see Arthur Wormhoudt, "*Diwan al Khansa*," translated from the text of Karim Bustani (Oskaloosa, IA: William Penn University, 1973).

36. Pierret and Cheikh, "'I Am Very Happy Here,'" p. 260, n. 69, point out that guns appear frequently as profile pictures for women supporters of IS.

37. The work has not been published in English, except in the Quilliam translation. Its principal target audience seems therefore to be internal, Arabic-speaking and Arabic-reading.

38. The works of the late Fatima Mernissi (who died in 2015) have done much to illuminate the roles of women in Islamic societies. She argued—not uncontroversially—that the Prophet envisaged a society with equality of the sexes, but that men in later generations subverted his message, pushing women into the background against the true spirit of Islam. See, e.g., Fatima Mernissi, *The Veil and the Male Elite: A Feminist Interpretation of Women's Rights in Islam*, trans. Mary Jo Lakeland (Reading, MA: Addison-Wesley, 1991), originally published in French, as *Le harem politique, Le Prophète et les femmes* (Paris: Albin Michel, 1987). The literature on women and feminism in Islam is enormous.

39. The justification for this is seen in the Prophet's marriage to his favorite wife, Aisha, who was nine at the time.

40. Nothing is said about the treatment of Christians who choose not to convert. See Chapter 6 for more on this topic.

41. The subject of female recruitment is immensely popular. See, e.g., Mia Bloom and Charlie Winter, "How a Woman Joins ISIS," *Daily Beast*, December 5, 2015, at http://www.thedailybeast.com/articles/2015/12/06/how-a-woman-joins-isis.html; Jayne Huckerby, "Why Women Join ISIS," *Time Magazine*, December 7, 2015, at http://time.com/4138377/women-in-isis/; Mia Bloom and Charlie Winter, "The Women of ISIL," *Politico*, December 7, 2015, at http://www.politico.eu/article/the-women-of-isil-female-suicide-bomber-terrorism/; Kate Storey, "The American Women of ISIS," *Marie Claire*, April 22, 2016, at http://www.marieclaire.com/politics/a20011/western-women-who-join-isis/; Nawar Fakhry Ezzi, "Why Does Daesh Recruit Women?" *Saudi Gazette*, January 14, 2016, at http://saudigazette.com.sa/opinion/why-does-daesh-recruit-women/; reposted at http://www.wunrn.com/2016/02/why-does-daeshisis-recruit-women/ February 15, 2016 (all accessed July 3, 2016).

42. Pedro Manrique et al., "Women's Connectivity in Extreme Networks," *Science Advances* 2, no. 6, June 10, 2016, at http://advances.sciencemag.org/content/advances/2/6/e1501742.full.pdf (accessed June 28, 2016). (Of the eleven authors, only four are women.)

43. This view is not confined to men (and women) of the Islamic State. In November 2015, an Indian sheikh in the state of Kerala described as "un-Islamic" the concept of gender equality and said that women could never equal men as "they are fit only to deliver children": Press Trust of India, at http://www.ndtv.com/india-news/kerala-sunni-leader-says-women-only-fit-to-deliver-children-1248727, November 28, 2015, and http://www.dnaindia.com/india/report-kerala-sunni-leader-says-women-only-fit-to-deliver-children-calls-gender-equality-un-islamic-2149865, November 28, 2015; also Shaju Philip, "Gender Equality against Islam,

Says Kerala Sunni Leader," *Indian Express*, http://indianexpress.com/
article/india/india-news-india/demand-for-gender-equality-against-
islam-and-its-culture-says-kerala-sunni-muslim-leader/; Sachin Jose,
"Kerala Sunni Leader Kanthapuram Says Gender Equality Is Anti-
Islamic, Stirs Row," *International Business Times*, November 28, 2015, at
http://www.ibtimes.co.in/kerala-sunni-leader-kanthapuram-says-gender-
equality-anti-islamic-stokes-controversy–657106; reports of his remarks
on YouTube at https://www.youtube.com/watch?v=hkpiEtBhfZ8 and
https://www.youtube.com/watch?v=TzZ3mGAJw9o (all accessed June
28, 2016). See also Neil MacFarquhar, "Chechen Leader's Advice on
Women: Lock Them In," *New York Times*, May 21, 2015. Of course, there
are non-Muslims with parallel views.

44. For a link to the video, see http://heavy.com/news/2015/12/new-isis
-islamic-state-news-videos-pictures-to-sons-of-jews-wilayat-al-khayr-chil
d-boy-soldiers-executing-shooting-spies-jewish-ancient-ruins-obstacle-
course-full-uncensored-youtube/ (accessed July 8, 2016).

45. Ahlam al-Nasr, the young woman who moved to the Islamic State from
Saudi Arabia, relates how she bought a gun in Raqqa and was trained in
the maintenance and use of her new "friend." "The playful character of
the shooting session places it somewhere between military training and
entertainment" (Pierret and Cheikh, "'I Am Very Happy Here,'" pp. 259–
260).

46. For the Palmyra shootings see the report on CNN, http://www.
cnn.com/2015/07/04/middleeast/isis-execution-palmyra-syria/. For the
December shootings, see http://heavy.com/news/2015/12/new-isis-
islamic-state-news-pictures-videos-execution-spies-traitors-shia-shiite
-homs-syria-saudi-arabia-war-declaration-full-uncensored-youtube-vide
o/. For the five-year-old, see Jay Akbar and Isabel Hunter, "ISIS Releases
Execution Video Showing 'New Jihadi John' Killing Five 'British Spies'
Accompanied by Young Boy with UK Accent Promising New Wave
of Terror Attacks," *Daily Mail* at http://www.dailymail.co.uk/news/
article–3382779/ISIS-releases-video-showing-execution-five-British-
spies-warning-David-Cameron-UK-bombing.html (all accessed January
31, 2016).

47. *Daily Mail* (London), December 4, 2015 (retrieved same date), citing the
Syrian Observatory for Human Rights. See also *Times of Israel*, same date.

48. See especially the writings of David Ayalon collected in *Outsiders in the
Lands of Islam: Mamluks, Mongols, and Eunuchs* (London: Variorum
Reprints, 1988); *Islam and the Abode of War: Military Slaves and Islamic
Adversaries* (Aldershot, UK: Variorum, 1994); also Patricia Crone, *Slaves
on Horses* (Cambridge, Eng.: Cambridge University Press, 1980).

49. Archive, specimens 6Z, 7P. See also specimen 13U, where the prizes on
offer include electronic devices, money, and domestic tools.

50. Archive, specimens 3W, 3X.

Chapter Six. Christians and Jews and . . .

1. See Adelle Nazarian, "Isis Kills Four Children in Process of Destroying Another Mosul Church," at http://www.breitbart.com/national-security/2015/07/09/isis-kills-four-children-in-process-of-destroying-another-mosul-church/ (accessed December 5, 2015). The writer here suggests that the Church of the Mother of Aid had stood there for "thousands of years"; this is presumably a slip for "hundreds."

2. See the Assyrian International News Agency, July 29, 2014, at http://www.aina.org/news/20140729100528.htm—and repeated at http://myocn.net/45-christian-institutions-mosul-destroyed-occupied-isis/—for a list of the properties and sites, classified by the different sects (both retrieved December 5, 2015). The use of a church as an arms depot will recall for some the use of the Parthenon, at the top of the Acropolis, as an explosives store by the Ottomans during the Venetian attack on Athens in 1687, with predictable results. The building pictured in the story by Nazarian seems to belong to the twentieth century.

3. Justin Welby, Archbishop of Canterbury, Christmas sermon, December 25, 2015, at http://www.archbishopofcanterbury.org/articles.php/5655/the-archbishop-of-canterburys-christmas-sermon (retrieved February 27, 2016).

4. For these writers see the entries in the *Oxford Dictionary of the Christian Church*, ed. F. L. Cross, 3rd ed., E. A. Livingstone ed. (Oxford, Eng.: Oxford University Press, 1997), pp. 850–851 and 1118–1119, with useful bibliographies.

5. Roland Broadhurst, trans., *The Travels of Ibn Jubayr* (London: Jonathan Cape, 1952), pp. 244–245.

6. See Jonathan Krohn, "Has Last Christian Left Iraqi City of Mosul after 2,000 Years?" NBC News, at http://www.nbcnews.com/storyline/iraq-turmoil/has-last-christian-left-iraqi-city-mosul-after–2-000-n164856 (accessed December 5, 2015).

7. See ibid.

8. It is available in translation at Archive, specimen S.

9. The words recur time and again in the Jewish liturgy for the Day of Atonement, when the entire book of Jonah is read.

10. For the Islamic Jonah, see the Quran, *sura* 10; see also the chapters on him in Muhammad ibn 'Abd Allah al-Kisa'i, *Tales of the Prophets (Qisas al-Anbiya')*, trans. William M. Thackston, Jr. (Chicago: Kazi, Great Books of the Islamic World, 1997), pp. 321–326; Abu Ishaq Ahmad ibn Muhamad ibn Ibrahim al-Tha'labi, *"Ara'is al-Majalis fi Qisas al-Anbiya" or "Lives of the Prophets,"* trans. and annotated by William M. Brinner (Leiden: Brill, Studies in Arabic Literature, 2002), pp. 681–688.

11. Archive, specimen S.

12. Ibid.

13. The text was available for some time online at http://justpaste.it.ejur. It has now been removed. It can still (as of December 7, 2016) be seen at http://www.memri.org/report/en/0/0/0/0/0/0/7859.htm, sourced to http://www.alarabiya.net/ar/arab-and-world/syria/2014/02/28/%D8%B5%D9%88%D8%B1%D8%A9-%D8%A3%D9%88%D9%84-%D8%B9%D9%87%D8%AF-%D8%B0%D9%85%D8%A9-%D8%A3%D8%A8%D8%B1%D9%85%D8%AA%D9%87-%D8%AF%D8%A7%D8%B9%D8%B4-%D9%85%D8%B9-%D9%85%D8%B3%D9%8A%D8%AD%D9%8A%D9%8A%D9%86-%D9%81%D9%8A-%D8%B3%D9%88%D8%B1%D9%8A%D8%A7-.html.

14. The alternative possibility, that the names of real Christian representatives were never there and that what we see are just invented names, seems implausible in the present context.

15. In fact the word *mithqal* (in Item No. 8 here) in Arabic means simply weight; and while it occasionally has other meanings related to particular weights, it does not designate a single fixed weight such as 4.25 grams. Further, the weight of the dinar was never fixed with the finality that this wording suggests.

16. There is a puzzle here, nevertheless: we get the impression that the Christians of Raqqa have had two days to consider their position, like their co-religionists in Mosul. Yet the date 20 Rabi II 1435 (February 20, 2014) in the first document represents the date of the second meeting between the Christians and the IS authorities, when the Christians have already had time to think over what to do. The date 22 Rabi II 1435 (February 22, 2014), on the second document, the pact itself, is two days later—but that leaves us to wonder why the signatures were not placed on a document whose contents were presumably known already at that earlier meeting on 20 Rabi II. Should this make us doubt the genuineness of this piece of source material?

17. An additional, scarcely noticeable, feature of modernity is that the IS document actually numbers the clauses of the contract. (For ease of reference later on? Because that makes a document look more formal in the modern eyes of those drawing it up?) The old Pact of Umar has no numbers.

18. For a rare study of the importance and significance of loudspeaker use in religious contexts in the Islamic world, see Brian Larkin, "Techniques of Inattention: The Mediality of Loudspeakers in Nigeria," *Anthropological Quarterly* 87, no. 4 (Fall 2014): 989–1015.

19. For (translated) texts of the Pact of Umar, see Bernard Lewis, *Islam from the Prophet Muhammad to the Capture of Constantinople*, vol. 2: *Religion and Society* (New York: Harper and Row, 1974), pp. 217–219; Norman A. Stillman, *The Jews of Arab Lands: A History and Source Book* (Philadelphia: Jewish Publication Society of America, 1979), pp. 157–158. The scholarly

literature on the Pact of Umar and on the situation of Christians (and Jews) under Islamic rule is enormous. For a study of the text of the pact itself, see Mark R. Cohen, "What Was the Pact of 'Umar? A Literary-Historical Study," *Jerusalem Studies in Arabic and Islam* 23 (1999): 100–157.

20. See Milka Levy-Rubin, *Non-Muslims in the Early Islamic Empire: From Surrender to Coexistence* (Cambridge, Eng.: Cambridge University Press, 2011).

21. For discussions of conversion, see Richard W. Bulliet, *Conversion to Islam in the Medieval Period: An Essay in Quantitative History* (Cambridge, MA: Harvard University Press, 1979); N. Levtzion, *Conversion to Islam* (New York: Holmes and Meier, 1979); Richard Eaton, "Approaches to the Study of Conversion to Islam in India," in Richard C. Martin, ed., *Approaches to Islam in Religious Studies* (Tucson: University of Arizona Press, 1985); David J. Wasserstein, "Conversion and the *ahl al-dhimma*," in *The New Cambridge History of Islam*, general editor Michael Cook, vol. 4: *Islamic Cultures and Societies to the End of the Eighteenth Century*, ed. Robert Irwin (Cambridge, Eng.: Cambridge University Press, 2010), pp. 184–208; and now Thomas A. Carlson, "Contours of Conversion: The Geography of Islamization in Syria, 600–1500," *Journal of the American Oriental Society* 135, no. 4 (2015): 791–816.

22. Archive, specimen 2X. The document is pictured at http://shoebat. com/2015/03/21/for-the-first-time-ever-evidence-surfaces-of-the-brutal-tax-jizya-that-muslims-are-forcing-upon-christians-right-now-the-same -tax-the-muslims-forced-on-the-americans-before-america-crushed-the-musl/ (accessed March 18, 2016), where it can be seen that it actually shows a payment of 27,200 Syrian pounds (almost one dollar more). The name of the taxpayer, an Armenian Christian, is shown there as Sarkis Yorkie Arakelian, and the date is given as 16 Safar 1436, equivalent to December 8, 2014.

23. In fact, the required payment is stated to be four dinars, and payment is required twice a year. Does this mean payment of four dinars by installments or does it mean four dinars twice a year? It is not clear.

24. M. J. Kister, "An Yadin (Qur'an IX/29): An Attempt at Interpretation," *Arabica* 11 (1964): 272–278; N. A. Stillman, *The Jews of Arab Lands: A History and Source Book* (Philadelphia: Jewish Publication Society of America, 1979), pp. 159–161, 180. For more recent examples see Aviva Klein-Franke, "Collecting the *Djizya* (Poll-Tax) in the Yemen," in Tudor Parfitt, ed., *Israel and Ishmael: Studies in Muslim-Jewish Relations* (London: Curzon, 2000), pp. 175–206.

25. It is also not always clear where persuasion ends and compulsion begins, where fear ends and conviction begins. In June 2016 a number of reports described an elderly man, one of the few remaining Christians in Raqqa, converting to Islam because he could no longer afford the cost of the

jizya. Close reading of the reports, however, which describe an IS video in which the man says he is converting to Islam, pronounces the shahada and says that he is doing it all of his own free will, suggests that, while lack of money or other problems related to being a Christian under IS rule may well explain his action, nothing in our evidence actually compels that sort of explanation. See Lisa Daftari, "Raqqa: Elderly Christian Forced to Convert to Islam: Cannot Afford ISIS Minority Tax," *Foreign Desk*, June 14, 2016, at http://www.foreigndesknews.com/lisas-desk/isis-forces-elderly-christian-convert-islam-raqqa/; Leah Marieann Klett, "Elderly Christian Man Forced to Convert to Islam because He Could Not Afford to Pay Minority Tax," *Gospel Herald*, June 15, 2016, at http://www.gospelherald.com/articles/64706/20160615/elderly-christian-man-forced-convert-islam-afford-pay-minority-tax.htm) (both accessed July 24, 2016; other reports basically repeat parts of these).

26. See Chapter 5.

27. In July 2016, Andrew White, who served for years as Anglican vicar of Saint George's church in Baghdad before being ordered by the Archbishop of Canterbury to leave that country for safety reasons, was being investigated over alleged ransom payments made by the charity to secure the release of sex slaves seized by IS. The religion of the women in question is not made clear, but they are likely to have been either Christians or Yezidis. See Anugrah Kumar, "'Vicar of Baghdad' Andrew White Suspended from Charity over Buying Back Sex Slaves from ISIS," *CP World*, June 30, 2016, at http://www.christianpost.com/news/vicar-of-baghdad-andrew-white-suspended-from-charity-over-buying-back-sex-slaves-from-isis–165857/; "Famed Christian Leader Accused of Paying Ransom to ISIS," Fox News, July 1, 2016, at http://www.foxnews.com/world/2016/07/07/famed-christian-leader-accused-paying-ransom-to-isis.html (both accessed July 8, 2016).

28. Anne Barnard, "Scores of Syrian [*sic*, for Assyrian—a different thing] Christians Kidnapped by Islamic State," *New York Times*, February 25, 2015; "Islamic State Frees 19 Christians as Ransom Paid: Activists," AFP, March 2, 2015.

29. David D. Kirkpatrick, "Islamic State Video Appears to Show Executions of Christians in Libya," *New York Times*, April 20, 2015.

30. A couple of examples: the *New York Times* of February 28, 2015, and March 18, 2016, both had editorials containing fairly ritualized condemnations of IS "genocide," "raw psychopathy," and "a sadistic battle for power and plunder."

31. "Christian Workers in Syria Crucified, Beheaded," at http://www.christianaid.org/News/2015/mir20151001.aspx (accessed March 18, 2016).

32. Melissa Barnhart, "5-Year-Old Christian Boy Cut in Half by ISIS Terrorists," at http://www.christianpost.com/news/5-year-old-christian-

boy-cut-in-half-by-ISIS-terrorists–124648/; Bob Unruh, "5-Year-Old Christian Boy Cut in Half by ISIS," http://www.wnd.com/2014/08/5-year-old-christian-boy-cut-in-half-by-isis/ (both accessed March 18, 2016).

33. See Haggai Erlich, "Islam, War and Peace in the Horn of Africa," in Terje Ostebo and Patrick Desplat, eds., *Muslim Ethiopia: The Christian Legacy, Identity Politics and Islamic Reformism* (London: Palgrave, 2013), pp. 185–195; and, at greater length, Haggai Erlich, *Ethiopia and the Middle East* (Boulder, CO: Lynne Rienner, 1994).

34. For the video, see http://www.breitbart.com/national-security/2015/12/04/islamic-state-video-shows-children-executing-spies-syria/ (accessed December 5, 2015).

35. Stillman, *Jews of Arab Lands,* offers plentiful evidence of this. The character and the significance of the Jewish experience under Islam give rise to manifold very varying interpretations; see for this Mark R. Cohen, "Islam and the Jews: Myth, Counter-Myth, History," *Jerusalem Quarterly* 38 (1986): 125–137; "The Neo-Lachrymose Conception of Jewish-Arab History," *Tikkun* 6, no. 3 (1991): 55–60; and *Under Crescent and Cross: The Jews in the Middle Ages* (Princeton, NJ: Princeton University Press, 1994).

36. It is no accident that one of the most important Jewish works of philosophy of the Middle Ages, known nowadays simply as the *Kuzari,* was entitled by its author, Judah Halevi, in the rhyming prose (in Arabic and, in this case, Judeo-Arabic) that was characteristic of the time, *Book of Argument and Proof in Aid of the Despised Faith.*

37. The latest report on the end of the Yemeni diaspora comes from March 2016. See Isabel Kershner, "Secret Rescue of Jews from War-Torn Yemen Concludes with Resettlement of 19 in Israel," *New York Times,* March 22, 2016, who reports that some nineteen Jews were brought to Israel in a secret operation, leaving around fifty who chose to remain in Yemen. For Afghanistan, see Jessica Donati and Mirwais Harooni, "Last Jew in Afghanistan Faces Ruin as Kebabs Fail to Sell," Reuters, November 12, 2013, at http://www.reuters.com/article/us-afghanistan-jews-idUSBRE9AB0A120131112 (accessed July 8, 2016). This is not, of course, to downplay the importance of, in particular, the Yemeni diaspora.

38. This is true under Article 64 of the current constitution.

39. *Jihad Watch,* December 26, 2015, at http://www.jihadwatch.org/2015/12/islamic-state-caliph-al-baghdadi-jews-soon-you-shall-hear-from-us-in-palestine-which-will-become-your-grave (accessed March 18, 2016).

40. See Isabel Kershner, "Stabbings by Palestinians Decline as Tactics Shift," *New York Times,* July 9, 2016, which reports that, according to the Israeli Shin Bet, the two Palestinians who attacked the Sarona café in Tel Aviv on June 8, 2016, were "inspired" by IS, but that "there was no evidence" that they "had been officially recruited" by IS or received support from it. This case is far from unique.

41. "Islamic State Threatens to Topple Hamas in Gaza," Reuters, June 30, 2015, at https://www.yahoo.com/news/islamic-state-threatens-topple-hamas-gaza–203927884.html?ref=gs (accessed July 9, 2016).

42. See Kate Brown's intriguing book, *A Biography of No Place: From Ethnic Borderland to Soviet Heartland* (Cambridge, MA: Harvard University Press, 2004).

43. Archive, specimen 8Y. Al-Tamimi notes and corrects a slip in the date at the top of the document; it is correct at the foot.

44. Archive, specimen 10W. The date is given as Saturday 19 Shaban, without the year—but 19 Shaban was a Saturday only in 2015.

45. Archive, specimen 5M. It must post-date the sharia sessions, announced on June 6, and it must be from before the next document to be considered, which is dated June 26, 2015.

46. Archive, specimen 6B. Tadmur is the Arabic name for Palmyra.

47. See the extensive report by Rukmini Callimachi, "ISIS Enshrines a Theology of Rape," *New York Times*, August 13, 2015, at http://www.nytimes.com/2015/08/14/world/middleeast/isis-enshrines-a-theology-of-rape.html?_r=0 (accessed July 12, 2016). For an announcement of a slave auction, in June 2015, with arrangements for submitting sealed bids, see Archive, specimen 13Y. (It is not clear that the women involved here are in fact Yezidis, because the auction was to take place in Syria.)

48. See "ISIL May Have Committed Genocide, War Crimes in Iraq, Says UN Human Rights Report," UN News Center, March 19, 2015, at http://www.un.org/apps/news/story.asp?NewsID=50369#.V4VY2_6V_IU, with a link to *Report of the Office of the United Nations High Commissioner for Human Rights on the Human Rights Situation in Iraq in the Light of Abuses Committed by the So-Called Islamic State in Iraq and the Levant and Associated Groups*, March 13, 2015 (accessed July 12, 2016).

49. For Shabaks see, besides the entry by M. van Bruinessen in *EI²*, IX, pp. 152–153, Amal Vinogradov, "Ethnicity, Cultural Discontinuity and Power Brokers in Northern Iraq: The Case of the Shabak," *American Ethnologist* 1, no. 1 (February 1974): 207–218; Matti Moosa, *Extremist Shiites: The Ghulat Sects* (Syracuse, NY: Syracuse University Press, 1988), pp. 1–9, with notes, pp. 451–453; Ali Mamouri, "IS Threatens Iraq's Minority Shabak Community," *Al-Monitor*, August 22, 2014, at http://www.al-monitor.com/pulse/ru/originals/2014/08/iraq-minorities-shabak-extinction-islamic-state.html (accessed July 12, 2016). For Kaka'is see Sozbin Celeng, "ISIS Threatens to Attack Kaka'i Religious Minority in Iraq," Ara News, March 20, 2016, at http://aranews.net/2016/03/isis-threatens-eliminate-kakai-religious-minority-iraq/ (accessed July 12, 2016). Ara News is a Kurdish news agency covering the semi-independent Kurdish-ruled area known as Rojava, and the broader Kurdish areas in neighboring countries of the region.

Chapter Seven. Apocalypse Now

1. Yaqut (a thirteenth-century geographer), quoted in Guy Le Strange, *Palestine under the Moslems: A Description of Syria and the Holy Land from AD. 650 to 1500* (Boston: Houghton Mifflin, 1890), p. 426.

2. Ibn Abd al-Munim al-Himyari (a fifteenth-century geographer), *Kitab al-Rawd al-Mitar fi Khabar al-Aqtar*, ed. Ihsan Abbas (Beirut: Librairie du Liban, 1975), p. 231.

3. *EI²*, IX, pp. 821–822 (by R. Eisener).

4. The Dome of the Rock, in Jerusalem, has an inscription naming the Abbasid caliph al-Mamun (813–833) as its builder. But when that caliph inserted his name in the existing inscription, he forgot to change the date, which still says 72 (of the Hijra, or 691–692 CE), which fits correctly with the reign of Abd al-Malik, the Umayyad caliph who actually built that wonderful monument.

5. Al-Himyari, *Kitab al-Rawd al-Mitar*, pp. 231, 473; also Yaqubi (a ninth-century historian), *Tarikh* (Beirut: Dar Sadir, n.d.), vol. 2, pp. 356–357. The name al-Saffah, with a base meaning of "pour out," can also mean "the Generous," but it is traditionally understood in relation to this caliph in the first sense. For the speech in which he calls himself by this name/title, see al-Tabari, *The History*, vol. 27: *The Abbasid Revolution*, trans. and annotated by John Alden Williams (Albany: State University of New York Press, Bibliotheca Persica, 1985), pp. 152–154, at the end of the speech. See also H. F. Amedroz, "On the Meaning of the Laqab 'al-Saffah,'" *Journal of the Royal Asiatic Society* (1907): 660–663.

6. *EI²*, II, p. 72, s.v. Dābiķ (D. Sourdel). For the battle, see Michael Winter, "The Ottoman Occupation," in *The Cambridge History of Egypt*, general editor M. W. Daly, vol. 1: *Islamic Egypt, 640–1517*, ed. Carl F. Petry (Cambridge, Eng.: Cambridge University Press, 1998), pp. 490–516, esp. the vivid detail provided in pp. 498–499, including how the aged Egyptian Sultan Kansuh al-Ghawri was surrounded by forty dignitaries descended from the Prophet bearing copies of the Quran on their heads. The Sultan fell off his horse, possibly from an attack of apoplexy, during the battle and disappeared, probably trampled to death. Edward S. Creasy, *History of the Ottoman Turks: From the Beginning of Their Empire to the Present Time*, 2nd ed. (London: R. Bentley and Son, 1878), p. 142, reports that according to Islamic tradition the tomb of the biblical king David lies on the plain.

7. Al-Amaq seems very likely to be identical to al-Amq, "the lowland," an area not far from Antioch. See Yaqut, quoted in Le Strange, *Palestine under the Moslems*, p. 71. It is of course no accident that this name is used as the name of the news agency that often communicates for IS.

8. For this passage see Muslim, *Sahih*, Fitan, 34 (no. 2897).

9. The naming of the city is actually rather more complicated. See the learned note of Halil Inalcik in *EI²*, IV, pp. 224–248, the entry for Istanbul, at p. 224.

10. This is one of the Thirteen Principles of Faith put together by Maimonides.

11. For blood moons and John Hagee's prediction based on them, see the Wikipedia entry "Blood Moon Prophecy," at http://en.wikipedia.org/wiki/Blood_Moon_Prophecy (accessed March 15, 2015). For the song "Moshiach Now," which is associated particularly with the Chabad movement of the Lubavitcher Rebbe, just Google the words.

12. The quotation is from Mercedes García-Arenal, *Messianism and Puritanical Reform: Mahdis of the Muslim West* (Leiden: Brill, 2006), p. 3.

13. Pew Research Center, Religion and Public Life, *The World's Muslims: Unity and Diversity*, August 9, 2012, at http://www.pewforum.org/2012/08/09/the-worlds-muslims-unity-and-diversity-executive-summary/ (accessed May 30, 2016), pp. 65–66.

14. David Cook, *Studies in Muslim Apocalyptic* (Princeton, NJ: Darwin Press, Studies in Antiquity and Early Islam, 2002); David Cook, *Contemporary Muslim Apocalyptic Literature* (Syracuse, NY: Syracuse University Press, 2005). See also Sandra Campbell, "It Must Be the End of Time: Apocalyptic *Ahadith* as a Record of the Islamic Community's Reactions to the Turbulent First Centuries," *Medieval Encounters* 4 (1998): 178–187.

15. See Quran, *sura* 17:4–8.

16. Wilferd Madelung, "Abd Allah b. al-Zubayr and the Mahdi," *Journal of Near Eastern Studies* 40 (1981): 291–306; "The Sufyani between Tradition and History," *Studia Islamica* 63 (1986): 4–48; and "Apocalyptic Prophecies in Hims in the Umayyad Age," *Journal of Semitic Studies* 31 (1986): 141–186.

17. Well noted by G. R. Hawting, *The First Dynasty of Islam: The Umayyad Caliphate, AD 661–750*, 2nd ed. (London: Routledge, 2000), p. 73 and p. 88, n. 3 (where for 8 read 18 and for 108 read 208).

18. Curiously, we are also told that he had over a dozen sons, but the list does not include the deceased intended heir, and none of them seems to have been considered as a substitute for him. See Yaqubi, *Ta'rikh*, p. 300.

19. For most of the details here see the entry on Sulayman in *EI²*, IX, pp. 821–822 (by R. Eisener), as well as the same writer's important longer study, *Zwischen Faktum und Fiktion: Eine Studie zum Umayyadenkalifen Sulaimān b. 'Abdalmalik und seinem Bild in den Quellen* (Wiesbaden: Otto Harrassowitz, 1987).

20. See especially the fascinating book of Bonnie Blackburn and Leofranc Holford-Strevens, *The Oxford Companion to the Year: An Exploration of Calendar Customs and Time-Reckoning* (Oxford, Eng.: Oxford University Press, 1999).

21. Quran, *sura* 9:35–37.

22. For the curious story of intercalation in Islam, see Alfred Guillaume, trans., *The Life of Muhammad: A Translation of Ibn Ishaq's Sirat Rasul Allah* (Oxford, Eng.: Oxford University Press, 1955), pp. 650–652, and

especially al-Biruni, *The Chronology of Ancient Nations*, trans. C. Edward Sachau (London: William H. Allen & Co. for the Oriental Translation Fund of Great Britain and Ireland, 1879), pp. 73–74, and 13–14, where the writer has interesting remarks on the loss of meanings to the names of the months arising from the prohibition on intercalation.

23. Interestingly in this connection, Salman Rushdie, in the story referred to earlier, clearly uses a solar year, not an Islamic one, when making the calculation of how long the Muslim Ibn Rushd spent in exile. His 1001 days are represented by Rushdie as two years, eight months, and twenty-eight days and nights: this comes to 1001 only if we use a non-Islamic year of 365 days.

24. It is certainly not accidental that the tenth-century writer Masudi, in listing the titles that he claims were taken by the Umayyad caliphs, gives the title al-Mahdi to Sulayman. Even if the story is as much an invention in the case of Sulayman as it is about the rest of the Umayyads, the specific choice of title in his case confirms the existence of a messianic tradition connected with this caliph. See also Chapter 2.

25. From the (eleventh-century?) *Kitab al-Uyun*, published in M. J. de Goeje and P. de Jong, *Fragmenta Historicorum Arabicorum*, vol. 1 (Leiden: Brill, 1869), p. 24; trans. by E. W. Brooks, "The Campaign of 716–718, from Arabic Sources," *Journal of Hellenic Studies* 19 (1899): 20–21 (adapted slightly here). M. Canard, "Les expéditions des arabes contre Constantinople dans l'histoire et dans la légende," *Journal asiatique* 208 (1926): 61–122, at 107, considers the prediction here as invented "no doubt to flatter the caliph," and as causing him to organize the expedition, though he also recognizes that it could have been invented after the event, in order to explain the expedition. But the historical context shows that it formed part of a larger program and must have been invented in advance in order to justify the expedition, not simply to flatter Sulayman.

26. For an example of the supposed significance of the year 100 of the *hijra* among Muslims, see also Tabari, *The History*, vol. 27, p. 148, where the "turn of the first century" (by which is meant the end of the first century of Islam) is described as a "turning point" for the Abbasids.

Conclusion

1. Some reports at the time of the 2016 Olympics suggested that IS was attempting to extend its reach there too.

2. For a sketch of the risks, see Sam Nunn and Andrew Bieniawski, "Foiling the Dirty Bomb: How to Head Off the Threat of a Radiological Weapon before It's Too Late," *Hoover Digest* 1 (Winter 2016): 55–57.

3. For a striking exposition of the notion that the West is being drawn into a clash, internal to Islam, between two positions, one that sees Islam as essentially antithetical to Western ideas and ideals and the other that sees

Islam as fundamentally compatible with the West, see Zeyno Baran, "Fighting the War of Ideas," *Foreign Affairs* 84, no. 6 (November–December 2005): 68–78. The intellectual descent of this idea from those of Samuel Huntington, author of *The Clash of Civilizations and the Remaking of World Order* (1996, an expanded version of an article published in *Foreign Affairs* in 1993), is clear.

4. Al-Qaida rejected IS as long ago as February 2014. See Liz Sly, "Al-Qaeda Disavows Any Ties with Radical Islamist ISIS Group in Syria, Iraq," *Washington Post*, February 3, 2014, at https://www.washingtonpost.com/world/middle_east/al-qaeda-disavows-any-ties-with-radical-islamist-isis-group-in-syria-iraq/2014/02/03/2c9afc3a–8cef–11e3–98ab-fe5228217bd1_story.html (accessed May 11, 2016).

5. See, e.g., "'Urgent Need' for Unified Arab Force to Counter Radicals," *Arab News*, March 10, 2015, at http://www.arabnews.com/featured/news/716291?quicktabs_stat2=0 (accessed May 10, 2016).

6. It seems worth noting here that "degrade" in this narrow military sense appears to be a recent U.S. contribution to the military, and hence the popular, lexicons. As so often occurs, such vocabulary changes tend to eliminate or obscure the human element.

7. See Remarks by the President at National Prayer Breakfast, February 5, 2015, at https://www.whitehouse.gov/the-press-office/2015/02/05/remarks-president-national-prayer-breakfast, where I have corrected the misprint (accessed May 10, 2016).

8. Julie Hirschfeld Davis, "Acts Committed in Islam's Name Betray Faith, Obama Says," *New York Times*, February 6, 2015.

9. See, e.g., Peter Ford, "Europe Cringes at Bush 'Crusade' against Terrorists," *Christian Science Monitor*, September 19, 2001, at http://www.csmonitor.com/2001/0919/p12s2-woeu.html (accessed May 10, 2016).

10. President Obama, September 10, 2014, at https://www.whitehouse.gov/the-press-office/2014/09/10/statement-president-isil–1 (accessed November 19, 2016).

11. For discussion of the view that IS is a cult and not a religion (and of what she sees as the difference), see Florence Gaub, "The Cult of ISIS," *Survival* 58, no. 1 (February–March 2016): 113–130.

12. For more on this event, see the May 10, 2016, article in the *Independent* at http://www.independent.co.uk/news/uk/home-news/police-apologise-for-making-fake-suicide-bomber-shout-allahu-akbar-during-counter-terror-exercise-in-a7022196.html (accessed May 11, 2016).

13. Quoted in Pippa Crerar and Nicholas Cecil, "Sadiq Khan: UK Muslims Must Do More to Root Out Cancer of Extremism," *Evening Standard*, November 19, 2015, at http://www.standard.co.uk/news/mayor/sadiq-uk-muslims-must-do-more-to-root-out-cancer-of-extremism-a3118801.html (accessed May 10, 2016).

14. See, e.g., John Gearson and Hugo Rosemont, "CONTEST as Strategy: Reassessing Britain's Counterterrorism Approach," *Studies in Conflict and Terrorism* 38 (2015): 1038–1064.

15. See *Independent*, January 18, 2016, at http://www.independent.co.uk/news/uk/home-news/backlash-as-david-cameron-announced-plans-to-teach-muslim-women-english-a6818496.html (accessed May 11, 2016).

16. See "Valls annonce des centres de réinsertion pour 'personnes radicalisées' dans 'chaque région,'" in *Le Monde*, May 10, 2016, at http://www.lemonde.fr/societe/article/2016/05/09/manuel-valls-doit-annoncer-ses-mesures-contre-la-radicalisation-djihadiste_4915701_3224.html (accessed May 10, 2016).

17. It is not clear how the obvious dangers to academic independence will be worked out and prevented from tainting such research. The memory of American psychologists working in support of "enhanced interrogation techniques" for the U.S. government remains uncomfortably fresh. See "New APA Policy Bans Psychologist Participation in National Security Interrogations," September 2015, at http://www.apa.org/monitor/2015/09/cover-policy.aspx (accessed May 11, 2016). But see also James Risen, "Critic of Psychologists' Role in Interrogation Is Asked to Reconsider," *New York Times*, April 15, 2016, at http://www.nytimes.com/2016/04/16/us/psychologists-torture-hoffman-report-rebuttals.html?_r=0 (accessed July 10, 2016).

18. More academic approaches from outside Islam are available too. See, for example, Alex P. Schmid, *Challenging the Narrative of the "Islamic State,"* ICCT Research Paper, June 2015, International Centre for Counter-Terrorism, The Hague, at http://icct.nl/wp-content/uploads/2015/06/ICCT-Schmid-Challenging-the-Narrative-of-the-Islamic-State-June2015.pdf (accessed June 22, 2016).

19. Reported by the *Times of India*, August 30, 2014, at http://timesofindia.indiatimes.com/india/Muslim-cleric-in-Kerala-issues-fatwa-against-ISIS-jihadists-sell-several-dozens-of-Yazidi-women/articleshowprint/41281217.cms (accessed May 11, 2016). This sheikh is the same one who in November 2015 said that women were "only fit to deliver children." See also Chapter 5.

20. See the reports in the *Times of India* of September 8, 2015: http://timesofindia.indiatimes.com/india/Over-1000-Islamic-scholars-condemn-killing-of-innocents-by-ISIS/articleshow/48873062.cms and in *The Hindu* of September 8, 2015: http://www.thehindu.com/news/national/muslim-clerics-issue-fatwa-against-is/article7629739.ece (both accessed May 11, 2016).

21. See the report by Joe Cochrane, "From Indonesia, a Muslim Challenge to the Ideology of the Islamic State," *New York Times*, November 26, 2016, at http://www.nytimes.com/2015/11/27/world/asia/indonesia-islam-nahdlatul-ulama.html?_r=0 (accessed May 11, 2016).

22. For these and related figures see Edward Delman, "ISIS in the World's Largest Muslim Country: Why Are so Few Indonesians Joining the Islamic State?" *The Atlantic*, January 3, 2016, at http://www.theatlantic.com /international/archive/2016/01/isis-indonesia-foreign-fighters/422403/ (accessed May 11, 2016).

23. For the fatwa see Richard Kerbaj, Tim Shipman, and Marie Woolf, "UK Imams Put Fatwa on Jihadists," *Sunday Times* (London), August 31, 2014, at http://www.thesundaytimes.co.uk/sto/news/uk_news/National/article 1453436.ece, available also at http://www.quilliamfoundation.org/press/ the-sunday-times-front-page-coverage-of-anti-is-fatwa-authored-by-dr- usama-hasan/ (both accessed May 11, 2016). For the figures see Ashley Kirk, "Iraq and Syria: How Many Foreign Fighters Are Fighting for Isil?" *Telegraph* (London), March 24, 2016, at http://www.telegraph.co. uk/news/2016/03/29/iraq-and-syria-how-many-foreign-fighters-are- fighting-for-isil/ (accessed May 11, 2016) and Edward Delman, "ISIS in the World's Largest Muslim Country: Why Are so Few Indonesians Joining the Islamic State?" *The Atlantic*, January 3, 2016, at http://www. theatlantic.com/international/archive/2016/01/isis-indonesia-foreign- fighters/422403/ (accessed May 11, 2016).

24. See, e.g., http://www.christianitytoday.com/gleanings/2016/january/ marrakesh-declaration-muslim-nations-christian-persecution.html; http://religionnews.com/2016/01/27/morocco-summit-pushes-muslim- clerics-improve-lot-religious-minorities/; http://www.catholicnews.com/ services/englishnews/2016/muslim-leaders-reiterate-support-for- minority-rights-in-islamic-nations.cfm (all these dated January 27, 2016); http://www1.cbn.com/cbnnews/world/2016/January/Morocco-Calls-for- Muslim-Nations-to-Protect-Christians-from-Persecution (dated January 29, 2016); http://www.nytimes.com/2016/02/03/world/africa/muslim- conference-calls-for-protection-of-religious-minorities.html?_r=0 (dated February 2, 2016) (all accessed May 16, 2016).

25. The Open Letter, in Arabic and with translations in various languages, as well as lists of signatories, is available at http://www.lettertobaghdadi. com/ (accessed May 22, 2016).

26. The dignitaries collaborating on the Open Letter number 126 (more have been added since the initial publication) and they come from all over the world: thirty-nine come from Egypt, seven from Yemen, four from Jordan, five from Jerusalem, while Nigeria, Sudan, and Morocco have three each. Other countries have only one or two each, with just one major exception: the United States, with twenty-one.

27. The Executive Summary is found at the head of the English translation and of all the other translations, but in non-English translations it is called simply a Summary (German: Kurzfassung; Bosnian: Sažetak; Hungarian: Rövid összefoglalás; French: Résumé; Turkish: Özet; etc.). In the Arabic original, it is called an Executive Summary (Arabic Mukhtasar

Tanfidhi), but, curiously, comes at the end—curiously, because an Executive Summary generally comes at the start of a document, offering an easy alternative to reading the main text.

28. People of the Scripture is interpreted here, unusually, as meaning only Christians. Jews are not included. The Letter describes "Arab Christians" as "not strangers to these lands, but rather, of the native peoples of these lands from pre-Islamic times ... For the past 1400 years, they have defended their countries against the Crusaders, colonialists, Israel and other wars."

29. The Open Letter has generated a useful commentary by a retired professor of Islamic history at the Hebrew University of Jerusalem: see Ella Landau-Tasseron, *Delegitimizing ISIS on Islamic Grounds: Criticism of Abu Bakr al-Baghdadi by Muslim Scholars*, MEMRI Inquiry and Analysis, no. 1205, November 19, 2015, at http://www.memri.org/publicdocs/MEMRI_IA_1205_Delegitimizing_ISIS_On_Islamic_Grounds-FINAL.pdf (accessed May 22, 2016).

30. The footnote at this point in the text gives a reference to the IS video of the incident.

31. For more on this app, see Bryan Clark, "ISIS Built an App with Cartoon Missiles and Guns to Teach Kids the Arabic Alphabet," TNW.com, May 13, 2016, at http://thenextweb.com/insider/2016/05/13/isis-built-an-app-with-cartoon-missiles-and-guns-to-teach-kids-the-arabic-alphabet/#gref (accessed May 1, 2016).

Glossary

Transliteration of Arabic here follows generally the patterns of my sources. The glottal stop (*hamza*), other than at the start of a word, and the *'ayn* are occasionally indicated (by ' and ', respectively). The Arabic definite article *al-* ("the") is (with a few exceptions) ignored in the alphabetization: thus, *al-dawla* will be found under d, not a.

ahl al-hall wal-'aqd—people of loosening and tying, hence people of influence, power
'alayhis Salam—peace be upon him (said of the dead)
alhamdulillah—praise be to God
Allahu Akbar—God is greatest (lit. God is greater)
amir (pl. *umara'*)—commander, prince
Amir al-Mu'minin—Commander of the Faithful, title of caliph
'aqida—creed
al-Aqsa—mosque in Jerusalem
ard al-malahim—land of slaughter
'ashara—ten
'asr to *maghrib*—(from the) afternoon (prayer) to (the) evening (prayer)
Assalamu 'alaykum wa rahmatuhu wa barakatuhu—Peace be upon you and His (i.e., God's) mercy and blessing
awwal 'aqd dhimma—first document of protection
baraka—blessing
bay'a—pledge of allegiance
Bayt al-Mal—Treasury
bid'a (pl. *bida'*)—innovation (in religion)
bid'a hasana—a good innovation
bunduqiyya—gun
dabbaba—tank

da'wa—call (of Islam)

dawla—turning, hence ruler/dynasty, hence state

al-dawla al-islamiyya—The Islamic State

dhimma—protection, name given to status of Christians and Jews under Islam

dhimmi—one who possesses the protection of the *dhimma*

Dhu al-Hijja—the twelfth month of the Islamic calendar

dinar—coin of high value, originally a gold coin

dirhem—coin of medium value, originally a silver coin

diwan—ministry

Diwan al-Hisba—Ministry of Morals

Diwan al-Ifta' wal-Buhuth—Department/Ministry of Fatwas and Research

Diwan al-Qada'—Ministry of Justice

Diwan al-Ta'lim—Ministry of Education

emir—see *amir*

fals (pl. *fulus*)—coin of low value

fatwa—a legal opinion

hadith—a tradition of the Prophet

hajj—pilgrimage

al-Haram al-Sharif—Arabic name for the mountain in Jerusalem where the Dome of the Rock and al-Aqsa mosque are situated; known also as the Temple Mount

hijra (in more old-fashioned English *hegira*)—the migration of Muhammad from Mecca to Medina, in 622 CE, from which the Islamic dating system begins

hudud (sing. *hadd*)—lit. limits; name for punishments laid down in the Quran

hukumat al-ridda—apostasy government (in language of the Islamic State)

imam—one who stands "in front," hence prayer leader, hence religious leader

in sha' Allah, inshallah, Insha'allah—God willing, if God will

'ishrun—twenty

isnad—chain of transmission (of a hadith)

isra'—nocturnal journey, hence the nocturnal journey of Muhammad to the seven heavens

Janna—garden, hence Paradise

jihad—struggle, hence holy war

jizya—special poll tax paid by Christians and Jews

Ka'ba—the huge black stone in Mecca, a center of Islamic rites especially during the pilgrimage

kafir (pl. *kuffar*)—infidel

khalifa—caliph

khamr (pl. *khumur*)—alcoholic drink

khamsa—five

khilafa—caliphate

khilafa 'ala minhaj al-nubuwwa—caliphate on the pattern of prophethood/prophecy *kunya*—by-name, in the form Abu + another name ("Father of . . ."), by which a person is normally known

la ilaha illa Allah—There is no God but God

mahram—a close male relative who, because he cannot marry her, may be with and see a woman as well as accompany her when she goes out

malhama (pl. *malahim*)—see *ard al-malahim*

mihrab—niche in mosque indicating the direction of prayer (*qibla*)

minhaj—program

mithqal—a weight

mufti—one who gives a fatwa

mujahid—one who strives, hence fighter in jihad

murtadd (pl. *murtaddin*)—an apostate

mushrik (pl. *mushrikin*)—one who practices *shirk*, polytheist

naskhi—a form of Arabic script

Nusayri—follower of a sect derived from the Shi'a, mainly in Syria

qibla—the direction of prayer

Quran—the holy book of Islam

radiyallah 'anhu—May God be pleased with him (of the dead)

Rafida—Shi'is in the language of IS

Rasul Allah—Messenger of God (Muhammad)

salat—prayer

sayf—sword

shahada—testimony, hence statement of faith of a Muslim (*la ilaha illa Allah Muhammad rasul Allah*—There is no god but God, Muhammad is the Messenger of God)

shahid—martyr (as in English/Greek, the root meaning of the word is witness)

shar'i—(religiously) legal

shari'a—religious law in Islam

shaykh—elder, title of respect

Shi'a—the second great division of Islam; short for Shi'at Ali, "the party of Ali"

Shi'i—a Muslim who belongs to the Shi'a

shirk—polytheism, idolatry, associating other gods with God

shura—consultative council, assembly

Sunna—see *Sunni*

Sunni—a Muslim who follows the Sunna, or way, of the Prophet

Sunnism—the larger of the two main streams of Islam

sura—a chapter of the Quran

tafsir—commentary (usually on the Quran)

takfir—declaring someone a *kafir*, infidel, in effect excommunication

tawba—repentance

tawhid—monotheism

umma—the community of Islam

wali—governor
wazir—minister, vizier
wilaya—province
wizara—ministry
zakat—a religiously prescribed charity

Index

Note: the Arabic definite article ("al-") is disregarded in the alphabetization. Transliteration of Arabic and of Arabic names generally follows my sources.

ISIS, ISIL, IS, Islamic State, as well as most occurrences of Iraq and Syria, have not been indexed.

"A Brief Guide to the Islamic State," 24
Abase, Amira, 122–124
Abbasids, 27, 39–40, 46, 177–178, 188, 195; coins of, 76
Abdullah, king of Jordan, 106
Abraham. *See* Ibrahim
Abu Bakr (first caliph), 31
Abu Sayyaf, 73, 91
Ad, 186
Adam, 34
al-Adnani, Abu Muhammad, 28
Afghanistan, 188
ahl al-hall wal-aqd, 35–36
Ahlam al-Nasr (pseudonym), 132–134
Ahmed, Shahab, ix
Aïda (opera), 115
Aisha (wife of the Prophet), 118, 241n39
Aitboulahcen, Hasna, 121–122
Alawis, 174
Ali (caliph), 52
All-India Sunni Jamiyyathul-Ulama, 204
alphabet app, of IS, 211

al-Amaq, 178
American Numismatic Society, 75
Antioch, 76
antiquities, IS sales of, 73, 81; U.S imports of, 79
apocalypse, 179–187
apostates, 30
Arab League, secretary-general of, 202
Arab Spring, 16
Arabic language, 8, 9, 46, 117, 179; courses, 123
Arafat, Yasser, and Quran, 35
archaeological objects, sales of, 78–79
Armageddon, Islamic, 178–180, 182–183
Asad family, 16, 61
Atatürk, Mustafa Kemal, 38
Awakening (Ar. *sahwat*; pro-government groups in Iraq), 30
Aya Sofya, 216–217n20

Baghdad, National Museum, 75
al-Baghdadi, Abu Bakr, 1, 27, 42–43, 46, 53–54
beards, 98, 105

Begum, Shamima, 122–124
Bible, 34
bida, 94, 108, 113, 115
billiards, 113
blood moons, 184
body parts, taken from living
    captives, 66
Bokova, Irina, 72
Bouazizi, Mohamed, 16
boundaries, 58
Britain, reactions to IS, 203, 205;
    Muslims, 203
Britani, Abu Rumaysah al (Siddharta
    Dhar), 24
Byzantines, 177–183, 186, 189

calendars, 60, 100–109, 192–193
caliph, 33–34; names and titles, 43–47;
    qualifications of caliph, 41–43;
    throne-names, 44–47. *See also*
    caliphate
caliphate, 48; nature of, 31–32;
    Ottoman, abolished, 38; proclaimed,
    27–38; succession to, 53–54
charity tax (*zakat*), 98
Charlemagne, 27
Chechens, 64
children, 140–145; and education
    under IS, 141–144; and *mamluks*,
    142–143; shooting Syrian soldiers,
    141;
Christians, 69, 70, 146–166; Ethiopian,
    in Libya, 163, 165–166; and
    Marrakesh Declaration, 206; in
    Mosul, 147–150; in Raqqa, 150–163
coins, 49–50, 73, 75–77, 80, 91; imports
    to U.S., 78–79; IS proposed, 107
Constantinople, 177, 182, 189, 194;
    besieged by Sulayman, 191
conversion, forced, 175–176
Cook, David, 185
cooking, for the mujahidin, 134
Cordoba, 40
crosses, 33

"crusader," ix, 61, 65
cult, IS as a, 252n11
cursing, 113

Dabiq, ix, 177–190, 194
Dabiq (magazine), 23, 186
Daily Mail, 90
Dajjal (Antichrist), 179
dalala (error), 115
Damascus, 194
Darwin, Charles, 214n3, 223n4
David (biblical king), 249n6
dawa (call), 39
Deir al-Zor (province), 22, 63
Delbrück, Hans, 82–84
Dhar, Siddharta (Abu Rumaysah al
    Britani), 24
dhimma, pact of, 153–157
diwan (ministry), 59, 61

education, 61–65; administration,
    63–67; fields of study, 64;
    suppression of fields of study,
    61–63
"Emergency Red Lists," 73–74
"enhanced interrogation techniques."
    See torture
evolution, 6

fasting, 9, 116
FATF, 88
fatwas, 96–99, 106–108, 119, 126–129,
    205, 208
festivals, 119
"fifth," caliph's share of plunder, 69
Final Hour, 178
fingers, position of, in prayer, 112
foosball (table football), 113
France, reactions to IS, 203–204;
    recruitment to IS, 206

al-Gaddafi, Muammar, 16, 49
gambling, 113
Gaza, Hamas leaders in, 168

genealogy (qualification of caliph), 41, 42
Geniza of Cairo, 22
Germany, recruitment to IS, 206
al-Ghazzali, 42
Golan Heights, IS advances in, 169
gold, 69, 90
graves, 33, 177–178

hadiths, 50–53, 99, 119, 178–180, 187–188; study of, 180–182, 188–189, 195
hajj, 191
Hawija, 98–99, 112
al-Hayat media center, 23, 28
health, 65–66
hijra, 190, 192
Hudhayfa ibn al-Yaman, 50
hudud (sharia penalties), 33, 98
Huntington, Samuel P., 15
Husayn, Taha, 34
Hussein, Saddam, 16, 45–46

Ibn Hanbal, Ahmad, 50
Ibn Hazm, 46
Ibn Jubayr, 101, 116, 147
Ibn Taymiyya, 108, 113
Ibrahim, 43, 91
ideology, of IS, and other forms of Islam, 197–212
imitation, of the infidel, 105
India, reactions to IS, 204–205; recruitment to IS in, 205–206
Indonesia, 205
Innovation. See *bida*
intercalation, 193
Internet, 25, 129, 139
Iran, 66; Revolution, 197
Iraq and Sham (Syria) (omitted from name of Islamic State), 37
Isa. See Jesus
Isaiah (prophet), 165
Ishmael. See Ismail
Islam, observance of, 7–8
Islam Online (website), 96
Ismail, 43

isnad, 188
Israel, IS and, 166–170; IS volunteers from, 168
Istanbul. See Constantinople

Jannah, 123. See also Paradise
Jerusalem, as center for Sulayman, 191
Jesus, 183
Jews, IS and, 166–170
jihad, 55
jizya, 70, 150–163
Jonah (prophet), 147, 149

Kaba, 52, 63, 91
Kagan, Ute Wartenberg, 75–77, 80
Kaka'is, 175–176
Kalashnikov, 128, 131
Kanthapuram, Sheikh Abu Bakr Ahmed, 204, 241–242n43
Karbala, 52
Kasasbeh, Muadh, 106–109
Keegan, Sir John, 3
Kerala, 204
Kesinovic, Samra, 124
khalifa, 47. See also caliph
Khan, Sadiq (mayor of London), 203
al-Khansa Brigade, 24, 134–139
khilafa. See caliphate
khilafa ala minhaj al-nubuwwa, 49–53, 113
Khomeini, Ayatollah, fatwa against Salman Rushdie, 96
Khorasan, and end times, 188
Kulthum, Umm, 15
kunya, 44
Kurdish language, 171
Kurds, 69, 98–99, 171–173

Lane, Edward William, 117
language (coded), 61, 200–201, 202–203, 208; translation, 207–208
law, Islamic, 95–96; U.S., forbidding mutilation or destruction of money, 91

Madelung, Wilferd, 18
Madina, 52
Mahdi, 17–18, 47, 194
mahrim, 66
Maimonides, 184
mamluks, 142–144
Mamluks, 189
Manasseh (biblical king), 165
Manchester (U.K.), 203
al-Mansur (Abbasid caliph), quoted, 81
maps, 62
Marrakesh Declaration, 206–208
martyrdom, 109, 163–166
al-Masisa, 177
al-Masudi, 46
Masyaf, 77
al-Mawardi, 42
Mecca, 52, 116; Grand Mosque
    takeover, 17; Mecca time, 233n22;
    Muawiya (first Umayyad), 52
medical treatment and women 66–67
Metropolitan Museum, New York, 73
mihrab, 111
Monaco, exports to U.S., 80
money, burning, 89–91
moon, new, 100–101
Mosul, Christians in, 147–150;
    museum, 72
Muhammad (Prophet), 31, 50, 91;
    succession to, 31; birthday of,
    106–109
mujahid (fighter for the faith), 41,
    61, 69
murtaddin. *See* apostates
music, IS and, 114–115
Muslim ibn al-Hajjaj (hadith collector),
    178
al-Mustasim (last Abbasid caliph),
    27, 45

nabi, 50
Nahdlatul Ulama, 205
Napoleon, 82
Nasser, Gamal Abdel, 16, 34

National Prayer Breakfast, 202
Netanyahu, Benjamin, 166
al-Numan ibn Bashir, 50–51
numbers, reliability of, 82–87, 89–90
Nusayris, 174

Obama, Barack, 202
Oberammergau, 18
Offa, king of Mercia, 76
oil, IS sales of, 81–88
Open Letter to al-Baghdadi, 206–211
al-Otaybi, Juhayman, 17–18
Ottomans, 189

Pact of Umar, 156–159
Palmyra, 75–76
Paradise, 10–12, 130–131
Paris, 121
Parthenon, 243n2
perfume, 119
Peter (disciple of Jesus), 48
Pew Research Center, 7, 11
Philby, H. St. John, 102
pigeons, keeping of, on roof, 128
plunder, 9, 98
prayer, 109–113; authenticity of, in
    Muslim eyes, 110; Christian, 109–
    110; Christian and Jewish women
    at, 111; Jewish, 109–111; language
    of Christian, 110. *See also tarawih*

al-Qahtani, Muhammad Abdallah, 18
al-Qaida, 17
al-Qaradawi, Yusuf, 96
Qaraqosh, 164
Quran, 6–9, 29–30, 33–35, 95, 104,
    116, 131, 144, 147, 149, 153, 186,
    193, 205; memorization, 132, 144;
    status of, compared to Bible, 34
Quraysh, qurashi, 42–43, 53

rafida. *See* Shi'is
Ramadan, 9, 30, 100–103, 115–119; in
    Sicily, 116; in summer, 116

Ramla, as local capital in Palestine, 91
Rania, queen of Jordan, 106
Raqqa, 186–187; Christians in, 150, 170
recruitment, by IS, motivations and success of, 199–200, 205–206
Red Arch, 78–79
"Red Lists," 73–74
responsum, 96
revenue, 68–93; antiquities sales, 73; donations from Saudi Arabia and Gulf countries, 69–70; taxes, 70–71
"Ruling on the Use of Christian Dates," 104
Rum. See Byzantines
Rumsfeld, Donald, 75
Rushdie, Salman, 96

sahwat. See Awakening
salat. See prayer
scouts, 144
Second Coming, 183–184
Selim I, the Grim (Ottoman sultan), 178
Selimovic, Sabina, 124
sexual activity, during Ramadan, 116
sexual norms, 66
Shabaks, 175–176
sharia, 9–10
Sharia Committee for the Observation of New Moons, 104
she'elot u-teshuvot, 96
Shepard, William, 5–6
Shi'is, 30, 61, 66, 173–174
al-Shishani, Omar, 23
shura, 35
singing, 115
Sisi, General, 202
Six Day War, 186
slogans of IS, 63
soccer, IS and, 114
Solomon (biblical figure), 194
Sotloff, Steven, 167
sources, 21–26

Spain, Islamic, 38–40, 45
Sulayman (Umayyad caliph), 47, 177–178, 190–192, 194–196
Sultana, Khadiza, 122–124
al-Suyuti, 108
Sykes-Picot Agreement, 58
Syria, 182–183, 189, 205

takfir, 211
Taliban, as harbingers of salvation, 188
al-Tamimi, Aymenn Jawad, 21
tarawih (supererogatory prayers), 115–119
taxation, 70–71; quranic, 70
teachers, 64; reformation of, 64–65
"This is the Promise of Allah," 29–30
torture, 253n17
Trinity, as shirk, 152
trousers, 98–99
Turkey, 66, 182–183, 189
Turkish Grand National Assembly, 38
al-Turtushi, 118
Twitter, 28

Umar (caliph), 35, 52, 118, 157
Umar ibn Abd al-Aziz (Umayyad caliph), 51, 53, 157, 190, 194–195
Umayyads, of Damascus, 46, 48, 51–53, 177–178, 190; in Spain, 39–40
Umm Kulthum. *See* Kulthum, Umm
ummah (Islamic community), 34
Unesco, 72
United Nations, 205; reactions to IS destruction, 72–73
United States, reactions to IS destruction, 73–74
Uthman (caliph), 35, 52

Vabalathus, 76
videos, IS, 99, 115, 163, 166
Vietnam, 82

Wahhabis, 103, 108–109

water, Sulayman piping, to Mecca, 191; quranic emphasis on in Paradise, 192

Welby, Justin, archbishop of Canterbury, 147

West Bank, illegal excavations in, 81

White, Canon Andrew, 165

widows, re-marriage of, 105–106

wizara (ministry), 59, 61

women, cooking, for the mujahidin, 134; correct behavior of, 134–139; and education, 137; and Internet, 139; and marriage, 137; and motherhood, 139–140; under IS rule, 125–140; writing by, 129–134

"Women of the Islamic State," 24, 134–139

Yazid I (Umayyad caliph), 52

Yezidis, 175; women, 125, 130

zakat (charity tax), 98

al-Zarqawi, Abu Musab, ix

Zenobia, 75–76